By George Vlahakis

Corporate profiles by Jackie Sheckler

Featuring the photography of Kendall Reeves and Rich Remsberg

Produced in cooperation with

The Greater Bloomington Chamber of Commerce

A Contemporary Portrait

Bloomington

A Contemporary Portrait

Bloomington

By George Vlahakis

Corporate profiles by Jackie Sheckler

Featuring the photography of Kendall Reeves and Rich Remsberg

Staff for *Bloomington: A Contemporary Portrait*

Sales Associate: Connie Ledgett

Executive Editor: James E. Turner

Managing Editor: Lenita Gilreath

Design Director: Camille Leonard

Designer: Katie Bradshaw

Photo Editors: Katie Bradshaw & Lenita Gilreath

Production Manager: Cindy Lovett

Contract Manager: Katrina Williams

Editorial Assistant: Robin Davies

Sales Assistant: Annette Lozier

Proofreader: Wynona B. Hall

Accounting Services: Sara Ann Turner

Printing Production: Frank Rosenberg/GSAmerica

CCI

Community Communications, Inc.
Montgomery, Alabama

James E. Turner, Chairman of the Board
Ronald P. Beers, President
Daniel S. Chambliss, Vice President

Part One
Table of Contents

Chapter 1
Perspective
An Introduction to This Place

Since being settled in the early 1800s as a frontier settlement, Bloomington has grown into one of the Midwest's most progressive cities, and yet also is a place for which residents and visitors remain nostalgic. While enjoying a healthy economy, this isn't at the expense of its beautiful, rolling landscape. While benefiting from many regional advantages, it is a place that puts tremendous value on a community spirit that serves as much of a foundation as the limestone found here.

Chapter 2
History
How We Have Gotten to Where We Are

Since being passed on by caretaker Indians to settlers headed west, Bloomington quickly emerged as a regional center for trading and industry and as home to one of the nation's leading research institutions in higher education, Indiana University, whose origins can be traced back to the city's founding. Opportunities were seen in Monroe County's rich abundance of natural resources such as limestone and timber, leading to the establishment of Ellettsville and other communities.

Chapter 3
Economy
Our Diversified, Knowledge-based Economy

Bloomington's economy derives much strength from its diverse nature. Its varied industrial base includes several employers with recognizable names such as General Electric, Columbia House, and Otis Elevator, and many others who produce or distribute things we see or use every day, such as Hall Signs' highway markers, Sunrise Publications' greeting cards, TASUS' auto moldings, and PYA/Monarch's food products. As the world's largest privately held medical device manufacturer, Cook Incorporated is playing a leading role in turning the area into something of a "Silicon Valley" in health care, through its numerous subsidiaries and other companies that have been attracted here. The presence of a highly educated workforce also is fostering an even greater shift towards a knowledge-based economy.

Chapter 4
Education
Our Lifetime of Learning

Few communities other than Bloomington genuinely can boast about having as much of a heritage of commitment to education. As home to Indiana University, the oldest state university west of the Allegheny Mountains, this southern Indiana city is forever associated with the state and nation's advancement. With the influence of IU and Ivy Tech State College, Bloomington has developed into one of the best educational environments in the Midwest.

Part Two

Table of Contents

Bloomington's Enterprises

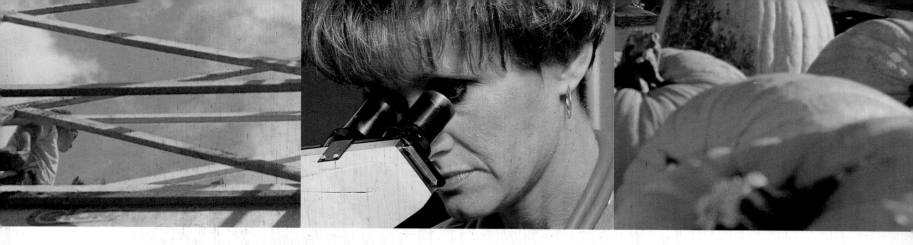

Foreword

Deciding to settle in Bloomington, Indiana, after a 36-year career that required us to move frequently was an easy choice for my family. We knew what we wanted. We had lived in 18 communities throughout the United States and overseas; in small towns and big cities; on the coasts and inland; downtown and in the country. Our experiences made us experts in what communities can offer, or, sadly, sometimes don't.

We sought the seemingly impossible: small town ambience, but big city amenities; seasons, but not seasonal ovens or deep freezes; civilization, but not at high cost to the environment; good roads, but not killer rush hours; symphony orchestras, but not to the exclusion of Bluegrass; human diversity, but not human strife; pavement, but paths as well; committed people, but with a eye to compromise; homes, not real estate investments; excitement, but not fear; close to large metropolitan communities, but not too close; sushi, but world-class pizza too; and growth, not sprawl.

Incredibly, we were able to satisfy our conflicting expectations. Combining the livability of a small Midwestern city with the sophistication of the home of a world-class university, Bloomington offers what can only be described as an extraordinary quality of life.

Working on this book has been very rewarding. The project has afforded me the opportunity to reflect on the good fortune that brought my family to this place. More than that, it has given me the chance to contribute to a project that will let others know how exceptional my adopted community is.

Perhaps this foreword is unusually personal. But Bloomington is a community that affects almost everyone on a personal level. I am confident that most members of the community would, if given the opportunity, approach writing this foreword in the same way. Each would want to explain why Bloomington, for them, is such a special place to live, work, and raise children. It is a community that becomes a part of what you are.

If you know our community, you already understand why I think Bloomington is the place to be. The photos and text of *Bloomington: A Contemporary Portrait* will remind you that your decision to live here was among the best you ever made.

If you have yet to learn about Bloomington, this book is a good place to start. Captured in these pages is a distillation of the essence of our community. You will learn about how Bloomington came to be, how it has grown, and what it offers. As you enjoy this book, you will begin to understand that this is indeed a special place. And, for some, this book will be a starting place for a decision to join us here either as a visitor, or a resident.

I am extraordinarily pleased to serve as the representative of the more than 1,000 members of the Greater Bloomington Chamber of Commerce in presenting *Bloomington: A Contemporary Portrait* to those who know how special our community is, or who will soon learn.

—Steve Howard
President, Greater Bloomington Chamber of Commerce

Preface

This may be the preface to my book, but these words were the last ones written for *Bloomington: A Contemporary Portrait*. Yet, it only seems appropriate that it be as such, because when I undertook the responsibility to write this book, I quickly realized what a difficult task it would be. This blossoming city is very special to many people, all of whom develop their own distinct visions of this place. They include my parents, who first brought me here in swaddling clothes, likely cream and crimson ones, a third of a century ago. Over the next couple of decades, we continued to make regular pilgrimages to this mecca, until I settled upon Indiana University for my college education and a cycle was completed. My father had successfully passed along his collegiate legacy to me.

However, unlike the many thousands who briefly resided here, I chose to return and now see this place much differently. I hope that the following pages offer some insight into why so many people make a connection with Bloomington, either as lifelong residents or as itinerant scholars. As local historian James Madison told me, writing about Bloomington is like the proverbial blind man striving to describe an elephant—it is a place where your perspective often depends on your vantage point. He was correct that it would be a great challenge to portray this community accurately in all of its many facets, and I'm not sure that I was completely successful.

Thanks should go my loving wife, Donna, a New Yorker turned Hoosier who convinced me that returning here would be the next logical step. I also want to express my appreciation to several people in the community whose support and suggestions helped me stay on course. They include Brian Werth, business editor at *The Herald-Times*; Steve Howard, president of the Greater Bloomington Chamber of Commerce; Robin Roy Gress, a transplanted Los Angeles scribe at IU; Jody Crago, curator of the Monroe County Historical Society; the librarians in the Indiana Room of the Monroe County Public Library; and my university mentors Julie Peterson, DeAnna Hines, and Ellen Mathia. Jackie Sheckler crafted all of the community profiles, and Kendall Reeves and Rich Remsberg provided the lovely photography that really causes people to pick up this book. Much of the credit goes to them. Lastly, thanks also go to our editor, Lenita Gilreath, who convinced and encouraged me that I could do this.

I hope that you enjoy reading this book and discover in it the many things that make Bloomington and surrounding Monroe County an extraordinary destination, and that it prompts you to come and see it for yourself.

—George Vlahakis
Author

Bloomington

Part One

Perspective

*An Introduction
To This Place*

*I cannot forget where it is that
    I come from
I cannot forget the people who
    love me
Yeah, I can be myself here in this
    small town
And people let me be just what
    I want to be.*

—Popular singer and Bloomington resident
John Mellencamp
from his song "Small Town"

"Above all things," wrote Henry J. Feltus, publisher of the *Bloomington Weekly Star*, in 1921, "we have the fish on the courthouse." Like most places, Bloomington has its lore and legends, including those about its storied metal fish that adorns the Monroe County Courthouse.

A fish might seem a strange symbol for a community located in south central Indiana, a couple of hundred miles away from the nearest Great Lake or a thousand miles away from the closest ocean. Some say it originally was installed by one of the city's earliest settlers, blacksmith Austin Seward, a Presbyterian church elder who chose the fish as a symbol of his Christian values. Others have said a fish simply was a good shape for a weather vane, which was its original purpose.

But the fish has always had a prime view of Bloomington, since at least 1826—although it hasn't always changed position with the breeze— and has become a symbol for Bloomington. More than 100 years ago, downtown businessmen chipped in to give it a coating of gold leaf.

When a new courthouse was erected in 1908, citizens raised strong enough complaints until the fish was regilded and placed back in its rightful place atop the rotunda. Today, the metal fish is still flying, and as Feltus noted, "Who has not returned to his hometown of Bloomington and said, 'That old fish on the courthouse looks good to me!'"

Progressive and Active

If that old fish could talk, what a yarn he could spin about a frontier settlement that has grown into one of the Midwest's most progressive cities, and yet remains a place for which residents and visitors remain nostalgic. Located about 50 miles south of Indianapolis and 100 miles northwest of Louisville, Kentucky, Bloomington is the county seat of Monroe County. Projected to have a population of 126,000 by the year 2010, the county includes the nearby town of Ellettsville, as well as several smaller communities. As symbolized by the fish overlooking its downtown, Bloomington is marked by intriguing contrasts and unique qualities usually not found in communities its size. With a city population projected to reach 70,000 early in the new century, it is a community that keeps looking forward without forgetting the past.

This is easily seen downtown, where revitalization includes saving several historic structures such as a former furniture factory for use as a city hall, research park, and offices. Urban renewal here means converting buildings constructed near the turn of the twentieth century for use as arts and performing arts centers, a convention center, offices, and for retailing.

This trend gained impetus with the county's decision in 1983 to preserve its courthouse, rather than replace it. Accomplished in the renovation was the reopening of a three-story rotunda that had been closed for about 25 years. Its renovation brought attention to downtown and spurred other similar projects.

Bloomington places a high value on preserving the natural beauty of its lush landscapes and verdant rolling hills. It's no secret why Bloomington frequently has been designated by the National Arbor Day Federation as a "Tree City." A peaceful, early morning walk through many parts of the city provides ample testimony. For more than 180 years, Bloomington and its surrounding areas have retained much of their natural beauty, enhanced with the development of three tree-lined reservoirs, including Lake Monroe, the state's largest inland lake.

In addition to working together to preserve green space, residents here often close ranks to see that young people, the elderly, and the needy are cared for—this includes nurturing the individual need for creativity. As one local official put it, people in Bloomington have created a living environment where self-realization is possible. As a result, in 1995, Monroe County was named the winner of

Educational and cultural groups interested in Tibet, the East Asian land now under Chinese military rule, are attracted to Bloomington's Tibetan Cultural Center. Tibet's spiritual leader, the Dalai Lama, is a visitor to Bloomington, such as when he came in 1997. Photo by Rich Remsberg.

the Outstanding County Achievement Award by the Association of Indiana Counties, and Bloomington is a two-time winner of "All-American City" honors.

A Community that Reaches Out

This same activism extends to how residents integrate Bloomington into the global scene. A not-for-profit volunteer organization, the Bloomington-based Sister City International, helped the city establish links with Lu-Chou, Taiwan, and Posoltega, Nicaragua. This also includes embracing newcomers, including Indiana University students from all 50 states and more than 120 countries. Away from the university campus, a large selection of international restaurants and groceries thrive. Hoosier hometown favorites such as Ladyman's Cafe, a good place for hot coffee and generous plates of dumplings, meat loaf, or fried chicken, sit comfortably alongside international dining spots. When the Dalai Lama, the exiled spiritual leader of Tibet, visits the United States, he often pays a visit to Bloomington. Here is the home of a Tibetan Cultural Center that attracts educational and cultural groups interested in the East Asian land now under Chinese military rule.

Many people were introduced to Bloomington about two decades ago, through the release of the 1979 Academy Award-winning film *Breaking Away*. The coming-of-age drama focused on four young men from Bloomington, called "cutters" for their many predecessors who worked in the region's limestone mills and quarries. This is an area rich in some of the highest grade limestone found anywhere on the planet. Rock harvested from a narrow belt of Salem limestone found in Monroe and neighboring counties can be found in many of America's best-known buildings and memorials, including more than 70 buildings in Washington, D.C., alone. It also is a legacy that includes an artistic tradition that has produced some of the finest stone carvers, cutters, and draftsmen anywhere.

In the film, the "townies" take their contempt for the university students onto a quarter-mile oval track and compete in IU's annual spectacular bike race, the Little 500, and learn about themselves and each other in the process. Among those inspired by the film were the thousands of bicyclists who have since made this area a Midwest haven for touring, as noted by *Bicycling* magazine. The journal ranked Bloomington among the top 10 places in the country for cycling.

Town and Gown

Since 1980, a large, two-part limestone statue designed by artist Jean Paul Darriau, *Red, Blond,*

A symphony of notable musicians, actors, and artists have found Bloomington to be fertile ground for creative development. They include top-selling rock singer John Mellencamp, who has chosen to remain in Bloomington, far away from the glitter and fast pace of southern California. Photo courtesy of Mercury Records.

Black, and Olive, has represented the cooperation that exists between government, university, industry, and community. Examples of the city's good relationship with the university are its programs to encourage the transfer of technology into off-campus commercial settings and its many task forces with strong campus participation.

More than 40 IU employees serve as elected or appointed officials in Bloomington or Monroe County government, and the city's mayor, John Fernandez, first came to Bloomington as an IU student. "What happens—and I'm probably a good example of this—is that people have a perception of Bloomington as a college town. As they mature and start to think about the kind of community they want to live in, people really fall in love with this place," Fernandez observed. "There's a tremendous sense of community. It's so easy to get involved, know people, and feel comfortable. It's like a big neighborhood."

Bloomington has been described in so many ways. *Psychology Today* called it one of the 25 lowest stress cities, based on its historically low rates of alcoholism, crime, suicide, and divorce. *PC World* and *Money* magazines describe Bloomington as one of the "best places for working at home," and ranked it ahead of major cities such as Cincinnati and Kansas City.

The New York Times, in naming it "among the Big Ten of college towns," commented, "Though small, Bloomington has pocket communities reflecting its artistic and athletic diversity." *Rand McNally's Retirement Places Rated* and *Modern Maturity* consistently rank Bloomington as among the top 10 places to settle down after a long career. In recommending the area as a great place to live, *Vegetarian Times* commented, "Bloomington makes these lists because of its terrific public school system, some of the most diverse music in the country, and its high social and environmental consciousness. It also will appeal to vegetarians because of an

(following page) Like other buildings in Bloomington's downtown, this former Masonic Lodge was restored and given new life. Today, One City Centre houses radio stations WTTS and WGCL and offices. Photo by Kendall Reeves.

(far left) Since 1980, a large, two-part limestone statue designed by artist Jean Paul Darriau, *Red, Blond, Black, and Olive*, has represented the cooperation that exists between government, university, industry, and community. Photo by Kendall Reeves.

(left) Bloomington has been described in so many ways. *Psychology Today* called Bloomington one of the 25 lowest stress cities. Photo by Rich Remsberg.

Located about 50 miles south of Indianapolis and 100 miles northwest of Louisville, Kentucky, Bloomington is the county seat of Monroe County. Projected to have a population of 126,000 by the year 2010, the county includes the nearby town of Ellettsville, as well as several smaller communities. Photo by Kendall Reeves.

A trend towards urban renewal gained impetus with the county's 1983 decision to preserve its courthouse, rather than replace it. Accomplished in the renovation was the reopening of a three-story rotunda that had been closed for about 25 years. Photo by Kendall Reeves.

eat-in co-op [with two locations] that takes the cake."

The emerging "knowledge economy" requires businesses to employ well-educated workers. Bloomington received a lot of national attention after a top business relocation consulting firm found that it had the fourth-highest percentage of four-year college graduates in the country. Of course, retaining an educated workforce involves more than the presence of IU and Ivy Tech State College, although it certainly doesn't hurt. Both on and off the IU campus, an impressive lineup of opera, theater, dance, live music, films of all kinds, and numerous opportunities for hands-on artistic expression makes for a well-rounded populace.

It even attracts major recording artists who come here to produce new albums. Singer-songwriter Kim Fox moved to Bloomington from New York

City because it provided fertile ground for her musical and personal development. "The combination of music school muses and the locals makes Bloomington a pretty amazing place," Fox told *Billboard* magazine. "You can see great music about every night. And the atmosphere is so relaxed. Living here, I've gained a new respect for music with a real simplicity—whether it's The Mysteries of Life [another Bloomington act with a national recording contract] or someone like John Prine." Her debut album for DreamWorks records featured a producer and musicians who were Bloomingtonians, including famed drummer Kenny Aronoff and a string section of IU music students.

The City's Intangible Assets
Simply put, Bloomington also benefits from a geographical advantage and excellent transportation

TO HONOR ALL WHO SERVED AND
HOSE WHO GAVE THEIR LIVES IN SOUTHEAST ASIA

		JOSEPH B. ZIEL	JAMES A. WORKMAN	JERRY L. BOOKER	ZETTIE J.C. DUGN
T. READ	DANIEL C. NICHOLS	EUGENE A. PARISH	ROBERT N. BROWN	KENNETH L. WALTERS	ROBERT M. SCOTT
M. SCOTT	RICKEY D. SOUTHERN	ALBERT W. WARTHAN	JOSEPH B. BRITTAIN	MARK W. SURBER	CHARLES F. EROT
T. NIGGLE	BOBBY WILSON		RONALD B. STILLIONS	STEPHEN E. HENDRICKS	ROGER W. CUMMINGS
W. SHAFFER	GENIE L. McDONALD	GERALD L. MILLER			

Monroe County has retained much of
its natural beauty, despite intrusions by
modern society. There are many places
like this one where folks come to
escape the cares of everyday life.
Photo by Kendall Reeves.

facilities. Eight trucking companies serve Monroe County, and two major rail haulers have daily schedules through Bloomington. The area also benefits from easy access to the nation's interstate highway system from several well-maintained state roadways. A proposed new interstate highway from Indianapolis to Bloomington will replace four-lane Indiana 37 and eventually provide a direct pathway between Canada and Mexico.

Many corporations and charter air services maintain their own aircraft and hangars at the Monroe County Airport. Its main runway was expanded and taxiways were improved in order to accommodate bigger jets and heavier payloads, and it boasts a fully equipped tower. One of Federal Express's top 10 customers, Cook Incorporated, is headquartered in Bloomington, and the shipping company's second-largest hub is at Indianapolis International Airport.

While many communities are still coming to grips with emerging technologies such as the Internet and the opportunities it provides for electronic commerce, Bloomington is well traveled on the information superhighway. Eight local companies and IU provide Internet access, and an ever-growing number of companies exist to help individuals and companies with web site design. IU also is connected to the National Science Foundation's high-speed research Internet—the very high performance Backbone Network Service that will form the basis for Internet 2, a national networking infrastructure that will sustain the American higher education community into the next century. The university also is among the top 10 "most wired" colleges in the country, according to *Yahoo! Internet Life* magazine. At least half of IU's students own computers, and 60 percent of its classes use the Internet for research and student assignments.

The city's telecommunications system features digital loop electronics that are supported by a fiber-optic network. The university offers ATM video conferencing, and nearby Crane Division Naval Surface Warfare Center is linked to the military network. With the help of federal funding, HoosierNet was established to provide many in the community, including small businesses and public service agencies, access to electronic mail and the World Wide Web.

When one considers how well poised Bloomington is for the twenty-first century, it is interesting to note how much it has changed in recent decades. Prior to World War II, its population was fairly homogeneous, and the city was much smaller than its present size. A large aerial photo of Bloomington in 1955 hanging at the

Monroe County Historical Museum shows the residential areas of Bloomington pretty much came to a stop at Saint Charles Catholic Church, located on Third and High Streets.

The high-volume retail activity now generated to the east, at College Mall and other shopping centers, would be years away. The same would be true for a tremendous amount of residential development to the east and south. Concerns existed over Monroe County's ability to sustain future growth. Man-made Lake Lemon soon would provide water to the city and much of the county, and Lake Monroe's creation in the 1970s would bring an end to the argument.

Reasons for living in and loving Bloomington are just as plentiful as the many stories surrounding the fish on the courthouse weather vane. Coming chapters present a contemporary profile of this place and some of the reasons it is so special. ⚓

Bloomington embraces newcomers, including Indiana University students from all 50 states and more than 120 countries. Photo by Kendall Reeves.

2

Our History

*How We Have Gotten
To Where We Are*

"*Whatever the challenge, be it lack
of water, rocky soil, or dense
forests, Monroe County continually
reinvents itself. The county just
seems to get busier, more diverse,
and more interesting with each
new challenge.*"

—*Jody Crago*
Curator of the Monroe County Historical Museum

While the area's limestone deposits date back

340 million years ago or more to the Mississippian period, its recorded human history only goes back a few centuries. Like the rest of Indiana, the territory that came to be known as Monroe County once was under dominion of the Miami and other Native-American groups. A vivid fossil record reveals that human society flourished in concert with the unspoiled environment of Indiana, as well as the rest of North America. Little can be fully understood about the state's first residents, except that they made enormous contributions still felt in today's economy. The rows of field corn and tobacco grown throughout southern Indiana involve plants that originally were domesticated by Indians. The same can be said for other common plants such as pumpkins, squash, and beans first cultivated by native Hoosiers.

In 1795, at Greenville, Ohio, Miami Chief Little Turtle—called by one historian "one of the most intelligent and renowned aboriginal Americans of any tribe"—had the vision to declare that his tribe owned all the land from Detroit south to the Ohio River and westward to the mouth of the Wabash River and the western edge of Lake Michigan. But in the years to follow the American Revolution, westward movement by settlers pushed other Indian tribes—among them the Pottawatomies, Delawares, Kickapoos, and the Piankeshaws— onto lands controlled by the Miamis.

Monroe County appears to have been on the boundary between the home and hunting grounds of the Delawares, Piankeshaws, Pecankeeshaws, and Miamis. Founded after an intense, nine-year series of skirmishes and treaties over a landmass encompassing much of the Midwest, the county was established by the Indiana General Assembly in 1818, two years after Indiana became the 19th state to enter the Union. Initially, it would be divided into two sections by an Indian boundary, extending southeast from Parke County to Jackson County. Land to the south of this boundary—often referred to as the "10 o'clock line"—was obtained through the treaty of Fort Wayne in 1809, in which

the United States obtained about 2.9 million acres of Indian land at a cost of approximately three cents an acre. The remaining area was ceded by Indians through the 1818 treaty of Saint Mary's, Ohio. The boundary line, legend has it, received its name because it ran parallel to the shadow cast by spears stuck into the ground at 10 A.M. on September 20, 1809.

Early Settlers

An initial survey of Monroe County lands south of the Indian boundary took place in 1812. Although its first Caucasian settlers could have come as early as 1810 or 1811, most of the families to settle Monroe County's first community and its county seat, Bloomington, arrived in 1815. Like the rest of southern Indiana, Monroe County was predominately inhabited by upland Southerners, a people of Scotch-Irish and German descent who initially had migrated to places such as the Blue Ridge Mountains and the Shenandoah Valley. Indiana was first settled by these Southerners who crossed the Ohio River and headed north as war and treaty opened Indian lands. On the basis of the 1850 census, it was estimated that 40 percent of the state's population consisted of adult Hoosiers

An abundant natural resource, limestone from Monroe and neighboring counties can be found in many of America's best-known buildings and memorials. Shown here are some of the tools used in the early days of the craft. Photo by Kendall Reeves.

In 1829, trustees of Indiana University convinced the Reverend Andrew Wylie—then president of Washington College in Washington, Pennsylvania, and a Presbyterian minister—to become the institution's first president. Today, IU is one of the country's leading teaching and research universities. Photo courtesy of IU Archives.

born in the South and their children.

The first African-Americans to settle in Monroe County also came early in the nineteenth century. Many had come from Virginia and North Carolina, where restrictions had been placed on their personal freedom. While Indiana eventually passed laws that restricted their lives as well, African-Americans were able to escape persecution by forming their own settlements. Among the first African-American settlers in Monroe County may have been Andrew

Ferguson, a Revolutionary War veteran who migrated with his wife to Indiana by 1822, pension records indicate.

Over the next 100 years, the face of Monroe County and the rest of southern Indiana changed very little. Census records from 1850 indicated that only 7 percent of the state's inhabitants were born abroad, and these had been German and Irish farmers and craftsmen, as well as diggers of canals and rail workers. Many of these immigrants soon would blend with those who came before them. When the census count was again taken in 1880, foreign-born residents accounted for only 7.3 percent of the population, a percentage far lower than any of the state's neighbors. Another great diversification of Monroe County would come much later, due to the influence of the state university.

Conditions in this pioneer wilderness were primitive, but initial growth was quick. Monroe County "was a wilderness filled with all varieties of wild animals inhabiting this latitude," wrote historian Charles Blanchard 70 years later. "By the time of the first land sale of Bloomington Township in 1816, there were a score or nearly so of families residing within its limits. . . .The settlement of the town was phenomenal. At the close of the year 1818, not less than 30 families lived in the town in hastily built log cabins or rude frame homes." Its population grew to nearly 300 by the 1820s.

Named for the fifth United States president, James Monroe, Monroe County was established on January 14, 1818, by the Indiana General Assembly. The new county's commissioners met for the first time that April 10, when they ordered that the county seat was to be laid out and named Bloomington. A public square was sectioned off for a courthouse, and the first land sales of city property took place. Proceeds of the sale totaled $14,326.85. Bloomington was chosen for the same reasons that led other settlers to the site—the elevated terrain seemed secure from floods and healthier than the lowlands. Farmers later would find that assumptions about the land being more suitable for agriculture would prove false. Depending on what one wants to believe, Bloomington was named either for one of its earliest settlers, William Bloom, or for the beauty of the area. Local legend has it that a group of pioneers, picnicking on an area hillside, were influenced by the blooming flowers and foliage below them.

In succeeding decades, other communities were established in Monroe County as more people came to settle, and often the opening of a new post office was a forerunner. For example, the town of Ellettsville initially was laid out in February 1837 and named Richland, for the township in which it

is located. When a post office was established there seven months later, the name was changed to Ellettsville, because another post office was named Richland in Rush County. The town was named for Edward Ellett, who had operated a tavern and other businesses there before dying in a cholera epidemic a few years earlier. Other Monroe County settlements included Harrodsburg and Unionville, founded in 1836; Fairfax, in 1837; Dolan and Smithville, in 1851; Hindustan, in 1853; Clear Creek, in 1854; Stinesville, in 1855; Kirksville, 1879; Modesto and Sanders, in 1892; and New Unionville, in 1906.

1820 to 1860

The history of Bloomington can't be told without discussing Indiana University. One condition placed upon the territory of Indiana in 1815 was that two townships be reserved for seminaries to provide education for the area. The following year, delegates to the new state wrote a constitution envisioning a public education system to "encourage the principles of humanity, industry, and sobriety." One seminary would be located in Monroe County, and it would grow into what is today one of the nation's leading public universities. "No other state in the Union

(top) In 1820, the Indiana General Assembly voted to establish a "state seminary" in Bloomington. Later to be renamed Indiana University in 1838, today the Big Ten institution is one of the nation's leading public universities. Photo courtesy of IU Archives.

The expansion of the railroads and the development of steam mining came at a fortuitous time for the area's limestone companies. Pictured here is one of the last remaining remnants of the historic Monon Railroad. Photo by Kendall Reeves.

In 1869, two brothers, James (shown here) and William Showers, capitalized on the easy availability of timber when they bought out their father's interest in a cabinetmaking business. After a fire destroyed their original factory, the Showers brothers built a new manufacturing facility on Morton Street with financial help from the city. Photo courtesy of IU Archives.

nearly two centuries of existence, the city and university have grown together.

One of the city's first products, in addition to college graduates, was liquor. Historian Blanchard writes: "One of the most noteworthy features of the town then was the liquor traffic. The most prominent of the merchants kept it on their counters free for their patrons, and a tavern or inn which did not keep it at the bar was a rarity, probably unknown in the early history of Bloomington. Among the liquor sellers were some of the best citizens, morally and temperately." A vigorous temperance movement drove liquor production away from the city during the 1840s. In addition, there were numerous factories of leather, domestic and farming implements, flour, tailor goods, oil, and numerous stores, shops, artisans, tradesmen, and professionals.

In 1827, the first limestone quarry in the state was opened by Richard Gilbert near Stinesville, which became itself a major center for limestone production in the 1880s. Gilbert understood the stone's initial applications for building footers and bridge foundations; however, it would be several decades before the railroads could make limestone more commercially viable.

The residents of Bloomington voted in 1827 to incorporate the community, but procedural requirements then were not met and the matter was deferred. By legislative action in 1845, the town was formally incorporated and officers later were elected.

Over the next few decades, business activity in Monroe County was marked by the establishment of salt and iron mines, numerous small factories of livery products, furniture, woolens, and a gristmill. The town's first bank was established in 1857, with assets totaling $20,000. The New Albany Railroad, built through Monroe County in the early 1850s, bolstered the local economy and increased the town's importance in the region. In 1856, Seward & Chase Iron Foundry doubled its operations, casting iron for use in stoves, plows, fry pans, axes, and parts for all kinds of machinery. Some people were put off by the progress Bloomington was making. "Expensive" changes in town streets to accommodate the railroad led to strong opposition to the continuance of the municipal government. In 1858—by a 115 to 101 vote—town residents decided to dissolve the municipality. The results of this close vote were short-lived, however, and after a year, Bloomington was reincorporated. In the mid-1860s, a referendum to become a city passed, but residents shelved the idea when it was determined that too few of the townspeople had participated in the vote. Finally, Bloomington did become a city in 1878, after yet another close vote.

In the county, several communities were established

had then incorporated into its constitution a declaration in favor of a university open to all alike," recalled a university history prepared in conjunction with the 1904 Louisiana Purchase Exposition.

This broad concept of education seems even more remarkable when a number of other factors are considered. At the time the legislative approval was given for establishing what then was known as the Indiana State Seminary, only about one quarter of the territory that would become Indiana had been purchased from the Indians. The only avenues for transportation were uncertain Indian trails, rough roads, and rivers and creeks. Only two or three small steamboats were traveling up and down the Ohio River to the south. By modern standards, most of the people could be considered illiterate or impoverished. But the people had a vision and appreciation for higher education. Thus, in their

By the early twentieth century, the Showers Brothers Co. was reputed to be the world's largest maker of bedroom furniture. Between 1869 and 1899, the factory was manufacturing a piece of furniture each minute. Photo courtesy of the Mathers Museum.

In 1940, Showers sold a portion of its complex to Radio Corp. of America, better known as RCA. In 1949, the plant produced the first black-and-white TV and, in 1954, the first color set. Before closing in 1998, the facility went on to become one of the world's biggest producers of TV sets. Photo courtesy of the Mathers Museum.

in response to local agricultural activity. Between 1835 and 1852, the village of Mount Tabor in Bean Blossom Township was arguably the leading trade center for grain and livestock in Monroe County, which caused some to briefly give it consideration as the county seat. As early as 1820, a sawmill was built over a dam constructed on Bean Blossom Creek.

In 1828, Mount Tabor was laid out with 66 lots, and businesses of various kinds soon were locating there. But the village's great boon was also short-lived. It benefited from seasonally high water access to the White River, which provided further trans-portation for pork and crops raised in the area. With the coming of the railroads, the once-thriving community—which once had 350 residents—was abandoned. Today, only a few foundations remain.

Harrodsburg, on the southern end of the county, is another community that had been prominent as an agricultural center. In 1853, hog producers generated close to $100,000 in business routed on flatboats from Harrodsburg. In April 1885, three men robbed the American Express Company's car on the Monon Railroad two miles north of Harrodsburg. One of the robbers, a county resident, was convicted after a second trial, and a second man admitted to the infamous robbery during a deathbed confession.

Five miles northwest of Bloomington is Ellettsville, which also grew from the establishment of a gristmill on a water source, at Jack's Defeat Creek, which was much broader then than it is today. Established with 14 lots, the community grew slowly until an English settler and experienced stonecutter named John Matthews was drawn to the area's limestone deposits and moved his family

to the area in 1862. As an apprentice stonecutter Matthews had helped to build London's Houses of Parliament, and his wife was a direct descendant of Sir Francis Drake. The Matthews Brothers Stone Co. became an important employer in the area, operating until it was sold to another local lime-stone company in 1978. Near the company's opera-tions is the Matthews' limestone mansion, which features the faces of four of his children carved above the entrance of the French mansard house.

By 1860, Ellettsville's population reached 250, and six years later, it was incorporated as a town. A major fire in 1886 nearly destroyed the town's business district, but a fortuitous shift in wind direction and rainfall saved a large part of the village. The determination of the people and the growing influence of limestone helped sustain its economy in the years to follow. Other communities in the county's limestone belt, such as Stinesville and Harrodsburg, underwent similar growth as that industry expanded.

The Role of Indiana University

The Indiana State Seminary—located at the present intersection of Walnut and Second Streets—was developing into an important source of new residents and economic activity for Bloomington. During the legislative session of 1827-28, an act was adopted to transform it into the Indiana College. Within a year, trustees convinced the Reverend Andrew Wylie—then president of Washington College in Washington, Pennsylvania, and a Presbyterian minister—to become the college's first president, with a $1,000 annual salary.

Commenting on the qualities of many students of the time, T. A. Wylie, cousin of the first president, observed: "Many of the students were young men brought up on farms and used to hard work. They came to Bloomington, generally on their own resources, depending on money they had earned or borrowed. It was not unusual for students to attend to their studies for a year and then absent themselves for the same length of time in order to earn money by teaching or otherwise, and to return to complete their college course."

Under Wylie the college prospered and gave Bloomington a degree of culture and intellectual refinement not present elsewhere in the new frontier. Within a decade, an effort to change Indiana College into Indiana University succeeded. "Without his determination and leadership, Indiana University might never have emerged today as one of the foremost American universities," Ohio State University historian George Chalon noted about Wylie. "Wylie nursed his institution through numerous harassments and attacks. He gained time for the educational institution that stood at the peak of Indiana's educational system." The relationship between the university and the community has been a symbiotic one, essential for their mutual success over the last 174 years.

1860 to 1900

During the Civil War, Indiana officially supported the Union. However, with many settlers having been upland Southerners, Monroe County and southern Indiana generally were torn by divided loyalties. "It's not that folks were necessarily in favor of the Confederacy, but it is that they were not in favor of the kind of war that President Lincoln and Indiana's governor, Oliver Morton, were pursuing," said IU historian James Madison. "The Civil War history here is the history of a community of upland Southerners, who had significant reservations about the war, even though lots of Monroe Countians went off to fight and went off willingly."

Even before the Confederate attack on Fort Sumter in 1861, county residents gathered that February and negotiated among themselves a resolution not to use coercive measures with the South. When news of Fort Sumter's surrender to Confederate troops reached the county that April 15, reactions were mixed. "It was true of Monroe County that, as many of the citizens had come from the South and had friends and relatives there, a strong sympathy was felt for the old home," noted historian Blanchard. Added Madison: "When Fort Sumter was fired upon, there was immense enthusiasm for the war, but it was for a war that would be relatively short and bloodless, and a war to preserve the Union. It was not enthusiasm for

the war that came to be, which in a year or two years was clearly a war that was going to be very long and very bloody and a war to end slavery."

At least 10 companies of militia composed of men from the region went off to fight, including some as members of the 27th Indiana infantry, which had the distinction of being the Union Army's tallest regiment due to a height requirement. But as the war raged on and other issues connected to the war emerged, Indiana had to institute a draft, over which there was much resentment. Some historians believe that sentiment turned decisively pro-Union after Confederate General John Morgan invaded Indiana in July 1863.

A number of escaped slaves passed through here on the underground railroad supported by members of the Convenanter Presbyterian Church, where the question of slavery had caused a rupture. Some of these religious people were among Monroe County's first settlers, and as a group they continued to come here until a few years before the Civil War, according to historian Henry Lester Smith. Among the prominent residents who took part in helping escaping slaves was Austin Seward, who operated a successful foundry and was active in local education matters. An important station of Indiana's underground railroad was immediately south of Bloomington at Walnut Ridge. A great many people in Bloomington harbored and fed the fugitives while they rested here. The escaped slaves then would continue through stations in Morgantown and Mooresville and north to Canada. The years following the Civil War began a period of economic growth for Bloomington, due to the expanded use of two of the area's natural resources—limestone and timber. Before 1870, inadequate transportation and the inability to mine large pieces of stone had inhibited the viable mining

---

"It is not egotism that causes a throb of pride to course through the veins of Bloomington citizens, when the subject of 'home town' is being discussed. Unlike natives of many small cities and towns, there is no hesitancy upon the part of Bloomington residents who happen to be visiting or having deported for various reasons from the place of their nativity, and taken residence in the larger cities; no shame is felt when asked that one question that always comes: 'Where are you from?' The answer is always promptly given, with no hum-hawing; no blush or timidity—always with that assurance that we are not going to be laughed at when we say: 'Bloomington, Indiana.'"

—Forest M. "Pop" Hall, 1922

of limestone. The expansion of the railroads and the development of steam power for mining came at a fortuitous time for limestone companies. Many major United States cities were expanding, as people began leaving farms for urban areas and as immigrants began coming in droves. Major fires in Chicago and Boston demonstrated the value of limestone as an ideal, fireproof medium with which to build, and the revival in popularity of Gothic and Romanesque styles also prescribed its liberal use. Between 1850 and the early years of the twentieth century, about 50 quarries, stone mills, and stone-cutting plants operated in the region. By 1909, Bloomington's quarries employed about 1,400 people. In 1918, stone from the region supplied 80 percent of the national building stone market, and demand for it remained high until the Great Depression.

As with limestone, residents discovered another abundant natural resource in area timber. In 1869, two brothers, James and William Showers, capitalized on the easy availability of timber when they bought out their father's interest in a cabinetmaking business for $300. After a fire destroyed their original factory, the Showers brothers built a new manufacturing facility on Morton Street with financial help from the city. By the early twentieth century, the Showers Brothers Co. was reputed to be the world's largest maker of bedroom furniture. Between 1869 and 1899, production had increased by 75 percent, and the factory was manufacturing a piece of furniture each minute. The Showers' influence even spread to residential real estate. A two-block area on North Washington Street remains the location of some of Bloomington's most beautiful historic homes, which the brothers built for family and friends.

1900 to 1950

The local economy was prosperous enough to merit construction of a new county courthouse dedicated in 1908, replacing the original one that had been remodeled in 1856-58. Other industries producing glass, baskets, and creosote opened. Showers Furniture Co. enjoyed its peak in 1928 and 1929, when gross sales exceeded $10 million. The Showers factory covered 22 acres, accounted for 25 percent of Bloomington's revenue, employed 2,500 people, and was the county's second largest employer. Both the furniture and limestone industries suffered during the Great Depression, but the hardships of the period were cushioned somewhat by the presence of the university.

Throughout its history, Bloomington has been plagued by problems involving another natural resource—water. In its early years, much-touted springs became suspect. Rainwater would drain through sinkholes and quickly flow through the limestone to the streams, largely untreated by natural purification processes. Drilling wells through the limestone was difficult, and often the water below would be found to be bitter tasting. A succession of reservoirs were built southwest of Bloomington between 1894 and 1915, but they often leaked through the limestone.

After another severe dry season in the early 1920s, the city quickly built Lake Griffy Reservoir, which was completed in 1924 and expanded in 1940. But Lake Griffy could not accommodate Bloomington's rapid expansion after World War II, so Lake Lemon, located nine miles northeast of the city, was built. Although Lake Lemon would boost the city's water supply by six-fold, it soon became evident that Lake Monroe Reservoir, completed in 1965, would be needed. Today, Lake Monroe abundantly serves the water needs for the area.

In 1940, Showers sold a portion of its then-200,000-square-foot complex to Radio Corp. of America, better known as RCA, which opened a factory that initially produced radios and later televisions. In 1949, the plant produced the first black-and-white TV and, in 1954, the first color set. In 1987, Thomson Consumer Electronics acquired the plant and the RCA name and eight years later marked the production of the plant's 65 millionth color TV. Within three years, however, the company succumbed to economic pressures and closed the plant and moved production operations to Mexico.

The factory would produce further innovation in the person of Sarkes Tarzian, the chief engineer of RCA's Bloomington operations. Tarzian left the company in 1944 to form his own company that would market an innovative radio system called Hi-Fam, a merging of the best features of AM and FM receivers. The market did not respond well to Hi-Fam, but did to another Tarzian product, the television tuner. By the end of the 1940s, his company was the nation's leading producer of TV tuners. On Armistice Day in 1949, Tarzian went on the air with the state's second television station, WTTV, which he based in Bloomington. The successful station since has been moved to Indianapolis and was sold by Tarzian for what was then the largest amount ever paid for an independent TV outlet, $26 million.

Since the end of World War II, Monroe County and Bloomington have undergone remarkable change, with the continued expansion of the university and the development of the city's "northern corridor," and its east and south sides, which were made possible by the creation of Lake Monroe. ⚘

Born in Bloomington in 1899, Hoagy Carmichael achieved international fame with compositions such as "Old Rockin' Chair," "Buttermilk Sky," and "Lazy River," and even as an actor in films such as *To Have and Have Not* and *The Best Years of Our Lives*. As an IU student, his favorite haunt was the Book Nook, a popular student hangout in the 1920s. Carmichael would hang out there for hours, pounding on the restaurant's piano. Photo courtesy of IU Archives.

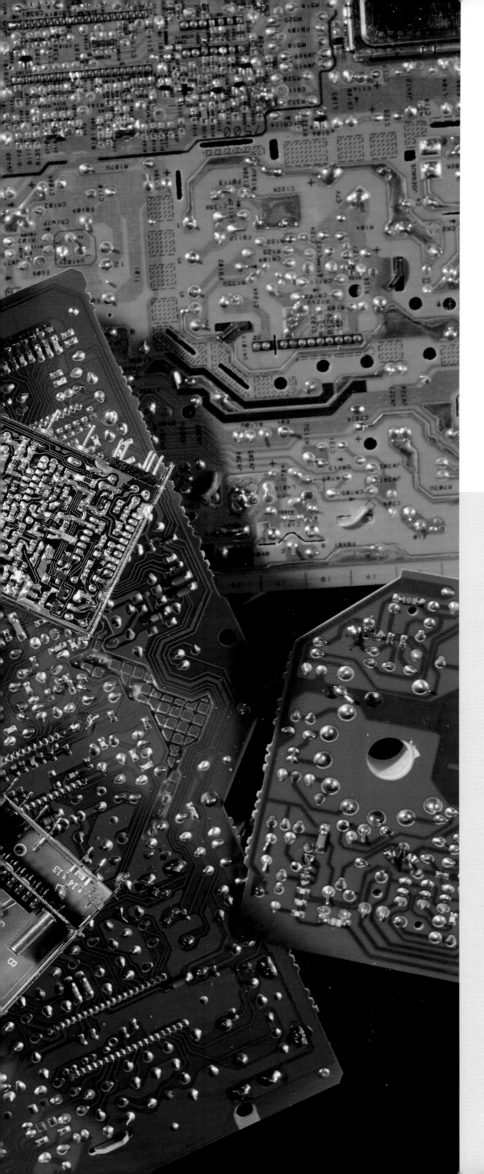

Chapter

3

Economy

*Our Diversified
Knowledge-based
Economy*

"One of the finest assets in this
community is its people, because of
their education and their wonder-
fully warm personalities. Before
coming to Bloomington, I had
about 200 people working for me
in Chicago and there was no com-
parison to the level of people you
find in Bloomington."

—Bill Cook
Pesident of Cook Group Inc.

HERE IS STILL PLENTY OF TIME TO

PLANT PERENN

HEY WILL PUT ON CO

THIS SEASON, MAINLY

SYSTEMS THAT WILL

BLOOMING PLANTS N

DAYLILIES

DAYLILIES ARE LONG-LIVED PERENNIALS THAT GROW ALMOST ANYWHERE UNDER MOST SOIL CONDITIONS AND REQUIRE LITTLE CARE... FEW DISEASE OR INSECT PROBLEMS

LONG, GRASS-LIKE FOLIAGE FORMS CLUMPS THAT MULTIPLY FREELY

SELECTING DIFFERENT VARIETIES GIVES AN EXTENDED BLOOM TIME...

LATE SPRING THROUGH FALL

SUN TO PARTIAL SHADE

PERENNIAL

SUN TO PARTIAL SHADE

DAYLILY

LONG-LIVED · HARDY · LOW MAINTENANCE

STELLA d'ORO

MINIATURE CONTINUOUS BLOOMER FOR BORDERS, CONTAINERS

15"

BLOOMS JUNE THROUGH FROST

$6

Indiana is a state where the production of durable goods serves as the foundation for its economy, and in the early 1960s, with the exception of the university, Bloomington's economy was very similar to those of other Hoosier cities. Production of television sets and radios was steady at RCA's enormous facility on South Rogers Street. Homegrown Sarkes Tarzian enjoyed a similarly strong demand for its tuners for TV sets.

Business was good at the Hotpoint and Westinghouse Electric factories on the city's emerging west side. New retail development to the east, later to culminate in one of southern Indiana's largest shopping malls, was well underway. Indiana University was nearing the peak of a remarkable expansion under the presidency of Herman B Wells. Considering the university's influences, it is not surprising that two new residents, who moved to Bloomington in 1963, a former medical products salesman and his wife, ultimately would have the greatest single impact on Bloomington as it approached the twenty-first century.

Bill and Gayle Cook, convinced that the hectic life of Chicago wasn't for them, began looking for a new place to live and grow a business in the spring of 1963. Bill already had been mildly successful with a start-up company that produced hypodermic needles. Gayle was an IU graduate with a fondness for Bloomington. In May, they

packed their Corvair, leaving Chicago behind. Two months later, they launched Cook Incorporated in a spare bedroom of their apartment. Beginning their company with an initial investment of $1,500, the Cooks began producing catheters, wire guides, and needles. With their first major sale to Illinois Masonic Hospital in Chicago, the Cooks and Bloomington turned the page on an interesting economic story that is far from over.

The Cooks' magic touch can be found all over Bloomington, as well as in nearby Ellettsville and Spencer. Cook Incorporated has spawned nearly 60 subsidiary companies worldwide, with products and services that include aviation, the production and worldwide distribution of medical instruments and fluids, plastic tubing, investments, real estate, charter transportation, and even professional sports and interior decorating. Though each company is independently responsible for its own physical resources, personnel, and financial performance,

In the spring of 1998, Cook Incorporated began construction on a new 70-acre corporate campus that it likens to Microsoft's or Nike's headquarters. The $30-million project will bring together a number of subsidiaries originally formed to meet a core need of the company, including Cook divisions in cardiology, radiology, critical care, surgical, and endovascular products. Shown here is a proposed rendering of the plant to be located in the Park 48 Business Park. Photo courtesy of Cook Incorporated.

Historically, Indiana is a state where the production of durable goods serves as the foundation for its economy, and with the exception of the university, Bloomington's economy is very similar to those of other Hoosier cities. Photo by Kendall Reeves.

each Cook firm benefits from shared technology and mutual product distribution channels.

One subsidiary, CFC Inc., has been involved in several major building renovations in downtown Bloomington, including Fountain Square Mall, which consists of buildings that were once the entire south side of Courthouse Square. The complex's 180,000 square feet house retail establishments, professional offices, and community rooms.

More Than Just a "College Town"

To the casual observer, Bloomington is a college town, and certainly IU is its largest employer. Nearly 6,400 area residents are employed by the university. Its annual budget is a gauge of IU's economic impact on Monroe County; in 1996-97 it neared $2 billion. The purchasing power of its 33,000 students of products, services, and housing also is vital to the economy. IU's workforce and other public sector employees account for more than a quarter of total county earnings.

Another important public employer is the Crane Division Naval Surface Warfare Center, which employs some 600 Monroe County residents, despite being about 25 miles away. The facility—which takes in nearly a third of Martin County—is seen by most in the region as another corporate leader in southern Indiana, as it encourages the rapid transfer of research and development into commercial as well as military products. Through a relatively new initiative, the "Buy Indiana" program, Crane has been inviting more southern Indiana firms to contend for the more than $300 million it spends each year.

"The economy is much more diversified than the people of Bloomington recognize it to be," comments Morton J. Marcus, director of the Indiana Business Research Center at IU. "The university is undoubtedly the biggest single unit because of its particular structure, and manufacturing is divided up into a lot of different companies, which obscures its importance. But these are important companies to this community, and that makes us much like the rest of the state. It also means that there is great cyclical sensitivity in that part of the economy."

Some of these employers have recognizable names, such as General Electric, Columbia House, and Otis Elevator, while others produce or distribute things we see or use every day, such as Hall Signs' highway markers, Sunrise/InterArt's greeting cards, TASUS's auto moldings, and PYA/Monarch's food products. The industrial base varies greatly, including several high-tech firms as well as traditional durable goods manufacturers.

For a community found deep in the heartland, Bloomington's companies have an international perspective, including more than a dozen with consistent export activity and eight that are foreign-owned. One locally based advertising company, Hirons & Co., has offices in Beijing and Shanghai, China, to serve other United States companies doing business in the rapidly expanding global market.

Recognized as one of the nation's leading universities, IU's enrollment has remained stable over the last several decades, which has made the university a steadying influence for the local economy. Monroe County historically has one of the lowest unemployment rates in the state.

City Unfailing in Facing Change

However, it does seem that Bloomington weathers a paradigm shift every few decades. Early in the twentieth century, the city's economy was greatly dependent upon two industries that took advantage of the area's abundant natural resources. Serving as a physical and economic foundation for Monroe and neighboring counties was limestone, a freestone abundant in the region that exhibits no preferential direction for splitting, and which can be cut and carved into a plethora of shapes and sizes. In the early 1900s, about 50 quarries, stone mills, and stonecutting plants operated in the region.

Skylines across the planet today continue to feature southern Indiana limestone, and it has found renewed popularity among building designers in recent years. Also in recent years, new commercial applications for limestone have been found in products ranging from windows to animal foods. A handful of stone companies continue to operate today in Monroe and neighboring Lawrence Counties. The other major employer, Showers Brothers Co., operated what was at one time the world's largest furniture factory, with its products made of wood.

However, World War II diminished the importance of the local limestone and furniture industries, when higher-tech manufacturers across the country were better able to take advantage of the war, in terms of technological advancement and innovation, capital accumulation, and profits. "I'm told that they actually made bombs out of limestone for air pilots to use to practice with," noted IU historian James Madison. Both limestone and wood were "natural resource-based industries, based on low technology and with low economies of scale, and not much return on investment."

Many corporations and charter air services maintain their own aircraft and hangars at the Monroe County Airport. Photo by Kendall Reeves.

After World War II, RCA and Sarkes Tarzian would be more technologically advanced, and several other manufacturing operations opened during the mid- to late-1950s. But within a few decades, market forces and economic realities that were becoming increasingly global in scope again had an impact on Bloomington.

First, Sarkes Tarzian, founded in Bloomington by a former RCA engineer, became one of the first American companies to move operations south of the Rio Grande River in Mexico in 1967. Strong competition from Japanese companies, however, forced the television components maker to divert more jobs away from Bloomington, and it ceased manufacturing operations here in 1977. Today, Carlisle Braking Systems, which produces braking products for motor vehicles, occupies the former Sarkes Tarzian plant.

In the late 1980s two of the city's largest employers were purchased by foreign concerns: RCA by French-owned Thomson S.A. in 1987 and Westinghouse Electric to Swiss-based Asea Brown Boveri (ABB) in 1989.

For ABB the acquisition of Westinghouse has proven to be a good fit, with the sole exception of its capacitor line. In 1993, ABB refined its operations, phasing out capacitors—which had been produced at the facility since the late 1950s—to focus on freestanding circuit breakers, reclosers, high-voltage fuses, and a new product—pad mounted switches.

Problems in the mid-1990s had fueled rumors that the plant would close, but relationships forged between its 250 employees and management have helped the company to position its Bloomington operations for a competitive global market, including trade destinations in South America and Africa.

February 13, 1997, was a day few in Bloomington will forget—the day Thomson S.A. announced that it would close its Bloomington television assembly plant and distribution center by April 1998, costing the city 1,300 jobs. Thomson would transfer its production of RCA and ProScan TV sets to Juarez, Mexico, joining many other companies that made similar moves. Until then, the RCA successor was the city's second largest manufacturer, operating the world's largest television assembly plant. Just two years before the announcement, the facility had produced its 65 millionth television, and four years before, the company had completed a 633,000-square-foot distribution center.

Located in the heart of Bloomington's Urban Enterprise Zone, Thomson had an annual payroll of more than $39 million. The company paid more than $1 million annually in property taxes and nearly $150,000 in county income tax revenue. But with Thomson's decision, the city suddenly found itself having to provide services and assistance to the displaced workers and immediately look for opportunities to replace the lost tax base and jobs.

Positioned For a New Century

"In many ways, Thomson was a defining moment for Bloomington, of where we are and what we're going to be like," comments Bloomington Mayor John Fernandez. "We have an opportunity to do this right, to take this site of the past 'industrial revolution,' and redevelop it into a site of future growth industries, knowledge-based, technology-oriented companies. If we can do that, then that's another major defining point in time for Bloomington as we go into the next millennium and a different economy. There's been a lot of discussion about the changing economy and this is really driving it home."

As of this book's writing, the 200-acre site and its 2 million square feet of manufacturing space had been placed on the market by Thomson in search of a buyer. Linda Williamson, director of the Bloomington Economic Development Corp., adds, "It was bad news for the people who worked there, but it allowed the community to step back and redevelop a site that had been declining. Everyone will come out stronger."

While the decision to close the plant came as a shock, it had been years in coming. Over its long history, the plant had employed as many as 7,000 people, but Thomson's labor force had been diminishing in size since 1980. At the same time, however, Bloomington's economy became more diversified, as evidenced by the varied kinds of products made here, as well as an eventual even ratio between industrial and nonindustrial employers. As a result, much of the growth in the local economy during this last decade has been broadly based.

Employment in health services, transportation, communications, finance, insurance, real estate, and construction have grown steadily in recent years. Bloomington Hospital, with a workforce approaching 2,400 people, is the city's third largest employer. Relatively new to Bloomington is Great West Casualty Insurance Co., which located a regional headquarters here in 1994 and has expanded its workforce nearly three-fold since then. High-tech related companies involved in computer services, products, and engineering account for 20 percent of all establishments in the city. Services account for 20.8 percent of local earnings, and durable goods manufacturing, 17.8 percent. During the first half of the 1990s, payroll employment in

Bloomington's eclectic variety of
stores, restaurants, and shops makes
it a strong regional draw for tourists.
Photo by Kendall Reeves.

(following page) For a community
found deep in the heartland, many
of Bloomington's companies have an
international perspective, including
more than a dozen with consistent
export activity and eight that
are foreign-owned. Photo by
Kendall Reeves.

Employment in health services, transportation, communications, finance, insurance, real estate, and construction have grown steadily in recent years. Photo by Kendall Reeves.

Skylines across the planet today continue to feature southern Indiana limestone, and it has found renewed popularity among building designers in recent years. Photo by Kendall Reeves.

Bloomington increased by more than 16 percent, much higher than the state's rate of 11 percent during the same period.

Fostering a Health Care "Silicon Valley"

The San Francisco Bay area and Seattle are known for their fast growing computer companies. Similarly Bloomington hopes it will be known for its contributions to medical treatment. Obviously, as the world's largest privately held medical device manufacturer, Cook Incorporated plays a leading role. In the spring of 1997, the company began construction on a new 70-acre corporate campus that it likens to Microsoft's or Nike's headquarters. The $30-million project will bring together a number of subsidiaries originally formed to meet a core need of the company, including Cook divisions in cardiology, radiology, critical care, surgical, and endovascular products.

In recent years, two new Cook products have hit United States and international markets with the potential for huge profits and market shares. One was Oxilan, a contrast medium fluid that, when exposed to fluoroscopic X-rays or a CAT scan, highlights blood vessels in patients. Cook also developed the first commercially available coronary stent, and in 1997 it received federal approval for a second-generation version. Coronary stents are stainless steel frames expanded with a balloon catheter inside an artery that has closed or appears likely to close following coronary angioplasty. By propping open the artery like a scaffold, coronary stents restore sufficient blood flow to the heart

muscle so that the majority of these patients do not need coronary artery bypass surgery.

Cook often has chosen to develop new companies to supply many of its needs, rather than go to outside suppliers in other parts of the country. For example, in 1969, Sabin Corp. was founded to produce and supply Cook with extruded plastic tubing. Today, Sabin itself is in an expansion mode, growing into a new 112,000-square-foot facility with additional room for expansion. When its medical products divisions are considered together as a group, Cook is the area's second largest manufacturing employer. But Cook also is beginning to serve as a magnet to other companies and initiatives involved in health care.

One recent example, KP Pharmaceutical Technologies, relocated to Bloomington to be close to IU and companies such as Cook and pharmaceutical giant Eli Lilly, which is based in Indianapolis. Formerly housed at the University of Kentucky, KP Pharmaceutical develops new formulations of prescription medicine for other drug companies, and consults with them on clinical research concerning supply, production, and dosage issues. Initial plans were to employ 40 people within three years, and eventually produce its own products. The company found appropriate facilities at the Bloomington Business Incubator STAR Center, just one of several area initiatives that help stimulate the start-up and expansion of light manufacturing and knowledge-based businesses.

Other Major Employers

Appliances were a major local product in the

Oliver Winery and Butler Winery have
cultivated well-established vineyards
that are enabling them to create
wines with a distinct southern Indiana
flavor and character. Photo by
Kendall Reeves.

1960s, and refrigerators are still made on the city's west side, although they now carry General Electric's nameplate and quality. The company is the area's sixth largest employer with about 3,200 workers, and its Bloomington facility became the world's largest side-by-side refrigerator factory after a $125-million expansion. Fortunately for Bloomington, side-by-side refrigerators are a growing segment of the market, thus boding well for the plant's future. The company used its Bloomington-made refrigerators to enter a difficult market for U.S. durable goods manufacturers—Japan. In 1995, GE signed a deal that marked the first time that an American appliance manufacturer would be selling products in Japan through an arrangement with a major retailer. Success in marketing Bloomington-made refrigerators has led GE to be able to market other products through Japan's second-largest appliance dealer.

Chances are the next time you ride up an elevator to your office or apartment, you will find the nameplate for Otis Elevator, a division of United Technologies. Otis, which employs 1,150 people at its Bloomington facility, is the world's largest manufacturer of elevators and escalators. Elevators made here have been installed in some prestigious locations, including the world's tallest building, the Petronas Towers in Kuala Lumpur, Malaysia; the 110-story World Trade Center in New York; the Eiffel Tower in Paris; and even in the Vatican in Rome. In 1997 the company was awarded a contract to provide energy-efficient elevators and escalators for the 52-story Conde Nast Building, the first major office tower built in New York in nearly a decade. The Bloomington plant will produce five elevators for what is being called the Big Apple's first environmentally conscious skyscraper.

PYA/Monarch, a subsidiary of Sara Lee Corp., in 1997 selected Bloomington as its new Midwest center for distributing its food products to national restaurant chains and eventually will employ more than 360 people. Columbia House, a mail-order business co-owned by Sony and Time Warner, recently completed a major expansion of its Bloomington operations. The company known for its music and video clubs has located its customer service center in a new $14-million structure near Cook's future headquarters, and its workforce will grow from 380 to nearly 1,050. TASUS is another growing company, producing plastic molded parts for the auto market.

In addition to Cook, several other companies have national headquarters in Bloomington. Sunrise/InterArt was founded in 1974 by three liberal arts college graduates who wanted to create and sell contemporary greeting cards. Today, the

company's cards and related products are marketed in the United States and Canada by a sales staff of more than 130. Sunrise contracts the work of more than 250 artists. Most recognizable among them is Mary Engelbreit, a Midwest artist who combines traditional values with a nostalgic approach that harkens to a simpler time, making her Sunrise's best-selling artist. In addition to cards, the company produces gift packaging, social books, stationery, and home decor accessories.

Contributing to Sunrise's success has been its creative approach to managing its workforce. It was one of the first companies in the area to offer flex-time and other benefits such as a four-day weekend once a month. At a time when the greeting card industry generally experiences few if any significant gains, Sunrise's sales are growing rapidly. Between 1991 and 1997, its sales tripled.

Since moving to a new 83,000-square-foot headquarters and manufacturing facility in 1996, Hall Signs, Inc. has expanded past its traditional core business as one of the nation's leading manufacturers of highway signs and accessories. The company has also moved into customized signs for private enterprises.

The Agency for Instructional Technology (AIT), a nonprofit organization originally founded with funding from the U.S. Office of Education in 1963, produces instructional materials such as videos and CD-ROMs and publishes a quarterly journal. AIT

Taking a leadership role for the city's business community is the Greater Bloomington Chamber of Commerce, which offers many services such as an annual trade show. Photo by Kendall Reeves.

decided to remain in Bloomington after an extensive national search for a new headquarters. Today it produces more than 2,500 titles for use in schools in the United States and Canada.

K&W Products, a producer of auto care products, relocated its headquarters here from California.

Tourism and Retail Trade

Tourism is important to Bloomington and the region's economy. According to one study, visitors to the area for its many festivals, concerts, sporting events, museums, and conventions poured an estimated $156 million into the local economy in 1996. One event that year, a national softball tournament, brought an estimated $556,000 into the economy. Nearly 4,500 local jobs are attributed to tourism, which accounted for an estimated total annual income of $73.6 million that year.

During the summer, the IU campus opens its otherwise vacant dormitory rooms for convention guests, including national gatherings of the Boy Scouts, Junior Achievement, and religious groups. This augments community efforts to attract the softball tournaments and other recreational sports events.

Valerie Peña, executive director of the Bloomington/Monroe County Convention & Visitors Bureau, points out that three-quarters of the revenue brought in by visitors comes from overnight guests. "We have a lot of research that shows that the majority of our visitors come five to six times a year. So Bloomington is more than a one-time destination," Peña said. "We believe that if we can get them here once or twice, we seem to do well in keeping them in the loop."

Similarly, people here recognize that arts and culture, while enriching everyone's lives, also have a significant economic impact. A 1995 study found that arts and culture contributed directly more than $20 million and indirectly more than $33 million into the local economy.

Bloomington's eclectic variety of stores, restaurants, and shops makes it a strong regional draw for tourists and those from nearby counties. Shopping and food purchases represent more than half of Monroe County's total estimated tourist expenditures, and the city traditionally has one of the highest per-capita retail activity rates in the state. College Mall, operated by Simon DeBartolo on the city's east side, has been a strong anchor for much of the community's retail activity since the early 1970s. Unlike other cities where large suburban shopping areas have killed the downtown, Bloomington has a vibrant commercial scene in the blocks surrounding Courthouse Square. Soon, another major shopping center, Whitehall Crossing,

will better serve residents to the west and those traveling along Indiana 37, a major four-lane highway that will become part of a new interstate route running from Indianapolis to Evansville. "This highway eventually will provide Bloomington with a direct transportation route to both Canada and Mexico, fostering its growing international market," said Steve Howard, president of the Greater Bloomington Chamber of Commerce.

Fertile Ground for Small Business

Back in 1963, when Bill and Gayle Cook formed the company that later became a corporate empire, they were able to approach the Greater Bloomington Chamber of Commerce and receive information on the region's opportunities, attractions, economy, and workforce. Today, even more community and university programs are available to new and existing members of the Bloomington business community, most of them small in size. "The vast majority of businesses here are small businesses. In fact, 75 percent of our members are small businesses," said Howard. "While large businesses and their financial impact are obvious, the small businesses are the unsung heroes of this economy."

A resource to small companies is the city's business incubator, the STAR Center, which is designed to help start-up businesses by offering space, shared services, and management assistance. Founded in 1994 as a public-private partnership, the center also houses the Small Business Development Center, which itself offers one-on-one consulting to existing businesses in areas such as business planning, marketing, and other aspects needed for success.

Taking a leadership role for the city's business community is the Chamber, which offers many services such as help in dealing with problems related to new technology. "The presence of a very well-educated populace has led to the development of many new businesses in Bloomington that focus on being knowledge-based rather than manufacturers. Particularly noticeable are the publishing and software industries," added Howard.

Three local small companies that are successful in quenching local thirsts are Oliver Winery, Butler Winery, and Bloomington Brewing Company. Over the last 25 years, the two wineries learned to produce with great success wines made from grapes or juice purchased outside the area. But in recent years, the two wineries have cultivated well-established vineyards that are enabling them to create wines with a distinct southern Indiana flavor and character.

Since November 1994, Bloomington Brewing Company has been making and selling five beers

and ales on site, as well as in other restaurants owned by its parent company, One World Enterprises, and other city locations. As part of a national trend, it is very likely that other brewing companies soon will join Bloomington Brewing Company in providing a tasty alternative to nationally distributed beers.

In 1996, IU consolidated a number of its community business outreach activities at its Research Park. It is also home to several companies—most involving computer software or hardware design applications—which occupy the former Showers factory in downtown Bloomington. The Industrial Research Liaison Program provides guidance and sometimes technical expertise to firms with research needs. The Indiana Business Research Center draws upon its extensive economic and population databases to provide information services for state and local governments and industry. The IU Center for Entrepreneurship and Innovation works with new companies and helps them benchmark success. On

the IU campus, many more programs are available in its nationally recognized schools of business and public and environmental affairs.

With the influence of forward-thinking people like Bill Cook and many others in the area and at IU, Bloomington is poised to take advantage of changes yet to come in science, medical knowledge, and technology. ⚚

Monroe County's abundant resources and quality of life make it a great place to raise a family, build a business, and call home. Photo by Kendall Reeves.

Chapter 4

Education

*Our Lifetime
of Learning*

"*In a community with an important,
nationally recognized university, a
forward-thinking state vocational
college, and two strong public
school systems, you would expect
the value on education to be quite
high. The climate for education in
Monroe County is good, and all of
the educational institutions both
reflect and contribute to that.*"

—John Coomer
   Superintendent of the Monroe County
   Community School Corp.

The Lilly Library houses one of the finest collections of rare books and personal papers in the world. Included among its exhaustive collection are rare Gutenberg and Coverdale Bibles, the writings of Martin Luther, and the complete series of scripts for each of the *Star Trek* television shows. Photo by Rich Remsberg.

Few communities can boast as long and as deep

a commitment to education as Bloomington. As home to Indiana University (IU), the oldest public university west of the Allegheny Mountains, this southern Indiana city is forever associated with the state's advancement. With the university's influence, Bloomington has developed into one of the best educational environments in the Midwest. Edward B. Fiske, former education editor of *The New York Times*, named Bloomington one of the nation's top 10 college towns, noting its "rich mixture of atmospherics and academia."

But there's more here than a great Big Ten university. Monroe County also is home to a thriving campus of Ivy Tech State College—the state's first statewide vocational technical college—2 high-quality public school systems, and 14 privately managed primary and secondary schools. Today, 90 percent of Monroe County residents have earned a high school education, and 60 percent have completed some college, with an average educational level of 14.2 years.

In 1997, the 179-year-old Monroe County Public Library was rededicated after being tripled in size. The following year, the Monroe County Historical Museum—itself the county's first public library built in the 1920s with Carnegie Foundation funds—reopened after a 20-month expansion project.

Education is so much a hallmark of this community that in 1997 *Fortune* magazine listed Bloomington as the fourth best-educated city in America. "More and more people from outside this community are recognizing the exceptional educational opportunities that Bloomington offers," says Myles Brand, IU's president. "The quality available here, at every level, makes it easier for us to attract top-notch faculty and graduate students. Though often said, it continues to ring true that we have the best of both worlds: an educated and cosmopolitan community in a beautiful and friendly small town."

From the county's beginnings, its citizenry has expressed support for education through action. In the same year that Monroe County was established—1818—children began attending school in the crude log county courthouse. Because the courthouse later would be needed to conduct governmental affairs, a

separate schoolhouse was built in 1819 near where IU later would be located. Yet, the public education infrastructure now in place could easily have been greatly diminished had early events gone differently.

The 1816 federal act providing for the admission of Indiana into the Union contained language designating Perry Township in Monroe County "for the use of a seminary of learning." However, the Indiana constitution inhibited the sale of any lands for school purposes for four more years, and when the legislature met in the winter of 1819, there was good reason for local concern about how much support the university really had statewide. Although another township, in Gibson County, had been designated for the earlier established Vincennes University, that institution lacked sufficient funds, teachers, buildings, and even students. A political feud had led to Monroe County's inclusion into Indiana's petition for statehood. Because Monroe County was attached to other counties for its representation, none of its citizens would be among those traveling to the state's first capital, Corydon, to vote on legislation about a state school. Historian James Albert Woodburn, in his history of Indiana University, recalled: "The men of Bloomington were not satisfied with the posture of affairs. . . . The people determined to have an agent from Bloomington on the ground—a member of the Third House, if you will."

That agent would be Dr. David H. Maxwell, a native Kentuckian who penned Indiana's first constitution, and who had turned his attention to Monroe County after the document's passage. He had been among those who acquired land at the

first sale of Bloomington lots in 1818, and had moved here a year later from the Ohio River town of Madison. "No record or tradition remains to tell the full story of what Maxwell did to secure legislative action in behalf of a state school," Woodburn wrote of Maxwell. But Maxwell, today considered the "Father of the Indiana University," must have been excited on that first Monday in December 1819, to hear Governor Jonathan Jennings express his support for the sale of land for what later became IU. Yet, after the bill's introduction and second and third hearings on December 31, the matter of a state school would not be discussed until January 11, 1820, when it was passed with "sundry amendments."

Four days later, in a Senate committee, Senator William Drew moved to amend the proposed legislation by removing from it the crucial provision that 2,000 acres of township land in Monroe County be forever reserved "as a glebe" for use by the seminary. Historian Thomas D. Clark reports that Drew "represented a considerable bloc of Indiana public opinion. He was a large landholder and lawyer, strong-willed and of impressive personality." A final committee vote on January 18 reveals how close the seminary bill came to failing passage: a five-five deadlock would be broken by a favorable vote cast by the president of the Senate, Lieutenant Governor Ratliff Boon. The bill subsequently passed back and forth between the Senate and House, with Drew aggressively seeking its defeat. "The celerity with which it was sent from chamber to chamber reminds us that there was a man on the ground especially interested in its final

success," Woodburn wrote. Interestingly, the version of the bill that passed on January 20, 1820, while providing for the organization of a state seminary, never actually discusses the school itself.

Its future rested entirely on decisions made by its trustees. Among them was Maxwell, whom the trustees elected as their board's first president. "The thing that interests me," said Thomas D. Clark, a University of Kentucky historian who was commissioned to research and prepare a history for IU's sesquicentennial in 1970, "is these people came out here in the woods, settled down near a land grant and kindled a flame of learning. It was a very weak, flickering flame, but they nurtured it and brought it to a big, significant flame." In 1838, Indiana College became Indiana University, and its board was expanded to ten members, including six Monroe County residents.

Since then, IU has been a case study in educational excellence. But its early years were troubled. A fire on All Fools' Day in 1854 destroyed the college building and its 1,200-volume collection of rare books. The fire occurred under suspicious circumstances, but town citizens, students, alumni, and faculty immediately set out to raise funds for a new building, which was completed in 1859. A second building for the science department, built in the late 1870s, was destroyed by another major fire—this time caused by lightning—in July 1883. That fire resulted in the loss of a 12,000-book library, an extensive collection of fossils, other valuable items, and a decision by university administrators to move the campus. A 20-acre tract—described as "unsurpassed in the state for

IU operates year-round with the Bloomington campus having nearly 325 degree programs, including 214 at the advanced level. About 7,500 degrees are awarded each year to graduates taught by nearly 1,540 faculty members. More than 70 of its academic programs are ranked in the top 20 by various publications and peer studies. Photo by Rich Remsberg.

its natural beauty and fitness for the purpose"—was purchased in Dunn's Woods and three buildings were constructed; they are now part of the university's historic Old Crescent section of campus. There had been talk of moving the campus since the 1870s, due to increased activity downtown. The new location would allow for the expansion that has come since 1888.

In its early years, women were not accepted into Indiana College or later into IU. A second seminary was founded in 1833 by county residents devoted to teaching young women, and it was the first school of its kind in the state, operating until 1863. In 1867, as IU trustees began to consider the admission of women on equal terms with men, Sarah Parke Morrison presented a petition without knowledge of the discussion taking place within the university. She was admitted the following autumn and became IU's first female graduate in 1869. "At that time, no other state university had adopted the system of co-education," commented the 1904 history of the university. "Indiana University was, among the state universities, the pioneer in this movement." Later, in 1895, Marcellus Neal would become IU's first African-American graduate.

During the winter of 1894-95, strong consideration was given to relocating IU away from Bloomington to Indianapolis. At a building dedication in January 1895, some local residents reacted angrily to students wearing badges supporting the move to the capital city. According to an excited report in the school newspaper, the *Indiana Daily Student*, residents removed the badges from the students there at the ceremony. Debate grew fierce on the issue, but the clinching argument for keeping IU in Bloomington was an existing covenant between university trustees and Monroe County. The agreement, ratified by state legislators in 1855, was a pledge that IU would remain in Bloomington forever. Early in the twentieth century, debate periodically resumed about moving the university, due to Bloomington's water shortage problems, but, again, the agreement was kept.

With the appointment of Herman B Wells as its 12th president in 1937, IU began its transformation from a modest-sized Midwestern state university into a major research and teaching institution. Under Wells, the university experienced its greatest growth and widened its scope to encompass the globe.

Even before the conclusion of World War II and the passage of the GI Bill, Wells realized that many returning soldiers would want to receive a college education. Between 1919 and 1950, the number of full-time students attending classes at IU Bloomington grew from 2,356 to 13,489, or an

Few communities can boast as long and as deep a commitment to education as Bloomington. As home to Indiana University, the oldest public university west of the Allegheny Mountains, this southern Indiana city is forever associated with the state's advancement. Photo by Kendall Reeves.

increase of more than 500 percent. Today, IU Bloomington has a total enrollment of about 34,000 students, but this probably would not have occurred without Wells' vision.

He appealed to European scholars when their countries were overrun by invading armies, and many of them took refuge in Bloomington, enriching the university community and fostering an international flavor in Bloomington that remains today. Thirty-six years after his retirement as president in 1962, Wells—who subsequently was given the elevated title of university chancellor—remains a beloved and visible figure on campus.

Over its 175-plus years, IU has gone from offering only courses in Greek and Latin to providing a varied and high-quality curricula covering nearly every area of knowledge not only at Bloomington, but also at seven other regional campuses statewide. Today, IU operates year-round with the Bloomington campus having nearly 325 degree programs, including 214 at the advanced level. About 7,500 degrees are awarded each year to graduates taught by nearly 1,540 faculty members. Sometimes called the "Mother of College Presidents," IU has had nearly 200 alumni appointed to the presidencies of colleges and universities, as well as many more

who have risen to become top executives at many of the nation's leading companies. More than 70 of its academic programs are ranked in the top 20 by various publications and peer studies. Its business, fine arts, journalism, music, optometry, and library and information science programs consistently rank among the top 10 in publications as varied as *Money*, *BusinessWeek*, and *U.S. News & World Report*. In fact, *U.S. News & World Report* regularly includes IU as one of the best values in higher education. "That's a fine university," sums up Hugh Davis Graham, coauthor of a recent national study, *The Rise of American Research Universities*, which listed IU eighth best in terms of research strength. Today, IU prides itself not only on the service it provides the state, but on how it has undergone a revolution to become "America's new public university," poised to meet the global challenges of a new millennium.

Nestled between Bloomington and Ellettsville is a regional campus of Ivy Tech State College, which offers a variety of associate and certificate degree programs designed to enhance job prospects for many Hoosiers. With an enrollment of about 2,300, the fully accredited Bloomington campus offers two-year degrees in accounting, business

In 1997, the 179-year-old Monroe County Public Library was rededicated after being tripled in size. Photo by Kendall Reeves.

Bloomington is a college town, and
through the university, it stays forever
young. Photo by Rich Remsberg.

With Indiana University's influence, Bloomington has developed into one of the best educational environments in the Midwest. Photo by Rich Remsberg.

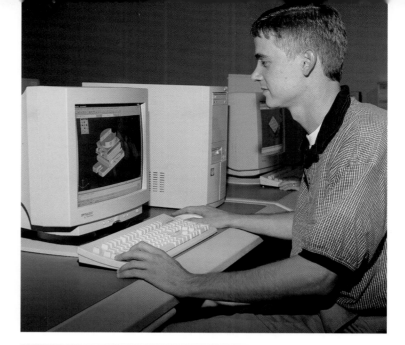

administration, computer information systems, electronics, industrial maintenance, nursing, and several vocational fields. For the majority of its students—area working people in their mid-20s to early 30s—the traditional college experience proved elusive after high school or simply was not desired. Thomas Jordan, the campus's executive dean, points to another surprising statistic: about 30 percent of those enrolled at the Bloomington campus already hold a baccalaureate or higher-level degree.

Jordan proudly tells the story of one recent Ivy Tech alumna who already had an MBA and a successful business career, but wanted to become a nurse. She was one of 30 people selected from hundreds of applicants for the campus's nursing program, successfully completed the two-year program, and today is caring for patients in a Florida hospital.

School placement records indicate that 95 percent of Ivy Tech graduates either find new employment or move up the ranks with their present employer, and in some programs that figure rises to 100 percent. The size of its student body has been growing at between 15 to 20 percent annually during the 1990s, making it the fastest growing campus among the 22 in the Ivy Tech system. Created through legislative action in 1963, Ivy Tech offered its first training program two years later, after the appointment of a state board of trustees and a president, but it would not be until 1971 that students at Bloomington would be awarded the first certificate degrees in nursing.

Several other programs were added during the 1980s, particularly after the Bloomington campus entered into a unique partnership with the Hoosier Hills Career Center, which serves high schools in six area school systems. Under the pilot project, a continuous curriculum was developed so students at Hoosier Hills could continue their vocational training without interruption at Ivy Tech, and programs in refrigeration, heating, and air-conditioning were moved to Ivy Tech. In 1997, the Ivy Tech system entered into a transfer agreement with Indiana State University so its associate degree recipients can go directly on to earn four-year bachelor's degrees from the Terre Haute-based institution.

In addition to its continuing education and vocational programs, Ivy Tech offers specialized training designed for employees of major area employers. For example, the college developed special classes in leadership, communication, and conflict resolution for at least one major manufacturer.

Rather than require these student-employees to leave the job site to attend classes, Ivy Tech offers the training program where it can best be applied—on the plant floor. Like IU, Ivy Tech is taking

advantage of emerging technologies, such as video conferencing and other distance learning tools, to offer students better access to the training and knowledge the international marketplace demands. In the next five years, the Bloomington campus of Ivy Tech will find a new home at Park 48, a corporate park it will share with the headquarters of Cook Incorporated, one of the world's leading producers of medical instruments and fluids.

At the secondary education level, the Hoosier Hills Career Center offers hands-on training in automotive body repair, building trades, food preparation, machining, and several other vocational areas. It allows students from four counties to earn academic credit towards a high school diploma while developing marketable skills that can lead to good-paying jobs.

The county's primary and secondary schools are another component of what makes Bloomington so attractive to those living here. In 1863, E. D. Hunter established the first graded school in Bloomington, with classes meeting in an old tannery building on South College Avenue. Prior to that time, children attended classes in various township schools, often in traditional one-room schoolhouses, private homes, churches, and the second stories of business buildings. As the city's population grew, so did the need for greater educational facilities. The tannery building was demolished for the construction in 1873 of Central School, a thoroughly modern building for the times. Kate Hight, one of the school's teachers, remembered its first day: "Long before the bell rang from the high tower, children

Monroe County is home to the thriving campus of Ivy Tech State College—the state's first statewide vocational technical college. Ivy Tech offers a variety of associate and certificate degree programs designed to enhance job prospects for many Hoosiers. In the upcoming future, Ivy Tech will find a new home at Park 48 Corporate Park. Photo by Kendall Reeves. Rendering courtesy of The Odle McGuire & Shook Corp.

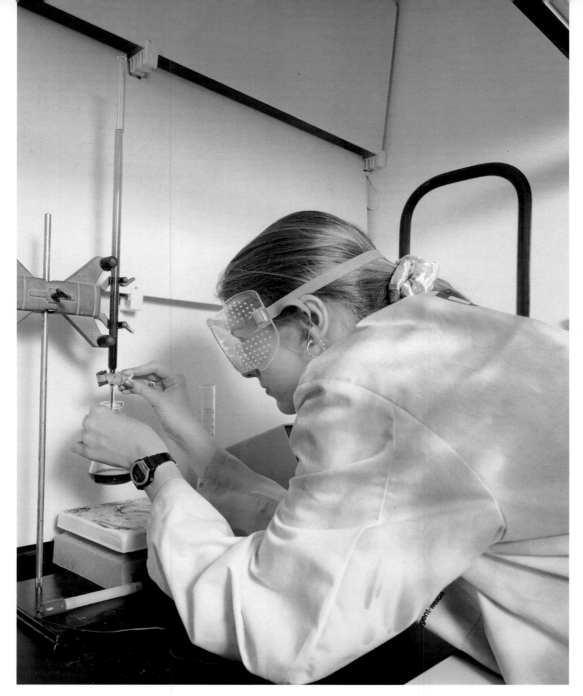

Indiana Department of Education statistics regularly show Monroe County Community School Corporation in the top 10 among the state's 293 school districts in terms of SAT scores, and more than 20 students are named National Merit Scholars each year. Photo by Kendall Reeves.

were coming from all directions, eager to see the splendors of the new building—the only school house in town. The children trouped up the grand stone steps to the big front doors, invitingly spread, breathlessly up the long iron stairs into the modern cloak rooms, with hooks for each and every child, and on into the spacious rooms to meet a smiling teacher." Central School, which served all grades through high school, had eight teachers and was considered by many to be the best school in the state, if not in the Midwest.

In 1897, Bloomington purchased IU's old Seminary Building—the university's original building—for use as its first high school. However, it would not be long before there would be a need for a new high school, and in 1914 a new one was built next to the Seminary Building. After a third Bloomington High School (today the site of Bloomington High School South) was built further south on College Avenue in 1965, the second high school was converted for use as a junior high school, only to be destroyed in a fire two years later. Today, much of the land where these

buildings once stood is used as a park appropriately named Seminary Square.

Today, the Monroe County Community School Corporation (MCCSC) is the state's 14th largest public school district with more than 10,500 students enrolled. The system, which includes 2 high schools, 2 middle schools, and 14 elementary schools, produces students who frequently go on to pursue higher education. Nearly 70 percent of MCCSC graduates are college bound, including many who remain in Bloomington to attend IU or Ivy Tech. Indiana Department of Education statistics regularly show MCCSC in the top 10 among the state's 293 school districts in terms of SAT scores, and more than 20 students are named National Merit Scholars each year. A report on the city's workforce commented, "The success of Bloomington's primary and secondary schools can be attributed to the community's acceptance of educational experimentation and dedication to lifelong learning." *Expansion Management*, a publication aimed at expanding businesses, agreed and has twice rated MCCSC one of the

best of 770 school districts it examined nationwide. In 1997, it was one of two school systems in Indiana given the distinction of a "blue ribbon" rating, extended to systems achieving high academic results without spending exorbitant amounts of money.

This isn't to say that Bloomington residents aren't making an investment in their future. During the 1990s, four elementary schools were replaced with multimillion-dollar buildings. Bloomington High School South underwent an extensive $32-million renovation, growing by 75,000 square feet and 29 new classrooms. An alternative high school was established in 1995 and expanded in 1997, and a third middle school is being built to further improve the attention given pupils by teachers. The average teacher in the system has more than 16 years of professional experience and three-fourths of MCCSC's 614 teachers have a master's degree. "I find in a college town an educational mind-set and that education is highly valued. That helps create a positive environment for public schools," comments MCCSC Superintendent John Coomer, who led school

systems in two other university communities before coming to Bloomington. Students respond through accomplishment—not only on the football field or basketball court, but also in national science olympiads and academic decathlons and international academic competitions. A team of students from Bloomington South gained international attention for their design of a bicycle that efficiently incorporates the use of solar energy. Shortly after winning a competition in Japan, members of the bike team already were at work improving their design for next year. "That's one of the things I like about high school kids," Bloomington South biology and physics teacher Paul Farmer told a reporter. "Their minds are always going."

Children living in the northwestern portion of Monroe County attend schools in the Richland-Bean Blossom Community School Corporation. While smaller, Richland-Bean Blossom schools pride themselves on offering a fundamental curriculum that, like MCCSC, pays attention to preparing graduates for the world of work. Organized in 1966, the district includes four schools: elementary, middle,

Honey Creek School, a one-room schoolhouse that was closed in 1945, was reopened in 1976 as a living history laboratory for Monroe County elementary age students, who attend all-day sessions to learn what learning used to be like. Photo by Kendall Reeves.

Each spring, students from the area spend a week at Bradford Woods, an IU camp located on 2,400 wooded acres in the gentle, folded knolls of Morgan County. It is home to the National Center for Accessibility, a leader in the movement to include people with disabilities in recreation, parks, and tourism. Photo by Kendall Reeves.

and high schools located in Ellettsville, and an elementary school in Stinesville.

Private schools in Bloomington offer educational options that are less conventional. The Bloomington Montessori School offers an alternative elementary school environment that focuses on the individuality of each child, allowing students to learn at their own pace. Harmony School is recognized by educators around the country for its successful programs and policies that prepare young people to play a meaningful role in society. Saint Charles School, which has been in continuous operation since its founding in 1923, prides itself on its low student/teacher ratio for the 450 children enrolled in kindergarten through eighth grade. For those with special needs, there is the Bloomington dePaul School, which offers intensive programs for those with dyslexia and other learning disabilities.

While both county school systems are well oriented towards academia, teachers, administrators, and local employers in recent years recognized a growing need to better prepare young people for the new and technological workplace. One successful program has been Tech Prep, an innovative program that provides high school students with academic and technological foundations for working in business, health, industrial, and applied science fields. Many participate in a graded internship program that gives students hands-on experience with area companies, including Otis Elevator and General Electric.

A newer initiative, School-to-Careers, is a federally funded effort that partners the school systems with area companies to improve students' preparation for secondary education or employment after graduation. David Frye, assistant superintendent for MCCSC, said his system's elementary school children learn about such "life skills" through exercises that are interwoven throughout the curriculum. They often focus on interpersonal communication, the concept of accountability and important values needed in life. "The effort to bring business into education has existed in the community for a number of years, so there's quite a bit going on," notes Diane Gregory, executive director of the Community Alliance for Lifelong Learning. "We emphasize to youngsters, that from the early grades they need to be thinking about someday when they will be in a career, and they need to be doing some planning for that," Coomer adds. "They need to be getting in mind the fact that what they're doing in school is preparing themselves for a career on down the line, both in their attitude towards attendance and punctuality as well as what they learn." Many area students from low-income families are pledging to remain free of drugs, alcohol, and involvement

in criminal activity, and get good grades. In exchange, they will get a college education, tuition-free, thanks to the state-funded 21st Century Scholars Program. "We are really trying to demystify the notion of kids being able to go to college and their parents thinking, 'This can never happen to my child,' because it can," says local program coordinator Debora Frazier.

In addition to what Monroe County's "lifelong learners" receive in the classroom, there are abundant educational resources available through Monroe County Public Library branches in Bloomington and Ellettsville, the Monroe County Historical Museum, and another outreach project, WonderLab. At present, WonderLab is a traveling, interactive, and hands-on museum that makes science fun for children and adults alike. Soon, it will be housed on property donated by the City of Bloomington that will, as WonderLab President Catherine Olmer puts it, help make the downtown "a family-focused area." It will be located within a few blocks of the newly expanded public library and historical museum. Today, a public library is more than simply books and periodicals, and Monroe County's library is no exception. The education section of *The New York Times* noted that its reference department is one of the best of its kind in the country, due to its computer on-line facilities. *Library Journal* cited the library for having one of the top 10 web sites for children in the country. It is a library that is very user-friendly— 64 percent of county residents have library cards— and it has the highest circulation rate of any library in the state.

The Monroe County Historical Museum, at the corner of Sixth and Washington Streets, reopened in September 1998, having grown from 8,000 to 20,000 square feet, and better able to relate the county's history and the activities of its people.

The opportunities for lifelong learning seem to be endless here, as offered by excellent primary and secondary schools, one of the nation's finest universities, and another college that offers training according to local needs. These excellent institutions are supported by a strong resource network that involves extensive libraries, creative museum programming, and a deeply ingrained belief that all of this is important. Bloomington is a community committed to learning and providing for the needs of future generations. ⚘

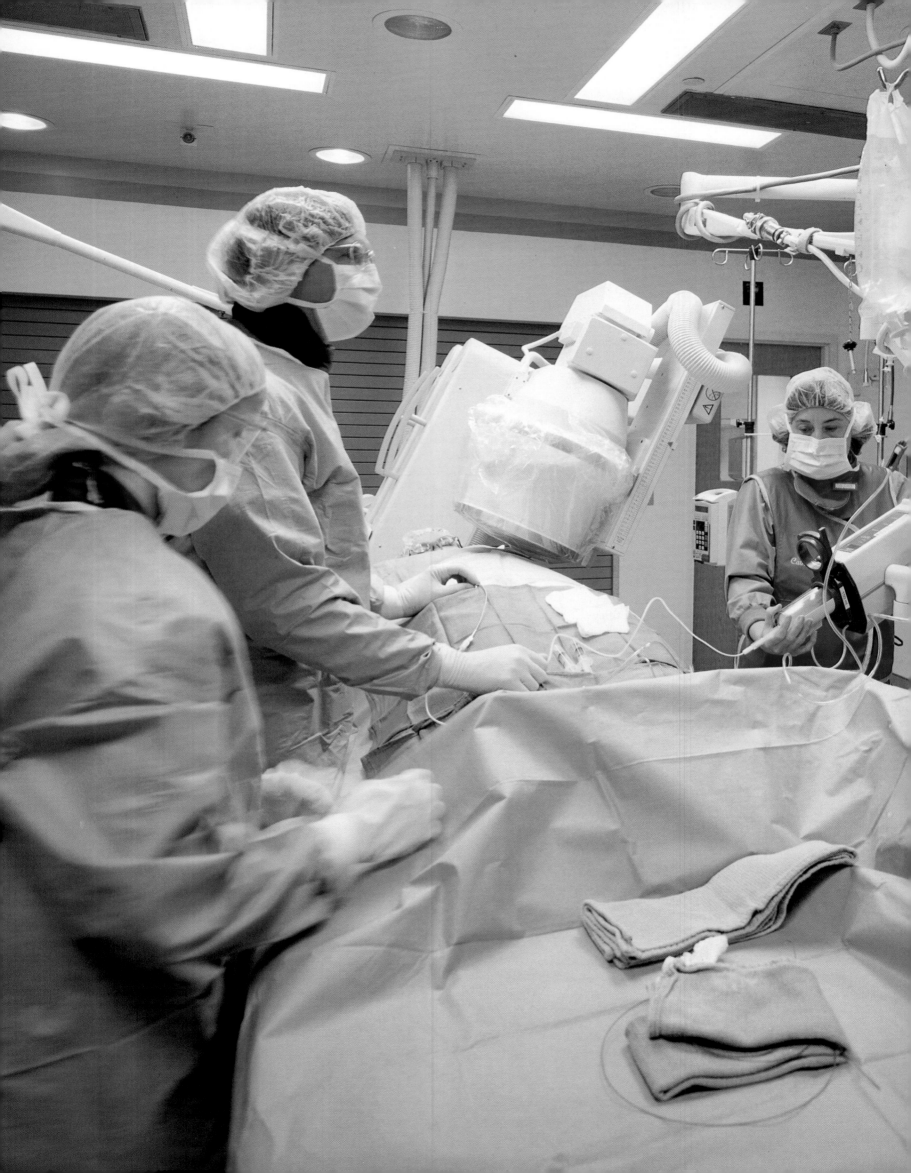

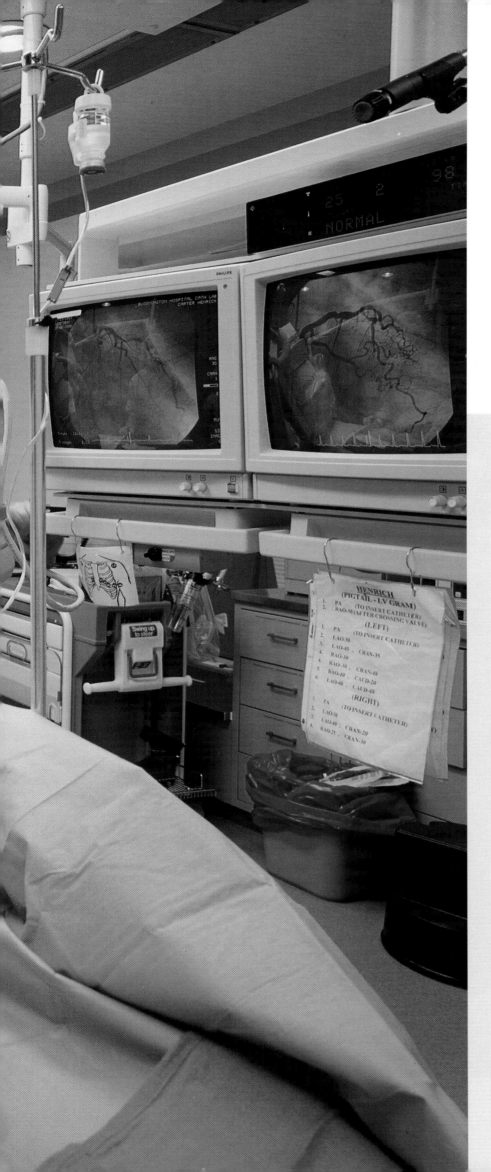

5

Health Care

*Caring for the Health Care
Needs of Our People*

*"I would have to say that, given all the
conflicting external pressures which
face the various providers of health care
services, Monroe County residents generally can feel assured that they have
access to an exceptionally high quality
of care that remains locally directed.
Nearly every medical specialty is represented by our local physicians—the
majority being board-certified.
Bloomington Hospital offers a full
range of acute care services. And there
continues to be competitive development by the hospital and others of a
variety of post-hospital services, including home health and long-term care.
Other opportunities exist, for example,
in alternative and complementary
medicine. But overall, I believe that the
current status of health care services in
Monroe County represents a strong
community asset."*

—*Nancy Carlstedt*
President of Bloomington Hospital

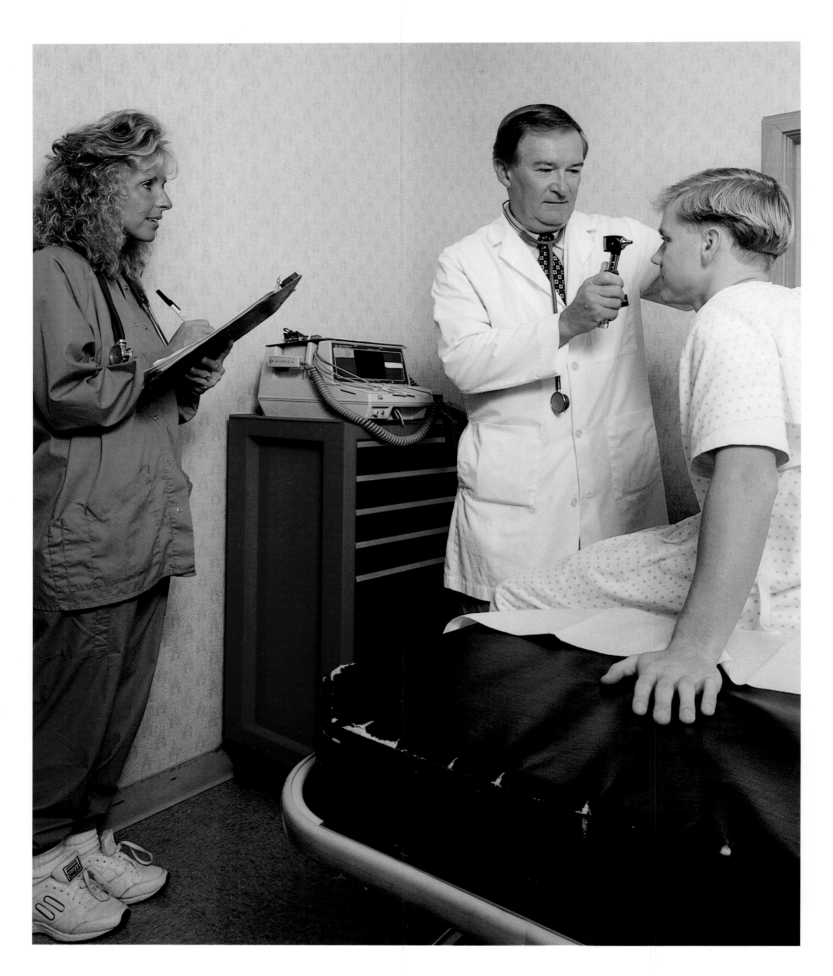

It was tragic news that the editor of the *Bloomington Telephone* had rushed to get into print, despite the fact that the paper already was filled with news of the upcoming presidential election. Early the night before, on October 31, 1904, a railroad cook named Lawrence Mitts had decided to walk to his family home in New Albany, Indiana, temporarily leaving his job in Owen County. While passing through the area near Bloomington along a railroad track, Mitts, who had been drinking, opted to take a rest and soon fell asleep. Sadly, a train came along, crushing the 32-year-old man's legs below the knees. "Railroad men tenderly cared for him and he was brought to the station," related a front-page article in the paper's November 1 edition. Dr. E. C. Harris happened to be at the rail station as Mitts was brought in on a train and subsequently was taken to Harris's office at the Avenue Hotel. There, he and another doctor worked all night to save Mitts, but by five o'clock that morning, the article said, "The spirit of one more unfortunate took its flight."

Local legend has it that Mitts's tragic death, which may have been avoided had there been a hospital in Bloomington, moved city residents to establish such a facility. Later the same day that Mitts died, the Local Council of Women of Bloomington voted to begin collecting funds for a nonprofit community hospital. A year later, in 1905, a two-story brick home and four acres of land on the city's west side were purchased, and a 10-bed hospital was opened. In 1918 a foundation was laid for a new 35-bed limestone hospital building. By 1965 and after two expansions, the original little brick house was torn down to make room for a new, five-story, 147-bed facility. Today, Bloomington Hospital remains the core for a fully modern, multifacility medical organization that serves as a regional referral center for residents in Monroe and eight surrounding counties. In addition, the city has several other progressive, high-quality treatment centers that are unparalleled in southwestern Indiana.

Like the Local Council of Women—who sold their stake in the hospital in 1987 but remain involved in how hospital assets are managed—residents here are more involved in health care issues than people in most cities. One recent example of this was the establishment of the Community Health Access Program (CHAP), one of very few clinics in Indiana that care for indigent patients without federal funding. The CHAP clinic was a broad-based response to health care needs for the poor and for those without insurance coverage. It evolved from various discussions between health care professionals, public officials, and private citizens in Bloomington, which all pointed to the need for an organized approach to indigent health

(previous page) Bloomington Hospital is a multifacility campus, providing high quality inpatient and outpatient care to residents of Bloomington, Monroe County, and the region. Photo by Kendall Reeves.

(left) For a community its size, Bloomington has a large number of highly skilled doctors, including several who are faculty members (and graduates) of the Indiana University School of Medicine in Indianapolis, which has been called by *U.S. News & World Report* one of the nation's best. Photo by Kendall Reeves.

care that also was cost-effective. Managed by the Public Health Nursing Association, it is a broad-based community response, because many area physicians contribute their time on a regular basis and greatly discount the cost of their services. Bloomington Hospital provides in-kind services such as radiology, lab testing, and its pharmacy—all very costly aspects of health care today. "It was a good community response to a need that was here, and it serves the population well," says Nancy Carlstedt, president of Bloomington Hospital. "I think the availability and the expertise of it are pretty well demonstrated. If we have a failure in the system, it's finding the right communication tools to let the people who need it know that it's available."

For a community its size, Bloomington has a large number of highly skilled doctors, including several who are faculty members (and graduates) of the Indiana University School of Medicine in Indianapolis. Several others are engaged in research and making medical advancements that could have an impact on patients nationwide.

For example, Dr. Matthew Parmenter, a foot specialist, has been developing a new technique to help those with slow-healing wounds. The treatment involves implanting antibiotic beads directly into wounds, and has been particularly effective with people whose bones have become infected or who have suffered severe skin loss. Used in concert with a new hyperbaric chamber installed at Bloomington Hospital's outpatient diagnostic center in the fall of 1997, the healing process gets an added boost. Patients placed in the chamber breathe 100 percent oxygen at two to three times the normal atmospheric pressure, thus increasing the amount of oxygen available for stimulating cellular wound repair.

Another example is Dr. Phil Serbin, a urologist who introduced a new, more effective way of treating prostate cancer, the second leading cause of death in men from cancer. The procedure, which involves implanting radioactive "seeds" in a patient's prostate to destroy cancerous tumors, was so new that doctors from the IU Medical Center came to Bloomington to observe the procedure. Also recently established was a new, second-generation lithotripsy facility, where urologists use sound waves rather than invasive surgery to remove painful stones that may have formed in the kidney, gall bladder, bladder, and ureter. The medical community here prides itself on offering services often available only in large cities.

Bloomington Hospital, a not-for-profit institution that has steadfastly remained that way, offers a full range of services, from family-oriented maternity care and emergency treatment to specialized procedures such as neurosurgery and open-heart surgery. Accredited by the Joint Commission on Accreditation of Healthcare Organizations, Bloomington Hospital has 297 licensed beds and 232 physicians on staff, trained in 34 different recognized medical specialties (95 percent of them board certified in their specialties). Another 1,700 staff employees round out a team of health care professionals whose goal is to provide personalized care to every patient. The hospital treats as many as 46,000 patients each year in its emergency room, and about 1,700 babies are born in its maternity facility annually. Its primary building underwent a major renovation in 1983 with the construction of a $26-million, 100,000-square-foot wing addition, but other, more recent, expansion projects have been for the hospital's outpatient treatment services—about 1.3 million outpatient procedures are performed each year—a cardiac care unit, an expanded emergency department, and a parking garage.

Since 1994, Bloomington Hospital has been the only facility between Indianapolis and Louisville, Kentucky, to offer a comprehensive range of heart treatment, including open-heart surgery and a

Bloomington has a proud heritage of providing the finest of health care options, but none so important as personal and compassionate service. Photo by Kendall Reeves.

Prevention of illness through wellness and fitness programs, like this one at the YMCA Family Fitness Center, is popular among residents of all ages. Photo by Kendall Reeves.

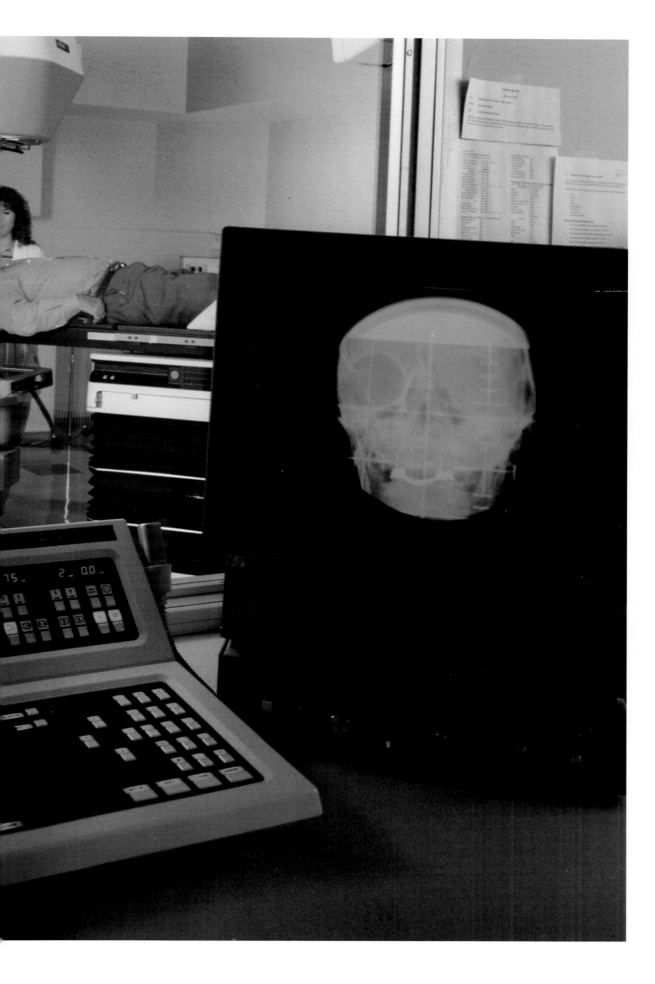

Bloomington Hospital serves as a regional referral center for residents in Monroe and eight surrounding counties. Photo by Kendall Reeves.

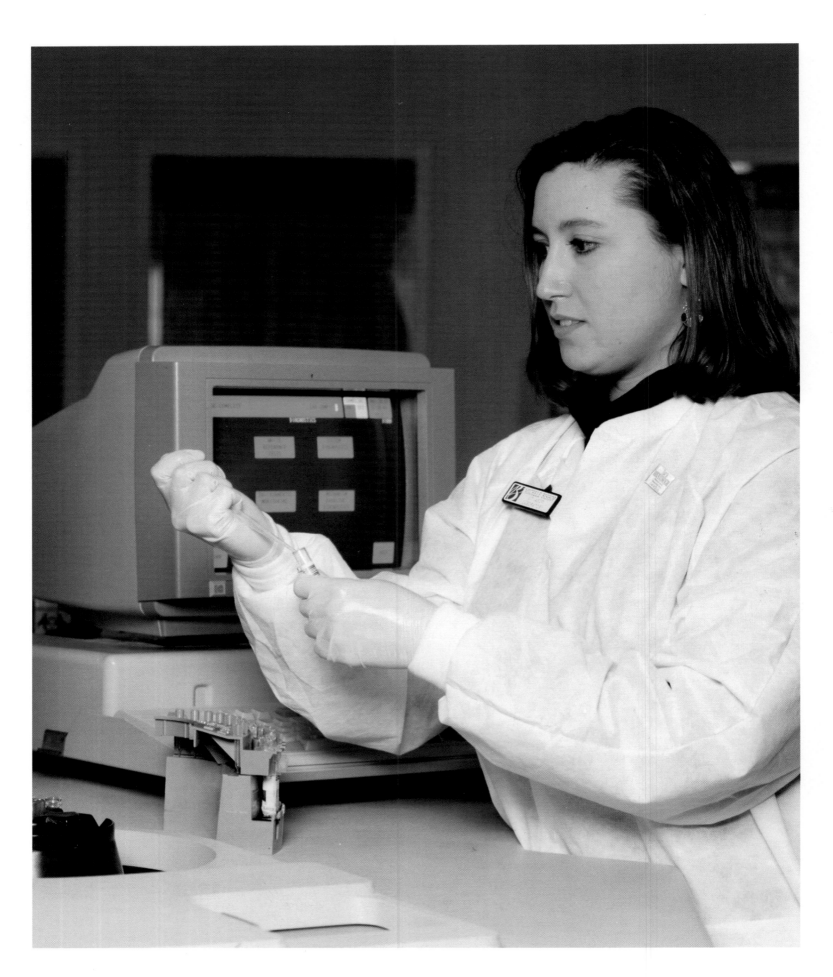

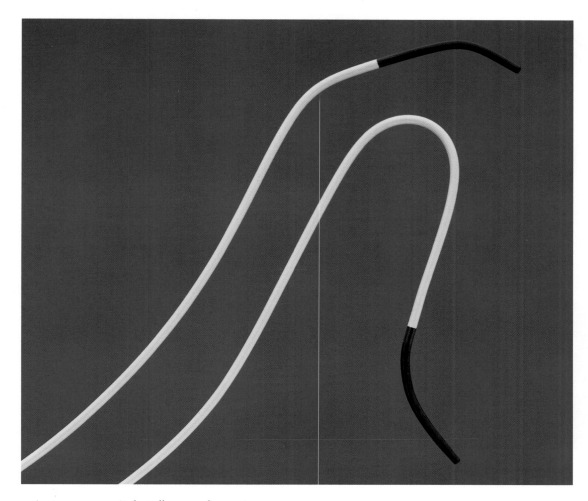

(far left) Bloomington Hospital, with a workforce approaching 2,400 people, is the city's third largest employer. Photo by Kendall Reeves.

(left) Many of today's medical breakthrough products resulted from the relationship Cook Incorporated cultivates with the medical professionals using its medical devices and products. Physicians and other health care providers depend on the Bloomington-based company for everything from industry-leading interventional and surgical devices to individual instruments custom-modified for the precise medical needs of a single patient. Photo courtesy of Cook Incorporated.

unique recovery unit that allows cardiac patients to remain under the care of the same nursing staff from admittance to discharge. For those who do not require surgery, there is the hospital's Cardiac Catheterization Lab, where cardiologists can take pictures of the heart to determine treatment and perform balloon angioplasty to open clogged arteries on an outpatient basis. The hospital's Cardiac Rehabilitation program marked its 20th anniversary in 1997; more than 2,200 survivors of heart trauma have taken part in its four-phase education and exercise plan.

Located on the city's southwest side is the Southern Indiana Surgery Center, a joint venture between Bloomington Hospital and an organization of area doctors that opened in 1993. The state-accredited ambulatory-surgery center has seven surgical specialties, including podiatry and orthopedics, gynecology, urology, and ophthalmology. It has become the anchor of a 35-acre medical park that also includes the hospital's Radiation Oncology Center, several specialty clinics, a diagnostic services center, and a rehabilitation clinic.

The hospital also operates a Children's Therapy Clinic that serves the needs of young people with a variety of disabilities through physical, occupational,

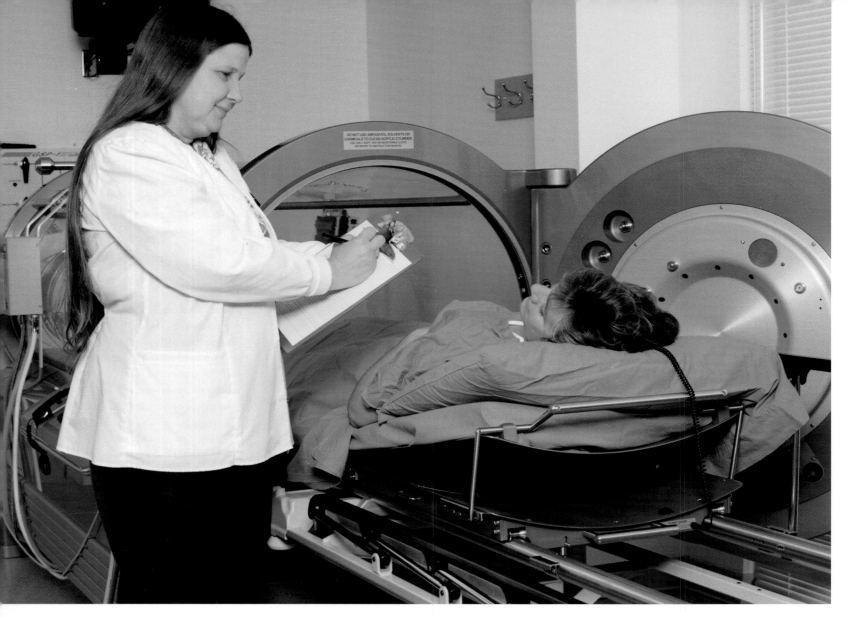

With a new hyperbaric chamber installed at Bloomington Hospital's outpatient diagnostic center in the fall of 1997, the healing process gets an added boost. Patients placed in the chamber breathe 100 percent oxygen at two to three times the normal atmospheric pressure, thus increasing the amount of oxygen available for stimulating cellular wound repair. Photo by Kendall Reeves.

and speech and language therapy. It is the only such program serving children in south central Indiana. Another service helping area families is the hospital's genetics counseling clinic, which advises expecting parents with concerns about the effect of medications, the likelihood of birth defects, and chromosomal disorders such as cystic fibrosis or muscular dystrophy.

Market forces reshaping health care have prompted Bloomington Hospital to branch into new areas. It merged with the Bloomington Convalescent Center and the Public Health Nursing Association to move into long-term care in Bloomington, nearby Bedford and Spencer, and into home health care. It also expanded its psychiatric services, including a new highly structured, short-term adolescent unit in Bloomington, and reached further into neighboring counties with clinics and programs.

Complementing the hospital are numerous medical practices, such as in the fields of neurology, obstetrics, ophthalmology, dermatology, urology, immunology and cardiology. Two locations of Promptcare Physicians Clinic, a care facility for non-life-threatening yet urgent ailments, complements the hospital's emergency facilities. Located about a half mile west on Third Street from Bloomington Hospital is the Southern Indiana Eye

Center, which offers comprehensive medical and surgical eye care. Founded in 1980 by Dr. Dan Grossman, the Eye Center is where cataract surgeries with implantation of intraocular lenses, glaucoma treatment, cosmetic and reconstructive eyelid surgeries, laser surgeries, and refractive surgeries are performed. Refractive surgery is a relatively new and quickly growing field that provides an alternative to eyeglasses and contact lens. It involves reshaping the eye itself to provide new functional ability for those with vision problems.

The IU School of Medicine may be located in Indianapolis, but some of the most exciting new treatments for cancer patients soon could be taking place on the Bloomington campus. At the time of writing, IU officials were pushing for funding needed to convert the IU Cyclotron and its proton beam generators for use in treating cancer and other eye diseases. Proton therapy is similar to conventional radiation therapy but involves precise delivery of subatomic particles to the affected area of the body. It has been useful for treating certain cancers, including prostate cancer, and eye disorders such as macular degeneration. The Midwest Proton Radiation Institute, a consortium of physicians and scientists from throughout the Midwest that would use the facility, opened a unit for the treatment of macular degeneration of the eye in 1998. They

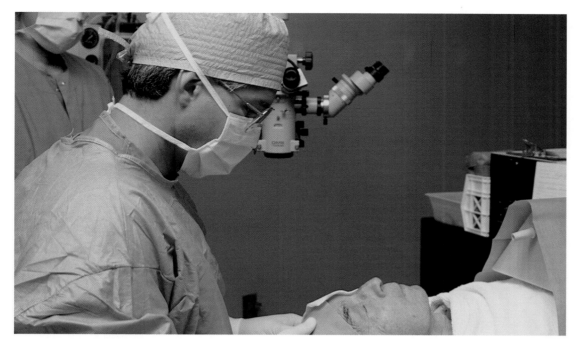

The Southern Indiana Eye Center offers comprehensive medical and surgical eye care. Photo courtesy of the Southern Indiana Eye Center.

hope the proposed facility will soon exceed that found at only two other places in the country, at Loma Linda, California, and Boston, Massachusetts.

The IU Health Center, on the university's campus, provides medical and psychological health services to IU students and their spouses and dependents. It includes a full-service medical clinic that offers lab tests and other examination services and a pharmacy. It provides specialized care in gynecology, reproductive health care, and allergies.

Since 1951, the IU School of Optometry has been one of the Midwest's leading educators of optometrists, ophthalmologists, opticians, and optometric technicians. In its clinics in the school's main building on Atwater Avenue, on the city's west side, and in downtown Indianapolis, it combines instruction with community service. The school's specialties include its ocular disease service, where highly trained specialists with the latest technology evaluate and treat patients with glaucoma, age-related eye disorders, diabetic and hypertensive eye disease, and other eye and vision abnormalities. Its binocular vision service helps those with problem eye movement, eye alignment, or visual perception. It also has special centers for children and sports injuries, and if care is needed after normal clinic hours, there is always an eye doctor on 24-hour call.

Several Bloomington-based organizations are helping those with emotional and psychological ailments. Since 1968, South Central Community Mental Health Centers have provided a full range of services, including counseling and therapy for those suffering from depression, stress, and alcohol and chemical dependency. In addition to offices in Bloomington, it offers treatment in neighboring Lawrence, Morgan, and Owen Counties.

Meadows Hospital of Bloomington, since 1992, has offered similar treatment services on both an

inpatient and outpatient basis and was the first such facility in the area to provide care designed specifically for children and adolescents. The 52-bed acute care hospital is located on seven acres of landscaped grounds on Bloomington's north side and features an outdoor Alpine Tower and challenge course. The challenge course uses simple elements such as ropes, ladders, poles, and beams to build self-confidence and esteem and teach the importance of trusting and working with others. Meadows Hospital is staffed by therapists who have completed master's degree research in social work and who are certified addiction counselors. Clinical supervision is performed by licensed doctors who are board certified in psychiatry. The staff also includes psychologists, psychometrists, and teachers.

Bloomington is home to the Children's Organ Transplant Association (COTA), an organization that, since its founding in 1986, has helped raise funds for hundreds of people needing an organ transplant. COTA was formed when a group of concerned Bloomington residents joined together to raise money for two-year-old David McConnell, who needed a liver transplant. About $100,000 was raised in two months for McConnell, who, sadly, died while waiting for his transplant. After his death, supporters decided to form COTA to help others in a similar situation. Today, the volunteer organization has grown and now has a full-time staff.

With all of these health care options available in Bloomington, it isn't surprising that Norman D. Ford, author of the book *The 50 Healthiest Places to Live and Retire in the United States,* ranked Bloomington 12th in the nation. ᴧ

The sport of basketball is highly revered in Indiana, and IU's hoopsters capture a lot of attention—every game at IU Assembly Hall is a sellout. The IU men's basketball team is coached by the enigmatic Bob Knight, who was selected in 1996 as the Big Ten Conference's top all-time coach and is a member of the Basketball Hall of Fame. Photos by Kendall Reeves.

IU's Student Recreational Sports Center (SRSC) and Wildermuth Intramural Center, and a handful of other gyms and fitness centers. You'll find people of all ages, from toddlers to seniors, enrolled in special swimming and wellness classes designed specifically for them at the YMCA, which features modern facilities for indoor swimming, weight training, and racquetball. IU's SRSC houses an Olympic-sized pool and diving wells, an indoor running track, and courts for squash, racquetball, and basketball, and similar facilities are also available at Wildermuth. The university also operates a tennis pavilion with eight indoor heated and air-conditioned courts that are open year-round, and more than 20 outdoor courts. IU facilities are open to the public at a nominal cost.

Public golf facilities offer a range in difficulty at reasonable prices. Eagle Pointe Golf Resort, located near Lake Monroe, recently spent $5 million to renovate its championship course and clubhouse,

and was ranked the sixth hardest course in the state by the readers of *Indiana Business* magazine. The Indiana University facility, which also features a par-three course and numerous practice areas, was called by *Golf* magazine a "first-rate experience." Also located in the city is Cascades Golf Course, a top-notch, city-owned facility. Rolling Meadows Golf Course is located on the Monroe-Owen County line and is the area's newest course. Golfers also are flocking to a new year-round practice facility on the city's south side, Tee-to-Green Driving Range, which has more than 70 covered and heated tee boxes. Five challenging courses in neighboring counties also help make Bloomington a destination vacation spot for many links players. Carved through mature forest, Salt Creek Golf Club in neighboring Brown County borders the state park and is one of the few public courses in the state to feature manicured bent grass on its tees, fairways, and greens.

IU's football team is no stranger to postseason play. In recent years, the team has had two Heisman Trophy candidates and gone to a half dozen bowl games. Photo by Rich Remsberg.

While people here are very active, they also appreciate action by others on the field, court, or even racetrack. The sport of basketball is highly revered in Indiana, and IU's hoopsters capture a lot of attention—every game at IU Assembly Hall is a sellout. The IU men's basketball team is coached by the enigmatic Bob Knight, who was selected in 1996 as the Big Ten Conference's top all-time coach.

Knight's teams have won three NCAA titles, postseason NIT and preseason NIT crowns, and numerous Big Ten championships. A member of the Basketball Hall of Fame, Knight has not only been successful nationally, but internationally as well. In 1979, he guided the U.S. Pan American team to a gold medal in Puerto Rico, and in 1984, he coached what may have been the best amateur basketball team ever assembled—the U.S. Olympic team. Knight's team, which included future Hall of Famers Michael Jordan and Patrick Ewing, easily won the gold medal in the XXIII Olympiad.

IU's football team, which also has been no stranger to the postseason, is coached by Cam Cameron, a youthful quarterback guru credited with mentoring leading NFL passers Gus Frerotte, Jim Harbaugh, and Elvis Grbac. In recent years, the team has had two Heisman Trophy candidates and gone to a half dozen bowl games. On Saturdays when the team is playing at home, cream and crimson are the predominant colors in town, as alumni, students, and fans converge on Bloomington. The traditional season climax is the game with Purdue University, when state bragging rights and the fabled Old Oaken Bucket are at stake.

In their third decade of varsity competition, the IU men's soccer Hoosiers are guided by four-time National Coach of the Year Jerry Yeagley. In over a quarter century, Yeagley has taken a program from the ground floor and built it into one of the strongest and most respected in the United States. IU owns more wins, has appeared in more Final Fours, and has a higher winning percentage in both regular season and postseason play than any other school in Division I soccer. His teams' victories include three NCAA Championships, and in 1997, his team had compiled a perfect 20-0 record heading into the NCAA tourney. Three of the starting players on the U.S. team in the 1998 World Cup were coached by Yeagley at IU.

IU is also a perennial contender in swimming, women's basketball, baseball, tennis, and track and field. IU's newly renovated Robert C. Haugh Track and Field Complex was host in 1997 to more than 1,000 of the nation's top athletes competing in the NCAA Division I Men's and Women's Outdoor Track and Field Championships, including several future Olympians.

When IU is playing at home, cream and crimson are the predominant colors in town, as alumni, students, and fans converge on Bloomington. Photo by Rich Remsberg.

More than 5,000 fishermen flock to Lake Monroe each summer in hopes of netting a fish tagged with a value of $5,000 during the area's annual "Crappiethon" contest. In addition, local and state fishing groups hold contests on the lake each weekend. Photo by Kendall Reeves.

Nearly a half dozen golf courses in Monroe and surrounding counties offer a range in difficulty at reasonable prices. Photo by Kendall Reeves.

Bloomington is a community of doers, where people of all ages do not elect to remain on the sidelines. Whether it is water aerobics, bicycling, or organized team sports, area residents support the many exercise and recreational activities offered by an ever-growing number of facilities. Photo by Rich Remsberg.

Monroe County's three high schools also field competitive teams in more than a dozen sports. In 1993 Bloomington High School South's Class 5A state football championship electrified the community during its title run. In 1997 Bloomington High School North did the same when it made history in becoming the final team to win the Indiana basketball championship in its original single-class format made famous in the movie *Hoosiers*. Judging from the excitement of this form of "Hoosier Hysteria," one would hope that Indiana goes back to single-class basketball.

While Indianapolis is home to the "Brickyard" and its "greatest spectacle in racing," Bloomington is not without ties to Indiana's auto-racing tradition. The Bloomington area is home to one of auto-racing's storied families, the Kinsers. The family's current torchbearer, Steve Kinser, is a 14-time national sprint car champion. Kinser stunned the racing world in 1994 when he won the International Race of Champions, competing against drivers Dale Earnhardt and Al Unser Jr. At age 42, he was a rookie driver in the Indy 500, capping off a career that began in weekend races at tracks like Bloomington Speedway, which continue here on Saturday nights throughout the summer.

Folks here are also big fans of professional teams including the Indianapolis Colts of the National Football League and the Indiana Pacers of the National Basketball Association. In 1996, the Indianapolis Indians, a AAA minor league baseball team, began playing in Victory Field, its beautiful new downtown stadium. All of these sports options are less than an hour away from Bloomington. ⚐

A number of local companies sponsor vehicles in the Mini Grand Prix race, a go-cart race through downtown Bloomington during Hoosierfest, one of its many festivals. Photo by Kendall Reeves.

Eight miles south of Bloomington is Lake Monroe, Indiana's largest man-made lake, which attracts more than 1.5 million fishermen, boaters, bird-watchers, and swimmers each year. Photo by Kendall Reeves.

Softball provides great recreation and is big business. One national softball tournament brought an estimated $556,000 into the area's economy. Photo by Kendall Reeves.

Bryan Park Pool is one of six swimming pools operated in the city by the Bloomington Parks and Recreation Department, the YMCA, and IU. Photo by Kendall Reeves.

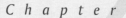

City Stages

Where We Perform

"I was too young to recognize the feeling for Bloomington that was growing within me. The compulsion to be there, to return there, to take from Bloomington the things it offered. Things I know now were more fundamental than kids and safe streets and broad meadows where you could run and fall panting in the thick cool grass as you gasped 'safe.' But I felt there were things there that I must have there and always I wanted to go back."

—Hoagland Howard "Hoagy" Carmichael
in his book The Star Dust Road

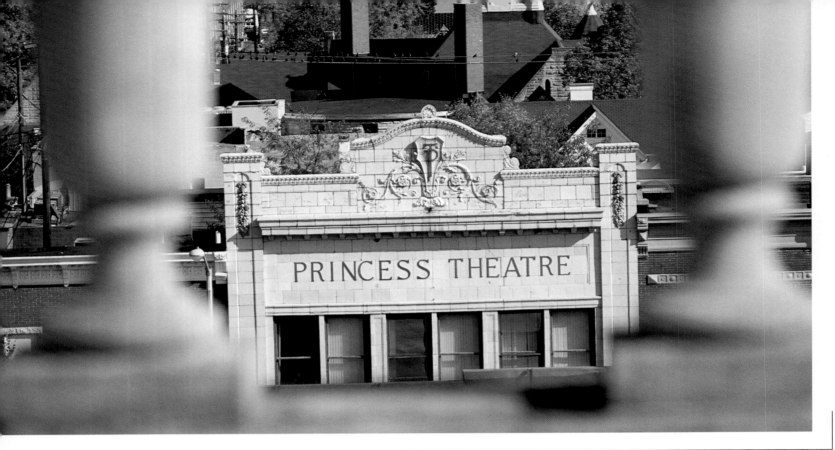

PRINCESS THEATRE

(previous page) The acoustics of the Musical Arts Center, on the IU campus, has been compared to the world's finest concert halls. The performance hall seats 1,460, and the stage compares in size and glamour with the New York Metropolitan Opera House. Since 1948, the IU School of Music's opera company has given more than 1,000 performances. Photo by Kendall Reeves.

(above) The Princess Theatre, built near the turn of the century, is another historic building in Bloomington spared from the wrecking ball. For decades, it enabled area residents and their imaginations to enter the world of Hollywood movies. Today, the restored venue serves the taste buds of those who come to the Princess Restaurant for Moroccan and Mediterranean cuisine. Bloomington is home to many excellent restaurants serving cuisine from all over the world. Photo by Kendall Reeves.

The IU Art Museum was completed in 1982. Designed by I. M. Pei, who modeled the museum building after the East Wing of the National Gallery in Washington, D.C., today, it serves as a distinctive setting for more than 25,000 objects in its collection, space for special exhibits, and a library. Photo by Rich Remsberg.

Like Carmichael, the composer of pop standards such as "Star Dust" and "Georgia On My Mind," a symphony of other notable musicians, actors, and artists have found Bloomington to be fertile ground for creative development. While many of these influential individuals have been associated with Indiana University and its nationally recognized programs in the fine arts and music, others have simply come from a long-standing community tradition.

"I think the university has had a major part in creating an environment that nurtures the arts," comments Frank Young, executive director of the Bloomington Area Arts Council and the John Waldron Arts Center, a focal point for much of the cultural activities in the city today. But Young adds that Bloomington "has an educated population that surrounds the university and is not necessarily part of the university that continues living here after being educated here." Included in the category of creative people who have made Bloomington home are the late Lotus Dickey and rock star John Mellencamp. Dickey was an indigenous poet and singer whose work was assimilated into the folk revival in the Midwest. Mellencamp is a top-selling rock singer who has chosen to remain in Bloomington, far away from the glitter and fast pace of southern California, the world's entertainment capital.

Of course, many luminaries came to Bloomington to study at IU and left their mark here. Janie Fricke, a two-time winner of the County Music Association's Female Vocalist of the Year Award, sang with IU's Singing Hoosiers and in the local hot spots. Other prominent alumni include two-time Oscar winner Howard Ashman, who created lyrics for the Disney films *The Little Mermaid, Beauty and the Beast*, and *Aladdin*. Theodore Dreiser, author of *An American Tragedy,* and Ross Lockridge Jr., writer of *Raintree County,* still are considered among America's most important novelists. Actors Kevin Kline, winner of two Tony Awards and an Oscar, and Charles Kimbrough, star of TV's *Murphy Brown,* each honed their skills in IU Theatre productions. Jeri Taylor has been a writer and producer of the various *Star Trek* series programs, and filmmakers David Anspaugh and Angelo Pizzo collaborated on the films *Hoosiers* and *Rudy*. Several orchestras of classical music virtuosos have studied in IU's internationally renowned School of Music, including violinist Joshua Bell, soprano diva Sylvia McNair, Hank

With an enrollment of 1,650 students and 145 full-time faculty, the IU School of Music is the largest and perhaps the best place anywhere to study music. Photo by Rich Remsberg.

Dutt and Joan Jeanrehaud of the inventive Kronos Quartet, and the concertmasters of Vienna, Austria, Baltimore, Cleveland, Houston, Montreal, Philadelphia, and San Francisco. The music school's Jazz Department also is top-notch and is directed by David Baker, who also oversees the Smithsonian Institution's jazz ensemble. Former jazz majors at IU, the duo of saxophonist Michael and trumpeter Randy Brecker—better known as The Brecker Brothers—developed and later formed arguably the most successful fusion band of the 1970s.

Perhaps Bloomington's appreciation for the arts can be symbolized by a sculpture located outside City Hall. The sculpture, a large fountain carved from Indiana limestone, was the first project funded under a unique city ordinance that sets aside one percent of large-scale capital project budgets for art. Several contractors already involved in renovating the former Showers Brothers factory were generous with their time and fees in order to hold down costs. Another major project, the renovation of the Indiana Theatre, a former movie house, into a performance center, also received much community support.

With an enrollment of 1,720 students and 156 faculty and scholars, the IU School of Music is the largest and perhaps the best place anywhere to study music. It attracts students from every state in the nation and 35 foreign countries. Nestled among the many trees found on campus, the school has been ranked number one in the nation by the *Chronicle of Higher Education, Change* magazine, and the *National Association of Music Executives in State Universities. U.S. News & World Report* ranked the school number one in 1994, along with the Eastman School of Music at the University of Rochester and the Julliard School in New York City. Three years later, the magazine ranked it second, along with Julliard, both a tenth of a percentage point behind Eastman. "Indiana University's School of Music has the most ambitious opera company anywhere in the country," commented Garrison Keillor, a writer and host of the national radio show *A Prairie Home Companion,* during a program originating from Bloomington. Added the *Chicago Tribune,* "The superb facilities of the Musical Arts Center and lofty professionalism of the faculty put the students in the big time from the start." Soprano Beverly Sills declared, "The music faculty at Indiana University is absolutely mind-boggling." Since its inception in 1948, the opera company has given more than 1,000 performances and has taken productions to Boston, Washington, D.C., Russia, and Paris. In 1981, IU music students presented the first performance ever by a university opera company at New York's Metropolitan Opera House, and today they continue to perform there regularly as individuals in annual competitive auditions. Annually, the school presents nearly 1,500 different programs and recitals in Bloomington.

One point frequently used in stressing the city's high quality of life is the thousand-plus performances held in the music school's recital halls and its Musical Arts Center, and the excellent theater productions on and off campus. An array of top entertainers also come to Bloomington each year to perform in the university's 3,700-seat auditorium, which underwent a thorough renovation in 1998-99, after more than 50 years of service. Soon, a completely restored, historic Indiana Theatre downtown will supplement the performance spaces available at the Waldron. Among its future tenants will be the Camerata Orchestra, a city-based classical music company consisting of local residents and members of the university community.

Over its history, Bloomington has continually nurtured local musicians. From as far back as the 1830s, the city has always had organized bands. In the early days, it was the custom to have bands head torchlight parades and play for campaign meetings of both political parties. Between the 1840s and 1870s, there were several bands, although accounts remain for only two of them, the Pinafore Band and a group consisting entirely of Bloomington's nineteenth-century version of the Von Trapps, the Sewards. Records indicate that when Theophilus Wyle brought his new bride to

Bloomington in 1838, he was met at the village boundary by a band led by Austin Seward. Fifty years later, when the couple celebrated their golden anniversary, the same family band serenaded them at their home, and playing the same clarinet at both events was James Seward.

In 1879, it is believed that Austin Seward formed his Silver Cornet Band, and in 1886, the first community band was founded with him as a member. The latter group later came to be known as the Bloomington Mechanics Band, since most of its members were mechanics, and it continued to exist under various forms until the 1940s, when it became a part of the Bloomington Public School System. In winter, musicians with the Gentry Brothers Circus would perform with the city band after their tours ended. When the circus later folded, many of these musicians adopted

The late conductor and composer Leonard Bernstein said of the IU School of Music that it was "extraordinary to have so many talented people in one place." Nearly 1,500 programs and recitals are presented each year. Pictured here, leading one of the school's orchestras, is Kurt Masur, music director and conductor of the New York Philharmonic. Photo by Rich Remsberg.

A recent *Gourman Report*, a national rating service, placed the Indiana University Theatre and Drama Program in the top two percent of all undergraduate theater and drama programs in the United States. The program produces at least a dozen plays each year, including during the summer at its Brown County Playhouse. Actors Kevin Kline, winner of two Tony Awards and an Oscar, and Charles Kimbrough, star of TV's *Murphy Brown*, each honed their skills in IU Theatre productions. Photo by Rich Remsberg.

Bloomington as their hometown. Local merchants supported the band, as would various types of special performances, ranging from minstrel shows at local theaters to processional music on Memorial Day, when it would play dirges going out to the cemetery, but circus music on coming out—reminiscent of New Orleans jazz funerals.

At the same time, another form of music was being forged that would be passed down informally through parents and grandparents. This was the folk music of southern Indiana, songs that would last and relate stories of love and heartbreak associated with establishing a home in the wilderness, or those of ancestors from the old country. Ethnomusicologist Alan Lomax traveled Indiana with his recording equipment in 1938, finding people still singing the folk songs their grandparents first heard as youngsters. In 1981, a retired construction worker and fiddler named for the Hindu Bhagavad-Gita teachings that associate the lotus blossom with purity and transcendence, Lotus Dickey, helped another generation to connect with this idiom of Indiana's musical legacy. Today, a vibrant folk music community, led by recording artists Grey Larsen, Janne Henshaw, and Malcolm Dalgish, pays its debt to Dickey at a world music and arts festival held in his name each fall that

attracts musicians from every color in the musical spectrum.

In the early 1900s, as the nation moved to the beat of Ragtime and Dixieland music, a group of young musicians in Bloomington was discovering "hot jazz." Paramount among them was Hoagy Carmichael. Born in Bloomington in 1899, Carmichael achieved international fame with compositions such as "Old Rockin' Chair," "Buttermilk Sky," and "Lazy River," and even as an actor in films such as *To Have and Have Not* and *The Best Years of Our Lives*.

Music critic Alec Wilder wrote of him: "I think it is unquestionable that Hoagy Carmichael has proven himself to be the most talented, inventive, sophisticated, and jazz-oriented of all the great craftsmen." He associated with other notable jazzmen, such as Bix Beiderbecke and Louis Armstrong, but often his songs were reminiscent of his Hoosier heritage.

As a child, his mother, a theater musician, tried to teach her son the piano, but Carmichael acknowledges that it was the great black jazz pianist Reggy Duvall who influenced him the most. "He showed me the art of improvising, using the third and sixth of the chord as the basis for arpeggios." He took the piano seriously as a teen, when

Bloomington's appreciation for the arts can be symbolized by the amount of public art found around the city. A unique city ordinance sets aside one percent of large-scale capital project budgets for art. These two friendly bears rest near a fountain outside the recently renovated Monroe County Library. Photo by Kendall Reeves.

he performed with a number of professional dance bands throughout central Indiana.

As an IU student, his favorite haunt was the Book Nook, a popular student hangout in the 1920s. Carmichael would hang out there for hours, pounding on the restaurant's piano. The late Angelica Poolitsan, whose family managed the restaurant, once recalled what happened after she bought a player piano. As the leader of a group of campus musicians, he was infuriated with the notion of a player piano and gathered friends together for a late-night raid on the restaurant. They dismantled the instrument, stored its automatic player equipment in the basement, and reconstructed the piano. Hoagy declared that "it was a fine piano," and played on it himself many times afterwards. The player attachment never was put back in. Legend has it that he wrote "Star Dust" on the piano of the Indiana Avenue establishment.

Recently, music began to emanate again from within its walls as a number of today's students perform in the same building, now known as The Gables. Carmichael's legacy remains intact in the IU School of Music. Its Archives of Traditional Music maintains the Hoagy Carmichael Room, which is designed as a memorial to the songwriter and

performing artist, with a portion of its extensive memorabilia collection on regular display. In 1998, a New Jersey man donated his extensive collection of 1,600 recorded versions of "Star Dust"—which he had gathered for more than 50 years—to the IU archieves. "The basis of it was he just loved the song," said his widow. "He thought it was the most beautiful song ever written." The room also is the setting for an ongoing concert series of live music from various ethnic and folk traditions. His music also is regularly performed by the school's Grammy-winning vocal group, The Singing Hoosiers, and in concerts presented by the school's jazz department.

As already mentioned, a thriving musical community exists away from the IU campus. Rocker Mellencamp is just one example of a number of music artists and groups who have found success either while in Bloomington or shortly after they left. These musicians find an audience while performing on the stages of Bloomington's downtown nightclubs, at university parties, and sometimes in less favorable places, such as parking garages. Local radio stations—including community station WFHB—are very supportive of a musical scene that *Billboard* magazine called in a 1996 front-page story "a new music haven."

The community shows its appreciation for the arts by ensuring an ample amount of venues for them to exist, including Indiana Theatre, which is being renovated for live performances. Photo by Kendall Reeves.

Recent success stories with ties to the Bloomington bar scene include alternative band The Mysteries of Life, folk singers Carrie Newcomer and Lisa Germano, country picker Junior Brown, and Kenneth "Babyface" Edmonds, an urban contemporary performer/producer who today has had more compositions published and performed than any other songwriter. Kenny Aronoff, a 16-year veteran of Mellencamp's band, is among the most sought-after drummers in the music business—having worked with Bob Dylan, Bob Seger, Melissa Etheridge, and John Fogerty among others—and yet he finds time to teach master classes in the IU School of Music.

Bloomington also is home to a musical organization with a background unlike any other in North America. The Star of Indiana was founded in 1984 by city businessman Bill Cook to benefit youth through enhanced music education. Since then, it has become a national power in drum and bugle corps performance, winning the world championship in 1991. In the fall of 1993, the organization created an entirely new musical genre: brass theater. Brass theater combines advanced lighting, costuming, and innovative stage techniques together with a diverse musical repertoire. Star of Indiana has performed with acts such as the Canadian Brass, in famed venues as the Hollywood Bowl, Lincoln Center, and on Public Broadcasting stations from coast to coast. In addition to music, these hundreds of young brass, percussion, and visual performers have learned valuable lessons about discipline, effort, and teamwork through Star of Indiana.

Bloomington also is known as a regional cultural center when it comes to the other performing arts. IU's Department of Theater and Drama consistently ranks among the best in the country and also is one of the largest. IU has more than 1,200 alumni who currently work in professional theater, teach in universities, or work in film, television, or related professions. Since the early 1880s, students have been able to get valuable experience in university productions. Today, nearly 40,000 people attend performances given throughout the year in the University Theatre, the Studio Theatre, T300 Theatre, and the school's version of "summer stock," Brown County Playhouse.

Away from campus, the Bloomington Playwrights Project develops new plays by talented young writers, including many from the area. The experimental Black Box Theater has been a good training ground for young directors. A considerable amount of serious theater is staged at the Waldron Arts Center as well. In the summer, the Monroe County Civic Theater presents the plays of William

Like the IU School of Music, the university's dance program attracts top faculty who enhance the quality of ballet taught here. Among them is Violette Verdy, an 18-year veteran of George Balanchine's New York City Ballet and former artistic director of the Paris Opera Ballet. Photo by Rich Remsberg.

Shakespeare in Third Street Park, although its productions are not affiliated with another organization devoted to the bard, the Indiana Shakespeare Festival, which recently relocated to Bloomington from Indianapolis.

A discussion of the arts in Bloomington cannot overlook dance. Among the newer faculty of the IU School of Music is Violette Verdy, an 18-year veteran of George Balanchine's New York City Ballet and former artistic director of the Paris Opera Ballet. She is an example of the kind of dance faculty the school is able to attract, thus enhancing the quality of ballet taught at IU. The school also invites principal dancers from leading United States dance companies for various public performances with students. Off campus, the Windfall Dancers celebrated their 20th anniversary in 1997. More participatory are a number of local groups that hold regular instructional dances for people interested in swing, old-time country, and even Texas-style line dancing.

In addition to the performing arts, there has always been strong support for the visual arts. Little more than a hundred years ago, one of the area's primary industries, limestone quarrying companies, had an impact in creating an artistically nurturing environment. After recognizing the stone's decorative attributes, several companies brought in master craftsmen from Italy in the late nineteenth century to carve the adornments for many of the nation's most outstanding buildings. These people came to work in the mills, designing pieces or executing the work of other sculptors from across the country. "That created another cultural environment that was focused on the arts and on the creative process. It was clearly a recognized part of the Bloomington area," said Young, himself a highly educated sculptor who grew up in Bloomington. Today, some descendants of these carvers remain in the area.

In subsequent decades, several prominent artists in various mediums gravitated to the area. Bloomington benefited from the presence of an artist colony in neighboring Brown County, where the "Hoosier Group" of painters had gathered to capture the pure beauty of southern Indiana's rolling, wooded hills. The first and most famous artist to take up residence in Brown County, T. C. Steele, was invited by then-IU President William Lowe Bryan to paint the IU campus in 1922. "Mr. Steele has no duties except to paint. He invites individuals and groups of students to his studio and gives occasional lectures," said Bryan in describing the artist's role. "Mr. Steele's position is analogous to that of the research professor, whose only duty is scientific investigation, with the difference that his

Since its founding in 1941, the IU Art Museum has grown to include more than 35,000 paintings, prints, drawings, photographs, sculptures, ceramics, jewelry, and textiles that represent nearly every art-producing culture throughout history. Photo by Kendall Reeves.

work is in the field of art." Many of Steele's paintings still adorn campus buildings today.

Art studies were still in their infancy then. Founded in 1895 as the Department of Freehand and Mechanical Drawing, today the school is considered the third oldest art department in an American college or university. In 1929, world-class ceramicist Karl Martz came to Bloomington as a young man and earned a degree from IU in chemistry. After being away from the area for a few years, he was lured back by Henry Hope, who came to IU in 1941 to transform IU's then-two-member art department into a fully modern school. Along with Martz—whose works are in the permanent collections of the Smithsonian Institution, the Tokyo Museum of Modern Art, and the Museum of Contemporary Crafts—Hope was able to recruit a full palette of world-renowned artists and scholars to teach and conduct research at IU. Others included George Rickey, a Hoosier native known as the father of kinetic art; David Smith, who is considered by some as the paramount sculptor in twentieth-century American art; and Phillip Pearlstein, who inspired the revival of figure painting in contemporary art. During Hope's 27-year tenure as chairman, the department grew into a school with more than 2,000 students and from a one-floor frame structure into a five-story limestone Fine Arts Building on Showalter Fountain Plaza.

Through visions of people like Hope, the IU Art Museum was completed in 1982. Designed by I. M. Pei, who modeled the museum building after the East Wing of the National Gallery in Washington, D.C., today, it serves as a distinctive setting for more than 25,000 objects in its collection, space for special exhibits, and a library. Another campus venue, the School of Fine Arts Gallery—commonly known as the "Sofa Gallery"—presents contemporary art produced in the last 20 years by significant regional and nationally known artists, as well as students in the school. They are complemented by the more than a dozen art galleries and exhibition spaces dedicated to local and regional artists. Many of them are located in downtown Bloomington, and a group of local artists and art supporters calling themselves the Alliance of Visual Artists has done a great deal to promote awareness of these spaces. The organization has held "coordinated open houses" to introduce people to places such as the Bellevue Gallery, Daisybrain Media Center, Phoenix, the Waldron's Rosemary Miller Gallery, and Dragon Gallery, and other spaces where local artists can show their work.

In addition, there is the Lilly Library, which has since 1960 housed one of the finest collections of rare books and personal papers in the world. Included among its exhaustive collection are rare Gutenberg and Coverdale Bibles, the writings of Martin Luther, and the complete series of scripts for each of the *Star Trek* television shows, complete with director's notes. The William Hammond Mathers Museum has one of the Midwest's largest collections of artifacts and photographs representing cultures from each of the world's inhabited continents. The materials have been collected and curated to serve the museum's primary mission in education. Its collection's strengths include traditional musical instruments and materials relating to Native Americans and greater Bloomington. The Monroe County Historical Society Museum, partly housed in an old Carnegie library built in 1918, recently underwent an expansion. It houses permanent and changing exhibits focusing on early settlers, Native Americans, and other aspects of the community.

The film scene is equally as rich as Bloomington's other cultural aspects. *The Ryder,* a local arts magazine, sponsors a series of classic, foreign, and art films throughout the year. Bloomington has more than 20 movie screens at various theaters, from the historic Von Lee Theater downtown to the Showplace Cinemas, which are equipped with the latest in digital stereo sound.

Bloomington truly is a destination for the arts. Although this fact is clearly obvious to the people who live here, community and university leaders hope to do more to shine the limelight on the area's musicians, actors, artists, and other cultural offerings. The coming years promise to be an exciting time, as a more unified town-gown effort to support the arts could result in new opportunities for artistic expression that appeal to an even wider audience. ◢

Bloomington is home to a musical organization with a background unlike any other in North America. The Star of Indiana was founded in 1984 to benefit youth through enhanced music education. Since then, it has evolved into a new performance venue, Brass Theater. Photo courtesy of Star of Indiana.

"The reputation of the Indiana University School of Music stands high and that of its opera theater especially so. Several times, I had to remind myself that these were student forces and not a professional group," wrote critic Nicholas Kenyon in *The New Yorker.* Among these former students is Sylvia McNair, today an internationally known opera star, pictured here. Photo by Rich Remsberg.

The John Waldron Arts Center,
operated by the Bloomington Area
Arts Council, hosts musical and
theatrical performances, holds art and
craft classes for all ages, maintains
two in-house art galleries, and serves
as the center of the city's art community.
Photo by Kendall Reeves.

Chapter 8

Hootenannies

*Our Festive
Celebrations*

"We're already a destination point
due to the presence of the university
and its multiple sporting events,
the beauty of southern Indiana,
and the many qualities which make
Bloomington attractive. You get
the best of a big city arts event, in
terms of quality, in a small town
setting. The hassles are far less
than going to Chicago or New
York to see a blues or classical
music festival, where you're
encountering parking problems,
traffic jams, and concerns over
safety. Those things are mostly
eliminated in Bloomington."

—Lee Williams
*Executive Director of the Lotus
World Music and Arts Festival*

The Courthouse Square serves as the site for many festivals and musical happenings throughout the summer, including an annual strawberry festival. Photos by Kendall Reeves.

Winters in Bloomington aren't too harsh. You rarely

see Weather Channel footage of Hoosiers pushing their cars out of snow

banks. Just the same, when the thermometer warms and the leaves start to

bud out, you find people out more. Nearly any reason to congregate—music,

theater, sports, and even food—brings the folks out in droves. Waiters

precariously bearing trays scurry down Bloomington streets in races against

each other and the clock. Some of the best recording artists from the

Midwest, nation, and even the world are regularly featured at festivals.

Chomp down a barbecue sandwich. Delicately savor some sushi. Don't forget

to include a cold beverage, including those produced at the local brew pub

or wineries.

The city and county play host to a myriad of annual events and festivals, as well as a number of weekly performances in local parks and even on the city's Courthouse Square. Even before the temperatures climb much, these activities begin with the Indiana Shakespeare Festival, a series of live performances, films, and workshops staged each February at the John Waldron Arts Center downtown. On the Indiana University campus, students rehearse for months their heavily choreographed, one-act musical productions in order to vie for top honors in the annual IU Sing. Spread over two nights, troupes of students cram as much high-energy music from Broadway and popular song in new, creative ways that center around the event's theme, but all within the time span of a few minutes. As a result, the pace remains fast, leaving the audience and performers exhausted by each night's end.

Connoisseurs of regional and national micro-brews gather early each spring at the downtown Convention Center to sample the products of more than 30 breweries, including fresh ales made by the city's own Bloomington Brewing Company. And the best part of the Big Red Beer Festival is that all proceeds go to charity. Later, during the summer,

Blues music and barbecue—what more would anyone want? As long as the sun is out and the beverages are cold, folks here in Monroe County need few other reasons to get into a festive mood. Photo by Kendall Reeves.

Oliver Winery sponsors a series of free music concerts at its beautifully landscaped 15-acre site, conveniently located close to the wine cellar.

While much of the nation has only recently discovered the excitement associated with basketball, "roundball" has captured the attention of Hoosiers for decades. While some might expect interest in the game to dim after the conclusion of the high school and college seasons, this isn't true in Bloomington, which is traditionally the first site of the national pilgrimage made by the Gus Macker three-on-three tournament each year. It all starts here with more than a thousand teams, which converge on the parking lot outside IU's Assembly Hall—itself a shrine to the game.

In late May the town of Harrodsburg celebrates its past and present when it comes together for its annual Heritage Days Festival. Many former residents and those whose ancestors settled this area descend upon this southern Monroe County town for an old-fashioned fish fry, homemade pies, gospel music, carnival rides, and a parade in which anyone can participate.

Since 1993, classical music lovers from across the Midwest have been flocking to Bloomington on Memorial Day weekend for the Bloomington Early Music Festival. Organizers have built upon the resources available through the nationally acclaimed IU School of Music to create a unique "town and gown" event involving people from throughout the community. In addition to solo, chamber, and orchestral concerts, workshops and round table discussions focus on the Medieval, Renaissance, and Baroque musical periods. Top performers have come from as far away as Europe and Russia to recapture the spirit of music dating back to the seventeenth century.

Complementing the Early Music Festival is a new event being launched in 1999, the Bloomington Music and Arts Festival. The event is envisioned to showcase the creative and artistic energy of IU and Bloomington's vibrant cultural scene. The proposed festival is intended to enhance Bloomington's reputation as a destination for the arts, and will feature outdoor productions by the IU Opera Theater in addition to performances of classical, contemporary, and international music on campus and around town. As envisioned, the "town-and-gown" organized festival will include educational components for all ages, such as workshops, master

Every Labor Day weekend, Fourth and Grant Streets are closed off for one of the Midwest's largest juried and best attended art festivals, the Fourth Street Arts Fair. You'll find original oil and acrylic paintings, breathtaking photography, textiles, wood crafts, and other artwork in booths along with those promoting local cultural and community organizations. Photos by Kendall Reeves.

The Fourth of July holiday is marked by a parade, fireworks, and an annual extravaganza concert of patriotic and popular music by the Bloomington Pops Orchestra. Photos by Kendall Reeves.

classes, lectures, and seminars for everyone from local band directors to church musicians. Artists and performers, including painters, sculptors, singers, and dancers, will offer pointers for neophytes and professionals alike. There will also be a host of special activities for children, organizers say.

Throughout the summer, the IU School of Music Summer Festival—which runs from June to August—features orchestral and opera performances, a chamber music festival, and soloist concerts by many of the finest young performers in classical music today. There's also "Jazz in July," a highly successful concert series at the IU Art Museum, that draws many of the area's best jazz performers on Friday nights, and IU Band concerts on Wednesday nights in Fine Arts Plaza. Many of these events are without charge. The city also gets into the act with performing arts series held at lunchtime Thursdays on the Courthouse Square, Sunday evenings in Bryan Park, and Fridays or Saturdays in Third Street Park. These provide a venue for families to enjoy the area's many pop, folk, and jazz music groups.

Benefiting Big Brothers and Big Sisters of Monroe County and child care programs at IU is the annual Fun Frolic, which has been bringing a county fair atmosphere in June to Bloomington since 1957. There are dozens of midway games, carnival rides, and food vendors set up in the parking lot of IU Memorial Stadium. Thousands from throughout southern Indiana get an early taste of elephant ears, cotton candy, and other fair staples.

In mid-June, two events are held concurrently in the heart of downtown, Taste of Bloomington and Arts Fair on the Square. Since 1982, more than two dozen of the area's finest eateries have been offering samples of cuisine varying from Japanese, Tibetan, Greek, Mexican, and Thai dishes to that familiar staple, pizza. Proceeds from the event benefit the Community Kitchen of Monroe County and the Hoosier Hills Food Bank, so more than the 6,000 annually in attendance are fed. Music performed by a varied lineup of local bands and races featuring waiters from various restaurants contribute to the atmosphere of the event. After eating, many Taste of Bloomington goers wander over to Arts Fair on the Square, which has offered area artists a showcase for their handmade jewelry, hand-blown glass, ceramics, and paintings since 1980. More than 50 artisans participate in the fund-raiser for the Waldron Arts Center.

The annual Summer Garden Walk is held each June by the Bloomington Garden Club on behalf of the Hilltop Garden and Nursery Center on the IU campus. Five distinctive residential gardens are selected annually that represent different aspects of horticulture. Included is a tour of the Hilltop Center, which features more than 50 varieties of perennials in bloom, herbs and vegetables, and fruit trees, all grown with environmentally sound gardening approaches.

July provides something of a breather for festival goers, as the month is usually given over to county fairs across the state. One notable exception of local interest is a four-day event south of Monroe County in nearby Bedford, the Limestone Heritage Festival. This festival celebrates the limestone industry's contributions to the region. Of course, it features a parade and music, but also has exhibitions in stone carving and tours of area quarries. Back in Bloomington, the Fourth of July holiday is marked by a parade, fireworks, and an annual extravaganza concert of patriotic and popular music by the Bloomington Pops Orchestra.

The Monroe County Fair in late July highlights the area's agrarian life. Local growers, livestock producers, and 4-H members bring their prized crops, animals, and projects to be judged. Canning, sewing, and conservation projects, art, photography, and homemade baked products fill the exhibition halls. Winners of the various local contests go on to compete at the Indiana State Fair in August in Indianapolis. Then, of course, there is the fair food; roasted ears of corn, pork chops, and tenderloins are favorites. Children of all ages enjoy the carnival rides and the midway games, which is proof that not everything changes.

In late August, the festival season picks up again with zeal and doesn't conclude until Christmas. Every Labor Day weekend, Fourth and Grant Streets are closed off for one of the Midwest's largest juried art festivals. The Fourth Street Arts Fair features the work of more than 100 artists and craftspeople from Indiana and other states, as well as music. You'll find original oil and acrylic paintings, breathtaking photography, textiles, wood crafts, and other artwork in booths along with those promoting local cultural and community organizations.

Hoosierfest, an annual event that celebrates the city's downtown, is held the first weekend in September. The festival also turns the downtown into a race course for bicycle and mini-Grand Prix

The Monroe County Fair highlights the area's agrarian life, and is always a good excuse to revert to your childhood on a rollercoaster, carnival rides, or midway games.
Photo by Kendall Reeves.

(following page) While many famous performers have been associated with IU and its nationally recognized programs in arts and music, others are simply part of a long-standing community tradition. Musician Grey Larson, pictured here with collaborator Andre Marchand, is a fixture in a thriving folk music scene.
Photo by Rich Remsberg.

In mid-June, Arts Fair on the Square offers area artists a showcase for their handmade jewelry, hand-blown glass, ceramics, and paintings. More than 50 artisans participate in the fund-raiser for the Waldron Arts Center. Photo by Kendall Reeves.

go-cart races. In recent years, the cart racing has gone high-tech, and some business-sponsored teams spend months and considerable money prepping their vehicles for what has become a serious event. Hoosierfest also has become known for the music it presents—past nationally known performers have included rock-n-roll performers the BoDeans, Fiona Apple, and Robert Bradley's Blackwater Surprise, in addition to singers and bands based in the area. Also in early to mid-September is the Monroe County Fall Festival in downtown Ellettsville, which centers on the pride its residents have for their community, and the Third and High Festival of the Arts at Saint Charles Catholic Church on Bloomington's east side.

Within just a few years, the Lotus World Music and Arts Festival has developed into one of the country's top international music festivals, growing from a two-night happening into a year-round phenomenon. It has attracted performers from Bulgaria, Ireland, Tibet, and other points across the globe for concerts in Bloomington throughout the year, but the October festival remains at the heart of this multicultural endeavor. Past festival audiences have been exposed to music from French folk singer Gabriel Yacoub, American female vocalists

Dar Williams and Laura Love, Louisiana zydeco band leaders Gene Delafose and C. J. Chenier, and Irish fiddler Martin Hayes, just to name a few. In addition to spotlighting music from around the world, the festival pays tribute to Lotus Dickey, a poet and singer whose music best exemplified the folk music revival that took place in Indiana during the 1980s. At its inception in 1994, festival organizers had hoped it would become an important regional festival, but already it has exceeded that purpose. With continued momentum, the Lotus World Music and Arts Festival could gain the prominence associated with the better-known Newport and Spoleto fests, while maintaining its casual, comfortable feel.

The Christmas season begins with the annual lighting of the city's trees and its "canopy of lights," an elaborate array spoking out from the courthouse to buildings bordering it on all four sides. In addition to numerous holiday concerts around the region, there are the Chimes of Christmas concert and madrigal dinners on the IU campus. New Year's parties all over town bring the year to a close, only for a cycle of activity that not only continues, but grows. ⚐

Within just a few years, the Lotus World Music and Arts Festival has developed into one of the country's top international music festivals, growing from a two-night happening into a year-round phenomenon. In addition to spotlighting music from around the world, the festival pays tribute to Lotus Dickey, a poet and singer whose music best exemplified the folk music revival that took place in Indiana during the 1980s. The festival attracts entertainers from all over the world as well as homegrown talent, including a capella sensation Vida. Photo by Kendall Reeves.

Community

We Get Involved

"To tackle the problems that we
have, what this community offers
is a wealth of resources and talents
that Monroe County needs and,
through them, is blessed to have.
The diversity of the people is really
what makes it work. We have a
broad base that we can draw from,
including many people from the
university, industry, and small business. The people in our community,
for the most part, realize that it's
important to give back."

—Dorothy Ellis
  *Active volunteer and former campaign chair and
  board member of United Way of Monroe County*

By definition, communities consist of people who are united by the social, economic, and political interests they hold in common. While such places may be known for their origins, culture, physical beauty, or other positive attributes, ultimately what distinguishes a city or town from other destinations is how it addresses its challenges—does it face them, or flee from them? In addressing these concerns, are the efforts organized, productive, and focused on the health, safety, and well-being of every resident? No society can solve its problems completely, but like other places that truly can be called communities, the people of Bloomington are not afraid of challenges, nor are they shy of banding together to address them, whether it be as individuals, through publicly—or privately—supported volunteer activities, social service agencies, or their spiritual centers.

One strength of the people of Bloomington is their tendency to address challenges head-on and with a zealous spirit that still amazes Peg Stice, executive director of United Way of Monroe County, 10 years after arriving in Bloomington. "There is no question that the spirit here is higher than it is in most places," Stice said. "How can we keep doing more things? It's because of our volunteers."

At state conferences for various philanthropic organizations, Bloomington chapters usually have mobilized more volunteers, people who aren't just participating but also are leading the break-out sessions and serving on committees. "There's a greater sense of ownership," Stice said. "That brings with it some challenges, because then everyone does have some goals in mind, in terms of what they want to see happen in the community. There's almost a fervor about the level of involvement and the need to do more. There's a quality issue that comes in, combined with the energy. It's not just a 'do' thing; it's an attitude that 'we want to be the best.'"

Many people draw strength from religious faith, as nurtured in their houses of worship. Unlike many other Midwest communities, religious

traditions here run the full spectrum, from the Catholic faith to numerous Protestant denominations, from Judaism to Tibetan Buddhism and Islam. People gather at country chapels, temples, kingdom halls, and even a mosque. There are three Catholic parishes in Bloomington, including Saint John the Apostle Parish, which will complete construction on a new church building in western Monroe County in late 1998. Between 500 to 600 Muslims in Bloomington gather for study of the Qur'an and prayer sessions scheduled five times daily at a mosque dedicated in 1996. For decades, Second Baptist Church and Bethel AME Church have served primarily the African-American community. Jews observe Shabbat services and Hebrew holy days at Congregation Beth Shalom. Bloomington Baptist Church, established in 1824, is just one of several churches that date back to the county's origins and demonstrate the breadth of the area's religious heritage. With help from hundreds of unpaid volunteer workers from throughout southern Indiana, two congregations of Jehovah's Witnesses built a new 70-by-70-foot kingdom hall in just five days.

While residents have their own places of worship, people in 27 congregations work together

(previous page) For most individuals, the civic pride often expressed and felt is not remembered as personally as when people help each other. Photo by Kendall Reeves.

A not-for-profit volunteer organization, the Bloomington-based Sister City International helped the city establish links with Lu-Chou, Taiwan, and Posoltega, Nicaragua. Photo by Kendall Reeves.

(left) The people of Bloomington work together to see that young people, the elderly, and the needy are cared for. Photo by Rich Remsberg.

The year 1998 celebrates the 10-year anniversary of Habitat for Humanity of Monroe County, which built 15 houses between 1988 and 1997 and expects to build that many more by the year 2000. Photos by Rich Remsberg.

through Monroe County United Ministries, a joint effort that focuses on helping the poor and disadvantaged. Governed by a single board of directors and financed by churches and individuals, the organization has more than 400 volunteers who contribute a total of 40,000 hours each year. The organization functions through three neighborhood centers and operates a learning center, a housing corporation, and several outreach programs. Another religious organization, the Salvation Army, offers emergency assistance, food and clothing, temporary shelter, and counseling.

The United Way of Monroe County is the corporate, university, and community face of compassion, providing direction and support to more than 25 public assistance organizations. In 1997-98, it raised a record $1.7 million for people in Bloomington and surrounding communities. Almost all of the monies raised stay in the community and assist organizations such as Stone Belt Center, which helps persons with disabilities to attain independence through developmental education, community-based employment, residential services, and other assistance.

In the past decade, the Stone Belt program has placed more than 1,100 people with disabilities into jobs, with an average job retention rate of 85 percent. This is consistent with the stated goal of the United Way of Monroe County, which is to "increase the organized capacity of people to care for one another." Other examples of this include the Hoosier Hills Food Bank, which is able to distribute food to people through more than 110 agencies in 6 counties, and the Public Health Nursing Association, which reports more than 5,100 visits to its Community Health Access Program clinic annually.

Every October, local restaurants get into the act by dedicating a week to donating a portion of their proceeds to the annual United Way campaign and feeding more than just the persons who come to dine. The United Way also cosponsors "A Week of

Caring," a coordinated effort in which businesses, churches, students, and other groups participate in hands-on volunteer projects at local service agencies. The annual event gives attention to the importance of volunteerism.

On a given day during the week-long event in October 1997, volunteers worked together to help renovate a 101-year-old Victorian home for Hannah House, a maternity home and crisis pregnancy center. In the meantime, on the other side of town, other volunteers were making needed improvements to a garden project that helps feed needy people. The city of Bloomington, through its Community and Family Resources Department, supports a volunteer network that encourages teenagers to help others. It regularly publishes a listing of opportunities at nearly 60 agencies and organizations throughout Monroe County.

Companies and their employees also are reaching out to help others. The Greater Bloomington Chamber of Commerce and the IU Alumni Association established the "Good Friends" mentoring program, which benefits young people who are at an uncertain time of their lives. General Electric allows its employees to take time off to

volunteer. Its Elfun Society involves employees at all levels of the Bloomington plant in a variety of projects each year, including their recent renovation of a home in Ellettsville for children with AIDS and other serious health problems.

"I'm overwhelmed by it. It's like you can't sleep at night; you can't believe all of these people were out there all the time," said the foster home's director, Deborah Launer, in a newspaper article about the project. Bank One, Indiana encourages its employees to take time off to volunteer. "We encourage it. We feel it's part of the job," said the bank's immediate past president, Bob Richards. More than half of the bank's 160 employees are involved in volunteer community service. Another financial institution, Monroe County Bank, closed its doors so its 60 employees could participate fully in "A Week of Caring." Several companies, including *The Herald-Times,* Hall Signs, and Sunrise/ InterArt, also have in-house philanthropy departments, working to make contributions to the community.

As the city's largest employer, IU also recognizes its responsibility to provide people and resources to address the challenges it has in common with the community. IU employees and retirees comprise

Community Kitchen, founded in 1983, serves free nutritious meals to anyone in need with no fees or eligibility requirements. Photo by Kendall Reeves.

Over its history, Bloomington has
continually nurtured local musicians.
From as far back as the 1830s, the city
has always had organized bands.
Photo by Kendall Reeves.

more than one-third of the membership in local
chapters of major service clubs such as Rotary and
Kiwanis. More than 225 IU staff members and students regularly participate in the "Good Friends"
program, and more than 200 campus volunteers
serve on committees for the annual United Way
campaign. Over 55 agencies have IU employees
serving as directors. One new initiative, a town-
and-gown committee formed in 1996, brings
together 10 university and community leaders to
identify and discuss challenges facing the area. On
one important issue—housing—the committee
sought expertise from IU's Center for Real Estate
Studies, a major national resource center for
commercial and residential real estate developers.

So rather than just distribute provisions, people
here seek solutions. Another significant example of
this is the joint effort between the United Way, the
Community Service Council of Bloomington and
Monroe County, and HoosierNet, a community-
based Internet provider. Working together and in
partnership with its United Way counterpart in
nearby Bartholomew County, they undertook the
Giant Step Initiative, an effort to increase the effec-
tiveness of the social service community through
computer networking technology. While in other
areas this might start with local companies donating outdated, "leftover" computers, officials here
believed success depended on being in the forefront.
As a result and with funding support from Lilly
Endowment, each United Way member agency is
"wired," complete with an e-mail address and a
World Wide Web presence. For people seeking help,
a comprehensive, book-sized directory that had
been the best available reference on local service
organizations has been distilled for the Web. In
addition, several other agencies were able to create
their own Web pages that inform and provide
further access to help.

The initiative also has made communication
among agencies more efficient. For example, just a
few years ago, if a major Bloomington employer
wanted to donate a large amount of office equipment or supplies, it might take days and many
phone calls to reach everyone with the good news.
Today, using new communications technology
usually described as being essential for businesses,
"working smarter" enables area agencies and
community groups to be reached almost
instantaneously by means of HoosierNet.

"They are now all in a network, so our little
not-for-profits in Bloomington have been communi-
cating electronically a while now, and greatly
reduced the inefficiencies that result from bad
communication," Stice said. "It's what any good
business would do, but what most not-for-profits

Reverend Dr. Ernest D. Butler has been pastor of the Second Baptist Church in Bloomington since 1959. Known as a tireless worker on behalf of the disadvantaged and disenfranchised, Butler has been recognized at the local, state, and national levels by religious and civic groups. Among his many honors, he has received JCPenney's Lifetime Service Award and the Monroe County Community Service Award. Photo by Kendall Reeves.

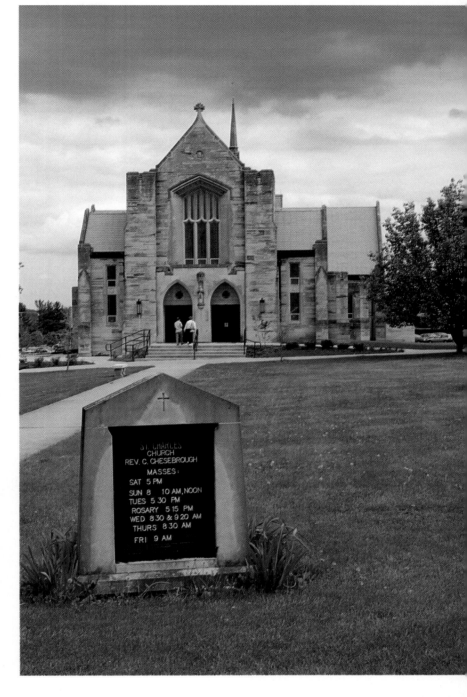

ST. CHARLES
CHURCH
REV. C. CHESEBROUGH
MASSES:
SAT 5 PM
SUN 8 10 AM, NOON
TUES 5 30 PM
ROSARY 5 15 PM
WED 8 30 & 9 20 AM
THURS 8 30 AM
FRI 9 AM

Many people draw strength from religious faith, as nurtured in their houses of worship. Unlike many other Midwest communities, religious traditions here run the full spectrum. While residents have their own places of worship, people in 27 congregations work together through Monroe County United Ministries, a joint effort that focuses on helping the poor and disadvantaged. Photos by Kendall Reeves.

(following page) Environmental, labor, and peace organizations are active in the community, as are senior citizen groups and youth groups such as the Boys and Girls Club of Bloomington, Girls Inc. of Monroe County, and the Boy and Girl Scouts. Many involve IU students, including women's basketball player Quacy Barnes, who went on to star in the WNBA. Photo by Kendall Reeves.

The Monroe County chapter of the American Red Cross provides relief to victims of fires and other disasters, offers courses in health and safety, and collects blood for use in hospitals. Photo by Kendall Reeves.

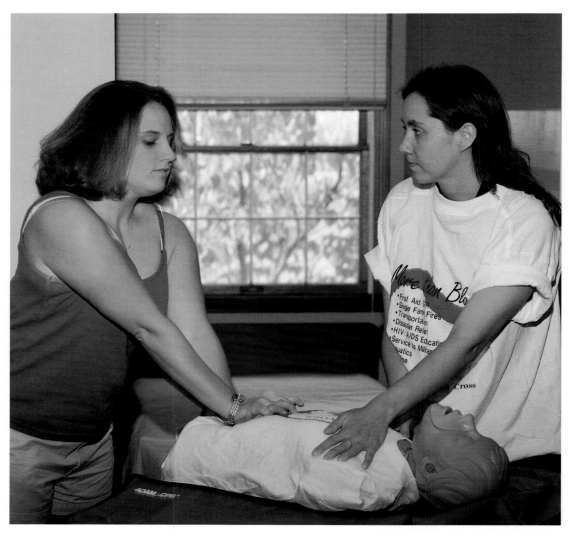

have not often been able to do." The computer network facilitates resource exchanges among agencies, cuts down on the number of time-consuming meetings, makes it easier for those in need to get answers quickly, and mobilizes people to work together on common problems.

Another key to addressing community challenges has been to establish public access sites at places like the Community Kitchen and the South Central Community Action Program for those who cannot afford a computer. An "all-ages" approach was taken in establishing public access sites—they include the Area 10 Agency on Aging and the Boys and Girls Club of Bloomington. "There are numerous examples, and we are developing what we're calling a 'cookbook' that will be a replicable model for other communities that are doing this," Stice said.

In times of crisis, this community pulls together. A good example of this is what happened in the days and months that followed a 1997 announcement by Thomson Consumer Electronics that it would close down its Bloomington operations and lay off 1,300 people in April 1998. City officials, who learned about the plant closing announcement a couple of days earlier, immediately brought

community service and education providers into the mix.

"We met that very next day," recalled Stice, "and we have been meeting every two weeks or so. . . . What the community did was to as quickly as possible identify what we could do early on." Local leaders immediately got in touch with officials in other, similar sized communities where similar closings had taken place. Indiana University worked with the city to serve as facilitator, offering connections to federal government officials as well as educational training.

The collected information was shared with local agencies and used to develop strategies. One such strategy was the establishment of a labor-management team at the plant that met once a week to organize and monitor programs designed to help workers. Peer counselors—persons chosen by labor and management in the plant—were trained to identify worker problems such as anger and substance abuse and to help workers access services that addressed them.

The Stand Proud Program was organized by IU business students, literacy program volunteers, and labor leaders, who worked together to train student volunteers to tutor Thomson workers. With the

The Hoosier Hills Food Bank distributes food to people through more than 110 agencies in 6 counties. Photo by Kendall Reeves.

A safe and secure atmosphere surrounds life in Bloomington. Photo by Kendall Reeves.

volunteers' help, many workers were able to pass GED examinations, learn to use a computer, and gain new skills that increased job opportunities. "The Stand Proud community response has been a win-win situation," comments Josh Cazares, AFL-CIO community services liaison. The efforts were an excellent example of how people here from all walks of life and backgrounds can work together to find solutions. Rather than wait to react to the closing's impact, people were proactive in anticipating problems early, "rolling up their sleeves" to soften the blow. The goal for the annual United Way fund drive was increased by 21 percent in expectation of community needs.

Area 10 Agency on Aging, which provides assistance to the homebound, operates Rural Transit, a transportation service that has 22 bus routes for residents in Monroe and Owen Counties. The Evergreen Project seeks housing solutions for older adults who continue to be active, despite some infirmities. The Monroe County chapter of the American Red Cross provides relief to victims of fires and other disasters, offers courses in health and safety, and collects blood for use in hospitals. Environmental, labor, and peace organizations are active in the community, as are senior citizen groups and youth groups such as the Boys and Girls Club of Bloomington, Girls Inc. of Monroe County, and the Boy and Girl Scouts.

The year 1998 celebrates the 10-year anniversary of Habitat for Humanity of Monroe County, which built 15 houses between 1988 and 1997 and expects to build that many more by the year 2000. "Many people know about Habitat's policy that prospective homeowners must contribute 'sweat equity' towards the construction of their home," said local Habitat President Scott Smart, who is also an IU business professor. "Beyond that, however, we rely on the continued support of partner families even after their required hours have been completed. Partner families are among our most dedicated volunteers."

The Monroe County Young Men's Christian Association (YMCA) has helped build healthy bodies and minds in Bloomington for more than 100 years. Its 85,000-square-foot, 17-acre facility on the city's south side is the largest and most complete family fitness center in Indiana. Built in 1981, it was expanded in 1985 and again in 1991. But in addition to having facilities needed for physical fitness, such as weight rooms, swimming pools, racquetball courts, and gymnasiums, the YMCA offers various self-help programs, such as those in stress management and nutritional instruction.

Throughout the pages of this book, much has been written about Monroe County and Bloomington—how the people rallied to confront water shortages, educational needs, the loss of companies and industries, as well as how they've nurtured an artistic vision that depicts the community's spirit. But for most individuals, the civic pride often expressed and felt is not remembered as personally as when people help each other. The problems experienced here are not unique, nor are the solutions. However, when people draw close as they sometimes do in Bloomington, their potential is limitless. ▲

The Monroe County YMCA has helped
build healthy bodies and minds in
Bloomington for more than 100 years.
Its facility on the city's south side is
the largest and most complete family
fitness center in Indiana. Photo by
Kendall Reeves.

Bloomington's
Enterprises
Part Two

Chapter

10

Networks

The Herald Times

A strong community newspaper with roots that run deep in the region's history, *The Herald-Times* places emphasis on local news, serving readers with information that is vitally important to the understanding of their community, neighborhood, local government, schools, and area business.

On May 12, 1877, two men lifted a sheet of newsprint from the ink-blackened bed of a second-hand printing press. Working carefully, Walter S. Bradfute and Frank Arnott gently folded that single sheet in half to form a four-page news pamphlet.

Printed in the back room of Arnott's mother's millinery shop, the publication would become Monroe County's longest continuously published newspaper. Casting about for something to name their neighborhood paper, the two looked at the recent invention of Alexander Graham Bell which was taking the world by storm. *The Telephone* newspaper quickly began spreading the news.

In 1943, *The Telephone* merged with *The Evening World* to become the *The Bloomington World-Telephone.* In 1950, *The World-Telephone* joined with the three-year-old *Bloomington Daily Herald,* and the first edition of *The Daily Herald-Telephone* was published on July 3, 1950. The word "Daily" was dropped from the name in 1977 when the H-T celebrated its centennial, becoming *The Herald-Telephone.*

The next big move came in 1989 when *The Herald-Telephone* changed its name to *The Herald-Times* and began morning delivery. Today, Schurz Communications, Inc. has branched out to include five newspapers, cable television, broadcast television, a shopper, broadcast radio, and KIVA Networking, an Internet service provider. Always on the cutting edge of technology, *The Herald-Times* recently launched a community Web site. HoosierTimes.com was created and developed by *The Herald-Times* to provide news, sports, and entertainment coverage important to all south central Indiana. *The Herald-Times* has partnered with local businesses and community groups to offer a broad range of information and ideas from a variety of sources.

A strong community newspaper with roots that run deep in the region's history, *The Herald-Times* places emphasis on local news, serving readers with information that is vitally important to the understanding of their community, neighborhood, local government, schools, and area business. The paper also serves as a complete source for news about the state of Indiana, regional concerns, and national and international developments.

Located at the center of a hotbed of collegiate athletics, sports also naturally plays a large role in the news package readers receive. In addition to Indiana University coverage, readers turn to *The Herald-Times* for reports on everything from local high school athletics to hunting and fishing. *The Herald-Times* takes seriously its responsibility of presenting clear and carefully considered opinion on its editorial page.

Under the direction of publisher Scott C. Schurz, the paper has had many successes, commercially and editorially. The newspaper is consistently recognized for journalistic excellence by professional organizations, including the Society of Professional Journalists, Hoosier State Press Association, Woman's Press Club of Indiana, Associated Press Managing Editors, and the National Federation of Press Women.

A spirit of civic duty is also demonstrated by participation in numerous community activities and organizations. H-T staff members may be found caring for animals at the Monroe County Humane Association, comforting youngsters at the Ronald McDonald House, baking cakes for a Harmony School fund-raiser, constructing a house for Habitat for Humanity, leading a Chamber of Commerce committee, planning an event with the Martin Luther King Jr. Celebration Commission, making crafts for the Apostolic Country Church, educating youngsters through its Newspaper in Education program, helping promote literacy with a weekly "Read Up On The News" column, or delivering clothing and food to a family whose home was destroyed by fire.

An integral part of the community, *The Herald-Times* helps area readers prepare for the day with coverage of all the important news, as well as places to go and things to do. As it has since its beginning more than a century ago, *The Herald-Times* continues to deliver.

The newspaper is consistently recognized for journalistic excellence by professional organizations, including the Society of Professional Journalists, Hoosier State Press Association, Woman's Press Club of Indiana, Associated Press Managing Editors, and the National Federation of Press Women.

Monroe County Airport

From its earliest beginnings in 1939, the Monroe County Airport has been an important cog in the region's economic development machinery. "A good airport is something you must have to ensure the economic well-being of a community today," says Airport Director Tom Boone.

It started when the City of Bloomington bought the Eller Farm four miles west of the city for development as an airport. During the early 1940s, Indiana University built an administration building and hangar at the airport site, and in 1943 the Bloomington Board of Aviation Commissioners was established.

In 1960, ownership of the airport was transferred to Monroe County government in order to increase the airport's tax base, and since then, a variety of construction projects has made the 850-acre airport what it is today.

Business flights make up the bulk of airport traffic. The airport houses 80 aircraft ranging from J-3 Cubs to Boeing 727s, using 48 T-hangars and 22 multiple aircraft hangars. The 24-hour-a-day, all-weather facility is the home base to corporate aircraft for over 20 local companies.

The economic impact of the airport is estimated at more than $25 million annually, according to figures from a 1995 economic impact study conducted by the Aviation Association of Indiana.

Other benefits can't be calculated in dollars and cents. Lives have been saved, thanks to air ambulances and the swift transport of time-critical medical supplies and donor organs. The quality of life for area residents is immeasurably enriched by the convenient and reliable transportation the Monroe County Airport affords.

As more and more business leaders discover Monroe County as a branch office or corporate relocation site, the sophistication of the airport plays a key role in their success.

"I was out at 6:15 this morning and here comes a big corporate jet," Boone says. "That kind of thing is happening all the time. You wouldn't have some of the big companies we have in Monroe County without a commercial airport."

Since the expansion of the Monroe County Airport's main north-south runway in 1994, large jets have been able to land here. And they do. Some are visitors—charter flights bringing football and basketball teams into the area. Some are musicians and entertainers—coming to perform or to study at the area's many entertainment venues and at Indiana University. Some are medical equipment technicians or computer experts—checking out new developments at local companies.

Some planes bring in politicians for a quick sweep to gather votes or check on government projects. Others are business executives wanting to see what south central Indiana has to offer their companies. To county officials and local business leaders, they bring the promise of a brighter future.

The airport also serves an important function in recreation. Pilot training and airplane storage is available. The Monroe County Airport also serves as the base for a Civil Air Patrol Squadron and Experimental Aircraft Association Chapter.

"We will continue to develop and expand the airport to meet the demands placed on it," Boone says. "We are committed to serving our customers with facilities that meet their needs now and in the future." ⚬

Bloomington's chapter of the Experimental Aircraft Association meets monthly at the airport.

Monroe County Airport is home base to over 80 aircraft.

Cook Aviation Inc.

The first impression some people have of the Bloomington area occurs while circling the Monroe County Airport, coming in for a landing. Thanks to the excellent service and dedication of Cook Aviation Inc., that initial experience is a positive one.

With its "red carpet treatment," Cook Aviation helps visitors get off on the right foot in this charming Midwest community. Cook Aviation employees specialize in Hoosier hospitality. "Service is our main priority," says President Rex Hinkle. "That's what this business is all about."

A Cook Group company, Cook Aviation is a fixed-base operator offering superior line service and a quick turnaround. Three fuel trucks provide efficient refueling at reasonable rates. An experienced staff takes care of the luggage, cleans the plane's interior, and has the aircraft ready to take off again in a short time.

Considerate touches inside the Cook Aviation terminal add to that warm welcome. Free coffee and ice are available, as are a pilot's lounge, and meeting and conference rooms. Courtesy and rental cars add convenience, as does a hotel reservation service with special crew hotel rates. Brochures and information about the Bloomington area help visitors figure out what to see and do on their visit, and the helpful staff is always happy to offer personal tips.

In at least one instance, Cook Aviation was instrumental in helping a corporation decide to locate its business in Bloomington. "When big corporations think of basing their companies here, they always look at transportation," Hinkle says. "Having a good airport that offers good service for corporate aircraft is very important."

The backbone of the enterprise, Hinkle says, is Cook Aviation's dedicated employees. Of the 10 staff members, a majority have been with the company since it started January 1, 1988. That adds a sense of continuity and experience that customers value. As part of the Cook Group, the people at Cook Aviation subscribe to the same philosophy that pervades the corporation: each employee is a valuable member of a team striving for a goal of excellence.

With more than 70 planes based at the airport and numerous gallons of fuel sold a month, Cook Aviation is a stickler for detail. Detailed record keeping is a must to keep the service functioning smoothly. When the Indiana University football team departs for a game, players and coaches know Cook Aviation will have everything on the aircraft ready to go.

Regular operation hours are 7 A.M. to 9 P.M., but Cook Aviation is on call 24 hours a day. Businesses sometimes need to operate beyond those scheduled times, and Cook Aviation is available to smooth the process. Medical emergencies also occur, such as when an organ for transplant needs transportation in the middle of the night. Cook Aviation is there to do whatever is necessary to speed the lifesaving procedure.

Some services can't be judged in dollars and cents, nor can they be found recorded in detailed maintenance reports. The net result of Cook Aviation is a better quality of life for people who work in, live in, and visit south central Indiana.

Cook Aviation's "red carpet treatment" helps visitors get off on the right foot in this charming Midwest community.

Cook Aviation is a fixed-base operator offering superior line service and a quick turnaround. Three fuel trucks provide efficient refueling at reasonable rates.

From a few people in a small office to 16 full-time staff members in a building all its own, *The Bloomington Voice* has grown to become a widely read weekly newspaper.

Back in 1992, south central Indiana was ready for an alternative newspaper when founders Bill Craig and Larry Rainey decided to take up the challenge. Keeping in mind the *Chicago Times* motto that "it is the newspaper's duty to print the news and raise hell," *The Bloomington Voice* has added a welcome viewpoint on issues ranging from city and county government to national and international policies.

Readers know they can turn to *The Bloomington Voice* for the story behind the story, the news that other mainstream media may be afraid to touch. When copies hit the stands each week, readers can look forward to in-depth cover stories dealing with such diverse topics as the march for Tibet's Independence, the shutdown of the local Thomson Consumer Electronics plant, the mayoral election, Single A baseball, and the disturbing legacy of a Nazi doctor.

Inside its 30 to 40 pages, *The Bloomington Voice* entertains with insider views on the local music and entertainment beats, amuses with cartoons, provokes with intelligent editorials, educates with an extensive calendar of community activities, and informs with letters to the editor.

And all of this information is contained in one neat package and it's free. Available at over 300 locations, plus the Internet, *The Bloomington Voice* is easy to pick up while running errands or relaxing over a steaming cup of cappuccino or a chilled glass of wine in a local restaurant.

"People are looking for something to read that is different," says editor and publisher Diane Aden Hayes. "We give people a voice that might not be heard otherwise."

Local businesses appreciate the wide range of readers attracted to *The Bloomington Voice*—as evidenced by a multitude of attractive ads created by top-notch advertising representatives and artists.

In 1997, the parent company of *The Bloomington Voice* was renamed NewVoice Communications and began acquiring other newspapers. The company bought the *Octopus* in Champaign, Illinois, and *The Illinois Times* in Springfield, Illinois. It also purchased CityScapes, a home page on the Internet's World Wide Web.

The Bloomington Voice also publishes *Dining Alternatives*, a comprehensive list of local restaurants, and the *Annual Manual*, a newcomers guide to the area.

The Bloomington Voice's commitment to service carries over to community involvement. It helps fund and support a variety of nonprofit organizations. The newspaper also sponsors events that enhance and celebrate the quality of life in Bloomington.

No matter the topic, *The Bloomington Voice* encourages readers to look at every angle and hear every voice. After all, that's the purpose of an alternative newspaper—to tweak the nose of "the establishment," point out the foibles of society, and make sure that every person has a chance to be heard. *The Bloomington Voice* does an excellent job of filling that role. Ⓐ

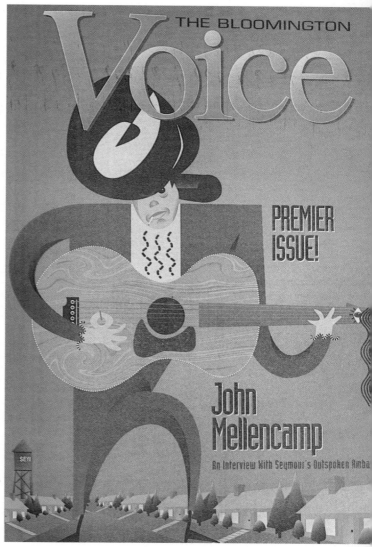

Readers know they can turn to *The Bloomington Voice* **for the story behind the story, the news that other mainstream media may be afraid to touch. The premiere issue of** *The Bloomington Voice* **featured an interview with John Mellencamp. Photo by Diane Aden Hayes.**

In 1992, south central Indiana was ready for an alternative newspaper when founders (left to right) Larry Rainey and Bill Craig decided to take up the challenge. Photo by Diane Aden Hayes.

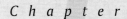

Chapter

11

Manufacturing, Distribution, and Technology

Otis Elevator Company

Otis Elevator Company has been steadily growing since its beginnings. In 1852, Elisha Graves Otis, a 41-year-old master mechanic, built a freight elevator with a safety brake for his employer, a bedstead manufacturing firm in Yonkers, New York. His invention was the world's first elevator that wouldn't plunge to the ground should the cable snap. To prove that point, Otis put

Otis's research and development initiatives have led to new components such as the High Performance Linear Induction Motor.

his reputation and his life on the line—he went up in his elevator and had the rope cut. The safety device held.

Less than a decade later, Otis died and his two sons, Norton and Charles, carried on the business, laying the groundwork for the elevator industry and receiving 53 patents between them. The elevator, more than any other modern invention, has shaped today's cities. The invention enabled architects to design taller and taller buildings, and people no longer had to climb stairs to reach the upper floors.

Today, 50,500 Otis employees work in more than 200 countries worldwide and speak more than two dozen languages. But they all share a common vision—to satisfy customers and employees by providing superior elevators and escalators.

The Otis Elevator Company in Bloomington is the only Otis manufacturing plant in North America. Since moving to Bloomington from New York in 1965, the company has maintained a position as one of the community's preeminent employers.

The Otis Elevator Company in Bloomington is the only Otis manufacturing plant in North America. Since moving to Bloomington from New York in 1965, the company has maintained a position as one of the community's preeminent employers.

In 1996, the manufacturing facility earned the State of Indiana Quality Improvement Award for quality initiatives and achievements. The award is presented each year to Indiana-based companies with extraordinary achievements in quality.

The facility's continuous improvement focus has enabled the Bloomington factory to significantly reduce defect rates.

Hand in hand with the reduction in defects is cost reduction, achieved through the facility's Preferred Supplier Program. This program is helping to identify suppliers dedicated to finding effective ways to reduce costs on products, from production materials to packaging and transportation, and it is helping Otis control cost, reduce inventories, and maintain high quality.

Otis offers its products for sale in virtually all countries in the world. Otis is the largest company in the manufacture, maintenance, and service of elevators, escalators, moving walkways, and other horizontal transportation systems. Otis is a wholly owned subsidiary of United Technologies Corporation. ⚠

Recently, Bloomington's plant gained acclaim as the manufacturer of elevators for the "world's tallest buildings"—twin towers in Malaysia, a $65-million elevator contract that is the largest ever awarded.

Another landmark contract gave the Bloomington plant the interesting task of producing 43 elevators for the 63-story World Trade Center in Bangkok, a $17-million job. The installation will be the first double-deck elevator installation in Thailand. A double-deck elevator consists of two cars constructed one atop the other in order to serve alternate floors simultaneously. These units reduce the number of elevator shafts needed in the building, thereby increasing the amount of rentable space.

The company is widely recognized for its quality initiatives. Bloomington honors include the 1994 Environmental Health and Safety Award for reducing hazardous waste levels, air emissions, and accident rates.

Otis Elevator Company has been steadily growing since its beginnings in 1852.

In 1996, the Bloomington manufacturing facility earned the State of Indiana Quality Improvement Award for its safety and quality initiatives.

Cook Incorporated

From its simple beginning, Cook Incorporated has grown into a multimillion-dollar, multinational corporation, and more importantly, it has transformed medical technology and saved lives.

Before Cook, no single manufacturer coordinated production of the devices required for the Seldinger procedure. Cook became the first company to meet the needs of early angiographers in the United States.

Cook Incorporated, started in 1963 on a $1,500 investment, epitomizes the American dream. What began as a single-room enterprise in a small Bloomington apartment has grown into a worldwide medical device organization meeting the needs of physicians and patients with less invasive and less costly health care options.

Cook offered the right products at the right time. From its simple beginning, Cook Incorporated has grown into a multimillion-dollar, multinational corporation. More importantly, it has transformed medical technology and saved lives.

Since the cardiovascular system, comprised of the blood vessels and the heart, does not show up on X-ray film, it is necessary to inject its parts with a radiopaque dye in order to visualize them. In that way abnormalities, such as vessel blockages or malfunctioning heart valves, can be diagnosed and corrective action taken.

It was not until a Swedish physician, S. I. Seldinger, in 1953 perfected the technique of guiding a small catheter through blood vessels, to the site where the dye needed to be injected, that cardiovascular catheterizations became a practical method of diagnosis, often eliminating exploratory surgery.

Dr. Charles T. Dotter of the University of Oregon and Dr. Walter E. Judson of Indiana University were among the American pioneers. When Cook Incorporated was founded in 1963, the catheterization procedure was still just beginning to receive widespread attention.

Before Cook, no single manufacturer coordinated production of the devices required for the Seldinger procedure. Cook became the first company to meet the needs of early angiographers in the United States, creating tremendous growth in the use of diagnostic procedures involving Cook products.

In the 1970s, physicians in fields other than cardiology and radiology began to recognize the value and ease of the Seldinger technique. Today the technique is applied to many disciplines of medicine, such as interventional radiology, urology, oncology, general surgery, cardiology, anesthesiology, and critical care medicine. As applications using the Seldinger procedure expanded into new areas, the market for Cook products also increased.

From that first step as a diagnostic tool, Cook was able to advance the technology even more. If the procedure could be used to diagnose a problem, then why couldn't it also be used to remedy the problem? The result of that approach can be seen today in such medical advancements as gall bladder surgery requiring only three tiny holes in the abdomen. Previously, gall bladder removal meant a major abdominal incision and a six-week recovery period for the patient. Now the patient typically goes home the next day.

Under president Phyllis McCullough, the firm has been adding employees steadily over the years. At 1,300, it is now the area's second-largest manufacturing employer. In late 1997, Cook Incorporated announced plans to construct a campus-like company headquarters west of Bloomington. The

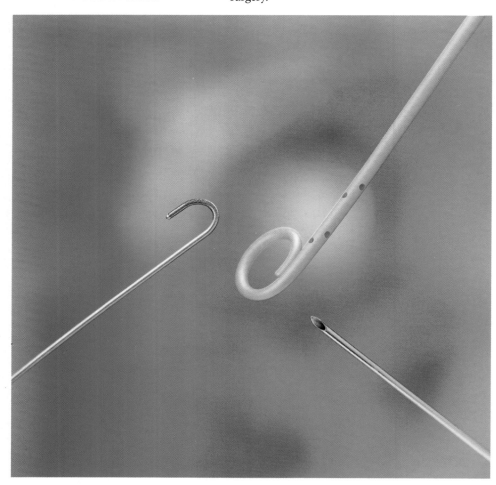

company purchased about 70 acres at the north end of Park 48 industrial park. Groups of buildings that will house manufacturing and research facilities will surround a large administrative office building at the hub of the new complex.

Over the years, Cook Incorporated has committed millions of dollars to product development to ensure continued growth. In 1997, Cook's GR II® Coronary Stent became the first new coronary stent cleared in three years by the U.S. Food and Drug Administration. Cook's earlier stent—the first approved for use in the United States—has been commercially available since 1993, with more than 100,000 United States implants.

Stents are small, round spring-like devices that are implanted inside arteries to prevent re-blocking of vessels after angioplasty dilation. The new stents allow access to blocked, narrow, and twisted arteries that were previously difficult or impossible to reach. Coronary stents now help thousands of heart disease patients who might otherwise require heart bypass surgery.

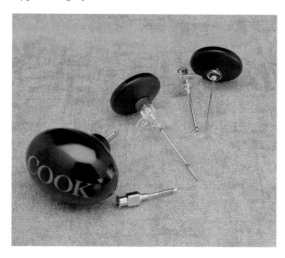

Medical products developed first by Cook are as follows: 1963—the first domestic Percutaneous Entry Needle, a needle for introducing a wire guide into vessels. 1963—the first domestic Percutaneous Entry Wire Guide, a wire guide for guiding catheters throughout the anatomy without surgical cutdown. 1963—the first domestic Percutaneous Entry Catheter, a catheter to follow the wire guide to various points in the vascular system to deliver radiopaque dye to diagnose abnormalities. 1964—the first Movable Core Wire Guide, which allows the physician to vary the stiffness of the wire guide during the procedure. 1965—the first Catheter Introducer Sheath Set, which allows nonsurgical placement of closed end catheters, temporary pacemaker leads, and cardiac output catheters. 1975—the first Angioplasty Polyvinyl Balloon Catheter, a catheter for dilating narrowed or obstructed

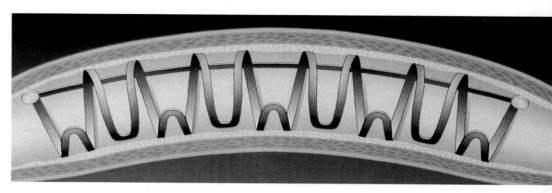

arteries. 1979—the first Peel-Away Introducer, a device that allows nonsurgical placement of catheters throughout the body. 1981—the first Cope Loop Drainage Catheter, a drainage catheter which has a suture mechanism for staying in place. 1987—the first "Screw Type" Intraosseous Needle, a needle screwed into the bone marrow for emergency replacement of fluids. 1987—the first Fallopian Catheter Set, a system utilizing a small wire guide to catheterize the fallopian tubes from the uterus. 1989—the first Bird's Nest Vena Cava Filter, a nonsurgically placed filter for trapping blood clots in the vena cava. 1989—the first Biliary "Z" Stent, a metallic stent for nonsurgical placement in the biliary tree to provide internal drainage. 1993—the first Coronary Stent.

Many of these breakthrough products resulted from the close relationship Cook Incorporated cultivates with the medical professionals using its medical devices and products. Physicians and other health care providers depend on Cook for everything from industry-leading interventional and surgical devices to individual instruments custom-modified for the precise medical needs of a single patient. It's all part of Cook Incorporated's commitment to saving lives. First, the company LISTENS to the needs of the world's medical professionals. Next, it works one-on-one with the practitioners using its devices to UNDERSTAND their needs. Finally, Cook Incorporated INNOVATES to address those needs by improving existing devices and creating breakthrough medical products that open new frontiers in health care. Listen. Understand. Innovate. A simple formula that has made Cook Incorporated one of the world's most recognized and trusted medical organizations. ⚕

In 1997, Cook's GR II® Coronary Stent became the first new coronary stent cleared in three years by the U.S. Food and Drug Administration.

In 1987, Cook manufactured the first "Screw Type" Intraosseous Needle, a needle screwed into the bone marrow for emergency replacement of fluids.

PTS Electronics Corporation

When PTS Electronics Corporation opened its doors in the early 1960s, it had a handful of employees, a commitment to quality, and a vision that spanned the globe. From that early workforce, two young men with drive and dedication emerged to guide the company to become a major force in the world of electronics.

As equal partners, Jack Craig and Jeff Hamilton determined when they bought the company that PTS Electronics would be the best at what it does. They vowed the company would offer "the highest level of quality and service to our customers in the electronics industry." That commitment would be achieved, they said, "by adhering to high ethical and moral standards, and creating an environment of trust and prosperity in partnership with our customers and employees."

Headquartered in Bloomington with plants in Tustin, California, and Denver, Colorado, PTS Electronics has grown to be a leader in the remanufacturing and rebuilding of tuners, modules, and mainboards; computer boards; monitors and terminals; cellular phone products; cable TV converters; and automotive electronics. Located in a quiet wooded area, PTS has ample room for expansion to serve its growing customer base.

The company's commitment to excellence is evident in its belief that its greatest asset is strong relationships with its customers. The entire PTS staff works to exceed customer expectations for quality service. PTS employees know how to listen to customers and respond to their needs with expertise unsurpassed in the electronic service industry. PTS uses teamwork to get the job done with customers becoming part of the winning team.

The PTS customer base includes major electronic manufacturers, independent electronic service dealers, national retail electronic chain stores, distributors, third party maintenance companies, and government and educational institutions. The list of major manufacturers that utilize PTS service reads like a Who's Who in the electronics field and

includes names such as Motorola, Pioneer, Emerson, GE, Goldstar, Hitachi, Magnavox, Midland, Mitsubishi, Alpine, Montgomery Ward, Panasonic, Radio Shack, RCA, Samsung, Sanyo, Sears, Sharp, Sony, Sylvania, and Toshiba.

PTS began as a television tuner service and replacement firm, and today this segment is still an integral part of the operation. PTS services all makes and models of TV, cable, and VCR tuners and has the nation's largest inventory available for immediate shipment. PTS's inventory allows customers to save up to 60 percent on the cost of television tuners when compared to manufacturer direct replacements.

In the mid '70s, PTS began servicing television modules and has developed a program to include mainboards and complete chassis from most major television manufacturers. PTS inventory provides a convenient source for a wide variety of mainboards and chassis. With over 300 individual test positions, PTS tests every mainboard in a live chassis before shipment to the customer. And if PTS doesn't have a module or mainboard in stock, the company can rebuild the nonworking unit.

The computer age has influenced and changed almost every aspect of business today. PTS knows how important it is to keep computer equipment and networks up and running. PTS's computer equipment repair program provides component level service on computer monitors, printers, personal computers, motherboards, and terminals. PTS also sells remanufactured equipment at a fraction of the original replacement cost. Many of the nation's large retailers and computer wholesalers

As equal partners, (left to right) Jeff Hamilton and Jack Craig vowed PTS Electronics would offer the highest level of quality and service in the electronics industry. That commitment has been achieved by adhering to high ethical and moral standards, and creating an environment of trust and prosperity.

PTS Electronics has grown to be a leader in the remanufacturing and rebuilding of tuners, modules, and mainboards; computer boards; monitors and terminals; cellular phone products; cable TV converters; and automotive electronics.

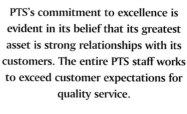

utilize PTS for their computer equipment service needs.

Over the years, PTS has gained the confidence of major manufacturers on a wide variety of projects. By utilizing its technical base and flexibility, PTS has the capability to start up production lines in a matter of days. Products serviced for the aforementioned manufacturers include cable TV converters, descramblers, and amplifiers; cellular phones; C-Band and DBS satellite receivers; appliance controls and modules; power supply boards; computer boards, monitors, and terminals; and electronic modules for the automotive, security, communications, and video industries.

PTS's belief in forming strong strategic customer/vendor partnerships can help accomplish four main objectives: reduce parts inventory, provide faster service, minimize labor costs, and increase profits. As part of PTS's winning team, clients are able to meet the challenges of today's service industry and be in a position to meet goals for tomorrow.

A high-tech, nonpolluting company, PTS attracts progressive people who have a strong desire to succeed and offers them a growth-oriented environment. Being located in Bloomington, with its high quality of life and wealth of natural attractions, is a main draw for attracting and retaining skilled employees.

"I would put our workforce up against any in the world," says Jeff Hamilton. "There's a lot of harmony among the people who work here, and we feel fortunate to have such an excellent workforce."

PTS Electronics knows that success in today's electronics industry requires the ability to be responsible to customers' needs and to adapt to new technology and market demands. PTS's technical and engineering personnel work hard to stay on top of new technology and training. PTS provides ongoing training for its employees, utilizing in-house training facilities, external management, and employee development firms.

PTS's emphasis on helping people and pursuing excellence extends into the community as well. The rapid growth and high retention rate of PTS are due in part to its ongoing commitment to the community it serves. The organization works hard to give back to the electronics industry and the local community.

Employees are encouraged to be active in the place where they live and work. Company management serves on the board of directors for such local organizations as the American Red Cross, Community Alliance for Lifelong Learning, Junior Achievement, Boys and Girls Club, and the Greater Bloomington Chamber of Commerce. PTS also provides financial support for area activities, such as a major grant to the Bloomington Community Foundation to help beautify Bloomington's entryways.

PTS Electronics is proud of its strengths—an outstanding portfolio of clients, high-quality service in rebuilding the world of electronics, dedication to its Bloomington birthplace, and a workforce second to none. PTS understands service, to its customers and to its community. After all, service is part of the PTS Electronics name. ⚸

PTS's computer equipment repair program provides component level service on computer monitors, printers, personal computers, motherboards, and terminals. Many of the nation's large retailers and computer wholesalers utilize PTS for their computer equipment service needs.

PTS's commitment to excellence is evident in its belief that its greatest asset is strong relationships with its customers. The entire PTS staff works to exceed customer expectations for quality service.

Sunrise/InterArt

Back in 1974, three liberal arts graduates fresh out of Indiana University were looking for jobs. Instead, they decided to make their own.

They rented a six-unit garage complex, knocked out a couple of walls, set up a second-hand press, and hammered together some racks. Thus was born Sunrise Publications, soon to become one of the largest greeting card publishers in the world.

The original concept was to design and produce contemporary greeting cards with a unique style of illustration and editorial content aimed at the baby boomer generation. According to Michael Fitzgerald, chief executive officer and one of the original founders of Sunrise, "We saw people's needs to express themselves. At the time the only cards available were 'grandmother cards,' simple florals with syrupy verses." And so Sunrise was born as an alternative card company for "people who would send a card—if only they could find one."

The trio never dreamed their little Sunrise operation would one day become a major player in the social expression industry. Millions of greeting cards bearing the name of "Bloomington, Ind." on their backs are sent each year. From its Bloomington address at 1145 Sunrise Greetings Court, Sunrise has expanded beyond greeting cards to include a wide variety of related paper products, such as gift bags, wrapping paper, stationery, photo frames, posters, journals, and other gift items.

"Sometimes the hair stands up on the back of my neck when I look at the people here and see

how far we've come," says Fitzgerald. "Sunrise is a very special place."

With all the growth and a desire to expand into new territory, a new name was needed: "InterArt." Sunrise continues to prosper as a social expressions manufacturer under the parent company of InterArt. Under the InterArt name, several sister companies have been created, such as InterArt Licensing, which represents Sunrise artists to manufacturers seeking the use of quality artwork in products other than greeting cards. Another sister company to Sunrise, InterArt Distribution is the first company in the American greeting card industry to distribute multiple product lines from a diversity of manufacturers. Today, InterArt employs over 600 people and covers 300,000 square feet with room to grow.

Licenses for Sunrise designs have been granted for distribution throughout the world. Over 325 field sales consultants and tele-sales representatives, all dedicated employees, market the products in the United States and Canada. Sunrise contracts the work of more than 250 artists worldwide, including popular illustrator Mary Engelbreit.

A long way from their initial primitive set-up, InterArt now maintains the latest technology in all of its operations. From manufacturing to product design, using state-of-the-art equipment and software creates endless possibilities in executing new design ideas.

The company's success can be attributed largely to the company's philosophy for dealing with people. To build a "people-first" attitude, InterArt provides a creative atmosphere that challenges people personally and professionally, and that encourages teamwork, communication, and information-sharing among employees. In keeping with this philosophy, Sunrise/InterArt has some of

Sunrise/InterArt maintains the latest technology in all of its operations. From manufacturing to product design, using state-of-the-art equipment and software creates endless possibilities in executing new design ideas.

From its Bloomington address Sunrise/InterArt has expanded beyond greeting cards to include a wide variety of related paper products, such as gift bags, wrapping paper, stationery, photo frames, posters, journals, and other gift items.

the happiest employees in Indiana. And for good reasons. Along with an attractive benefits package, each month employees get a four-day weekend, or two paid days off. Between four-day weekends, personal time, and vacation time, each employee receives 40 paid days off a year.

Another unique benefit that InterArt offers to its employees is the InterArt Career Development Center, which coordinates educational seminars and workshops on timely subjects, ranging from advanced computer training to improving public speaking to management techniques. The Career Development Center also includes an extensive library of resources as well as two key programs, Wellness and Parenting. Armed with the belief that a happy and healthy employee results in a more efficient workforce, InterArt offers optional wellness classes on topics such as "How to Quit Smoking." The Parenting program presents workshops on parenting issues, maintains a parenting resource library, and provides assistance to Sunrise families with problems. InterArt also offers a Parenting Resource Guide with instructions for other businesses that may be interested in creating a similar Parenting program.

InterArt's commitment to people extends beyond its corporate boundaries and into the community. In addition to helping other local companies develop their own parenting training for employees, Sunrise/InterArt supports literacy programs, employs physically and mentally handicapped citizens, and sponsors festivals, including the popular Lotis World Music and Arts Festival. Local schools and other organizations also have benefited from extra paper stock and greeting cards donated by Sunrise/Interart for arts projects.

With a strong belief in protecting the earth, InterArt is committed to a comprehensive recycling program. Starting in the 1980s, Sunrise decided to get the recycling ball rolling. Instead of paying people to take paper to the county landfill, Sunrise initiated a paper collection program and hired people to transport its waste paper to recycling mills. Between buying recycled paper products for office use, using recycled-content paper for nearly 100 percent of Sunrise greeting cards, and recycling vast amounts of waste paper, InterArt hopes to do its part in helping the environment. Taking the efforts a step further, InterArt also experiments with using tree-free paper made from kenaf, a fast-growing, rapidly renewable plant and an environmentally positive alternative to wood-based paper.

During its swift climb in the marketplace, Sunrise has never forgotten its roots or the community that has helped it prosper. Sunrise remains a strong example of Bloomington's artistic community and entrepreneurial spirit. ⚼

Sunrise/InterArt's goal is to design and produce contemporary greeting cards with a unique style of illustration and editorial content aimed at the baby boomer generation.

Sunrise/InterArt employs over 600 people. Its facilities cover 300,000 square feet with room to grow.

Carlisle Braking Systems

Bloomington, Indiana, is home to the worldwide headquarters of Motion Control Industries, a subsidiary of Carlisle Companies, Inc. The Bloomington facility produces braking products for the off-highway market.

Carlisle Braking Systems produces its brake products using the latest in flexible turning and machining center Computer Numerically Controlled technology. Most materials can easily be machined with workpiece sizes ranging from that of a pocket calculator to a kitchen oven.

Dedicated to supplying high-quality off-road braking components, Carlisle Braking Systems (CBS) has built its stellar reputation by remaining totally committed to supplying and serving its markets. At the same time, Carlisle strives to always be a good employer and well-respected member of the business community in the Bloomington area.

The Bloomington facility is home to the worldwide headquarters of Motion Control Industries, a subsidiary of Carlisle Companies, Inc. Principal products produced at the Bloomington site include caliper disc brakes, actuators, adjusters, full-power hydraulic brake valves, manifolds, and pressure switches, making Carlisle a full-system brake manufacturer.

These products have been manufactured for nearly every major type of off-highway heavy equipment and have provided superior quality, ease of maintenance, and long-lasting performance for over 30 years.

The Bloomington operation has undertaken aggressive strategies targeted at developing its people, processes, and systems into a flexible, responsive, and very competitive organization. Supporting this effort is the strength and commitment of Carlisle Corporation, available capital resources, and a workforce willing to do "whatever it takes" to get the job done.

Carlisle came to Bloomington in 1990, when it bought the B. F. Goodrich plant, formerly the Sarkes-Tarzian television tuner company, which closed in the early 1970s. But the history of the Carlisle corporation goes back a long way. It is a story of growth and success based on a quality product and customer satisfaction.

Carlisle's focus on rubber, plastic, and transportation-related products dates to its founding in 1917 as a maker of automobile and bicycle inner tubes. During World War II, its production, by then including tires, was converted to synthetic rubber.

As the company has grown, rubber products have continued to be an essential part of its business. Over the years, however, growth has also come from acquired businesses that have broadened the markets Carlisle serves.

Through a decentralized management system, Carlisle businesses now manufacture roofing systems, food-service permanent ware, high-performance wire and cable, specialized trailers, rubber and plastic automotive components, refrigerated shipping containers, heavy-duty friction and brake systems, specialty tires and wheels, and in-plant processing equipment. Carlisle Companies Incorporated is comprised of three operating segments—construction materials, transportation products, and general industry. Each year, Carlisle spells out a series of long- and short-term objectives whose achievements are considered critical to the company's success. Setting ambitious goals and pursuing them aggressively is Carlisle's way to achieve the growth and profitability its shareholders expect.

One key to Carlisle's growth and evolution has been to preserve businesses that have developed a competitive advantage or market leadership, add new capabilities to serve new markets, and shed those few businesses that have not built value.

The ideals which have fueled Carlisle's success extend to its role in the community as a corporate citizen. By supporting such programs as United Way and the Community Kitchen, Carlisle employees make a difference in Bloomington. Taking its community involvement a step farther, Carlisle hires employees from the Stone Belt Center for people with developmental disabilities. "It is good for them and it is good for us," General Manager Rob Heinrich says.

Carlisle offers a full package of employment benefits for its employees, but it also offers the "extras" that make it a desirable employer. A 401K plan, with the company paying a two-third match,

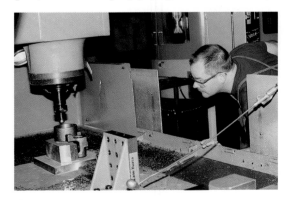

is available, as is the option to purchase company stock—an excellent investment since the stock almost tripled from 1991 to 1996.

An aggressive recycling program at Carlisle Braking Systems has reduced waste and helped protect the environment. Long a recycler of scrap metal, Carlisle also recycles office paper, computer paper, aluminum cans, and other metals.

Much has changed since Carlisle first opened its doors in 1917 with a single product and domestic focus. Carlisle now reaches out from 59 locations in 13 countries to service, construction, transportation, and general industrial markets.

But the driving impetus behind Carlisle still stands. Carlisle Braking Systems' mission is to be the leading provider of selected engineered braking components, leveraging its brake and friction expertise while focusing on niche markets.

Its goal is to optimize financial performance, provide superior customer service, and promote an environment that will foster mutual commitment of its human resources. Carlisle pledges to pursue technical and business innovations for aggressive growth as the leading brake components supplier to the commercial/industrial vehicle markets.

Along those lines, the Carlisle Braking Systems objective is to enhance present long-term relationships as well as establish new ones with customers who share a common vision for a progressive tomorrow. ⓐ

Carlisle Braking Systems has a progressive quality assurance organization represented by the latest in inspection techniques. Pictured here is a Carlisle employee utilizing a coordinate measuring machine used for checking critical dimensions on machined parts.

Carlisle Braking Systems employee utilize various state-of-the-art computer systems to monitor products through various stages of production, from design to shipment.

Hall Signs, Inc.

From a garage workshop in downtown Bloomington almost a half-century ago to a new state-of-the-art manufacturing facility, Hall Signs has grown to be one of the nation's leading manufacturers of traffic control signs.

How did the small one-man business become such an impressive success story? The answer is simple: the company was founded on good, old-fashioned principles. It was committed to a focused vision—that Hall Signs would have a positive impact on society through innovation, process refinement, and quality core values rooted in Christian beliefs.

Back in 1949, Wayne F. Hall started with a $1,000 investment and a conviction that he could supply America with quality sign products at competitive prices. Hall persuaded his wife to quit her job and become secretary/treasurer for this new venture.

In the 1960s, the business moved to Bloomington's west side. Building a large warehouse and increasingly turning its efforts toward sign manufacturing, Hall Signs began purchasing aluminum coil from major aluminum producers and transforming it into chemically treated cut shapes for the burgeoning highway market.

By the mid-1970s, Larry W. Hall left his career with the 3M Corporation and joined his father and mother in business. The company leveraged the younger Hall's experience by instituting new silk screening and printing operations, further establishing the company's reputation as a full-service sign manufacturer.

Today, Larry Hall is the president of the company that his father started nearly 50 years ago. Hall Signs, Inc. sells signs and related equipment in every state in the nation and to foreign countries in the western hemisphere. However, the company isn't content to rest on its laurels. "We are always willing to try new things," Larry Hall says. "We think it's more fun to set the pace and have others chase our dust clouds."

On July 4, 1996, Hall Signs moved into its new 83,000-square-foot facility, which allows the company to grow, together with customer needs, into the twenty-first century. With about 65 employees, Hall Signs is an industry leader in the manufacture of aluminum signs, as well as the world's largest manufacturer of cast aluminum sign brackets. The company mass produces these sign supports, something few of its competitors can do.

The enhanced capabilities of the new facility make the move into custom commercial sign products a logical development. Hall Signs creates custom signs destined for spots along America's roadways, as well as for major business enterprises in need of quality signage. The company has moved beyond supplying signs only to state and local governments. Its expanding customer base includes Fortune 500 companies, large utility firms, private developments, subdivisions, and the nation's largest shopping malls.

"We want to build upon our reputation for quality products in our traffic division with custom products for the private sector," says General Manager Greg Otter.

Hall Signs' graphic design artists can help customers select the perfect shape, size, style, and material necessary for their custom sign projects. Hundreds of options such as clip art, special borders, or custom colors can be incorporated quickly and inexpensively. As a full-service sign manufacturer, Hall Signs stocks large amounts of raw materials, allowing the company to respond quickly to a customer's request.

As part of their customer service program, Hall Signs can provide material samples and a color proof of the finished product. The goal is total quality manufacturing and guaranteed customer satisfaction.

Hall Signs leads the industry in innovation. For example, at the Soldiers and Sailors Monument in Indianapolis, Hall Signs manufactured the over-sized street signs at Monument Circle and, as a

President Larry Hall stands with custom signage designed by Hall Sign's art department and produced through the commercial design division.

Two and a half tons of coiled aluminum are being processed on the "cut-to-length" line.

The landscaped entrance reflects the friendly and courteous service customers receive from Hall Sign employees.

result, developed the specialty sign brackets which hold them.

A most important aspect of the company's success is a respect for the value of employees and the importance of a corporation's people. That sense of value runs deep at Hall Signs. Quite simply, the company believes in teamwork—one employee working with another, department with department, suppliers with manufacturers, and companies with customers.

That is how the beautiful new facility was planned and constructed. "For a year or so, we asked our employees what they would like to see in the new building," Larry Hall says. "Their ideas and suggestions helped make this such an impressive facility."

The company operates under a philosophy emphasizing open lines of communication with management. Part of this philosophy necessitates creating committees with employee members, involving management in employee training, and listening to employee solutions to problems. No idea or suggestion is overlooked.

The family of Hall Sign professionals has—through their talents, energy, and hard work—helped build a company that is a great source of pride. "Some of our people have been with the business for 20 years or so," Hall says.

To help in job growth, Hall Signs offers to pay tuition for employees to gain job-related skills at Indiana University, Ivy Tech State College, and other educational facilities. Also, amenities at the plant show the company's genuine concern for its employees—a comfortable kitchen and break room, picnic tables nestled under a canopy of trees on the well-tended lawn, a computer training room, and that familiar Hoosier accessory, an outdoor basketball goal.

Hall Signs also takes seriously its commitment to its hometown, particularly young people and families in need. A Charitable Contributions Committee helps decide where company resources should be distributed. Some programs have become a yearly tradition. For instance, the company supplies Thanksgiving baskets for those in need by purchasing turkeys, and the employees donate the canned goods and other food items.

Likewise, Hall Signs provides backpacks filled with school supplies at the start of a new school year to children living in a local shelter. Close to the heart of Larry Hall is the Bloomington Boys and Girls Clubs, where he serves on the board of directors. Larry and his wife, Patsy, were able to help the clubs by donating a passenger van to assist in transporting the children.

Hall Signs' employees participate in picking up litter and beautifying a section of highway north of Bloomington under the state's Adopt a Highway program. The company also designed the identifying signs for this statewide program.

From the Hall family through the extended family of employees to the families who turn to them for quality products and great service, Hall Signs is a company that has built a reputation for caring and quality. With a firm appreciation of its past, Hall Signs looks forward to the future and the new millennium with a commitment to carry on the family's vision. ⚲

Finished printed stock traffic signs are on the rack, ready for packaging and shipping.

A Scanning Auger is used to locate imperfections measured in angstroms in tiny microcircuits.

Crane Division

Naval Surface Warfare Center is a national asset located in the Hoosier heartland. One of the biggest employers in southern Indiana and a major contractor in the state, Crane has grown from a center that employed just three civilian employees when first orders were received there in 1941, to over 3,400 employees with an annual payroll of $150 million.

The size of Crane is mind-boggling: 185 miles of paved streets and highways, 226 miles of unpaved roads, 75 miles of perimeter fence, 170 miles of railways, an 800-acre lake, 2 smaller lakes, and 2,892 buildings. Crane is a city unto itself. In fact, it is larger than the District of Columbia.

Gently rolling hills covered with hardwood forests and small man-made mounds cover the landscape. Crane has 1,800 of these grassy mounds filled with 600,000 tons of ammunition and weapons. That was the early role of Crane, hence the nickname "the ammo depot." But the base does a lot more than that.

The Crane story starts back in 1934 when the federal government's Works Progress Administration project included plans for a 32,000-acre state forest in the southwestern part of Indiana. Since the area had been pretty much cleared of trees by the railroad and timber industry, the government brought in 700 workers who, between 1934 and 1938, planted 4.5 million hardwood trees for the park.

Then along came World War II, and priorities changed. Six days before the bombing of Pearl Harbor, the proposed state forest opened as a Navy ammunition depot, where ammunition was manufactured and stored. The initial mission was to prepare, load, renovate, receive, store, and issue all kinds of ammunition, including pyrotechnics and illuminating projectiles, and to act as a principal source of supply at a most critical time—the early days of World War II. Although it might sound strange that a Naval base would be located in southern Indiana, it was a perfect site in 1941. In addition to meeting the requirement of being far enough from the Eastern seaboard to minimize the danger of enemy air attack, the site was remote and free from congested areas. The land also could be easily obtained, and the area offered a suitable manpower pool.

The Naval Ammunition Depot, Burns City, was commissioned on December 1, 1941. In May 1943, the depot was renamed the Naval Ammunition Depot Crane, in honor of Commodore William Montgomery Crane, the Navy's first Chief of the Bureau of Ordnance. During World War II, civilian employment reached almost 10,000, and more than 1,300 Navy and Marine Corps personnel were assigned to the installation.

In 1970, recognition of the extent and diversity of fleet support efforts resulted in changing the name of the depot to the Naval Weapons Support Center, Crane. The new name more accurately reflected Crane's true function and, with attendant mission statement changes, established Crane as a research, development, test, and evaluation center.

Crane Division covers just under 100 square miles of northern Martin County, or roughly half again as big as the District of Columbia.

In 1977, another major change occurred with the designation of the Army as the single service manager of conventional ammunition. This resulted in the establishment of a tenant command, the Crane Army Ammunition Activity.

Today, Crane serves a modern and sophisticated Navy as a recognized leader in diverse and highly technical product lines such as microwave devices, acoustic sensors, small arms, microelectronic technology, and more. Crane stands as an industrial leader in providing better methods and technology in the production of modern naval combat weapons systems. All five of the armed services—Army, Navy, Air Force, Marines, and Coast Guard—are represented at Crane. Crane covers 62,463 acres in a remote rural area in Martin County and small portions of southern Greene and Western Lawrence Counties, about 25 miles southwest of Bloomington.

The natural beauty of Crane is spectacular. High hills, deep valleys, rock outcropping waterfalls, springs, scenic vistas, and even several caves all combine to create some of the best wildlife habitat to be found anywhere. Coyotes, foxes, bobcats, wild turkeys, and deer roam the Crane forests. The base also has several pairs of eagles and "condos" for Indiana brown bats.

Included among Crane's 50,000 acres of woodlands are two 200-acre stands of white oak trees, being grown for harvest to replank the Navy's *USS Constitution*. There are 29 old family cemeteries scattered around the Crane grounds, with more than 3,000 graves. Crane workers maintain the cemeteries and allow family members access to visit.

Not only is Crane a very important component in the area economy, but it is also a "good neighbor" in the community at large. The base supports a variety of endeavors that help make the area a better place in which to live and work. Improving education is a top priority, and Crane excels in this area. The center's partnership with about 40 schools in the south central Indiana region encourages students to get involved in science and technology.

Outreach programs include an annual science fair, tutoring of students at their schools in math and science, career counseling, and summer internship programs for teachers to stay in tune with state-of-the-art technology. Crane also keeps people from having to move to urban areas to find decent jobs. The center encourages young people to continue their educations beyond high school and gives some of those who do an incentive to come back home.

In another move to give back to the community, Crane sponsors a "Buy Indiana Business Fair" at the base. The venture was created to acquaint Indiana businesses with Crane's streamlined purchasing methods and the kind of products and services the base is in the market for. Each year Crane spends more than $300 million on a broad spectrum of goods and services. Crane believes that using as many of the products and services as possible from local businesses will not only benefit the area's economy, but will also provide customers within Crane with greatly improved services in terms of vendor responsiveness, product quality, and timely maintenance and repair.

An integral part of the community, the Crane center has changed from one that was virtually closed to anyone who did not have business there to one where tours for students and other groups can be arranged, and sportsmen are invited to hunt and use beautiful Lake Greenwood on the center at various times throughout the year. Armed Forces Day open houses, bicycle rides, fall foliage tours, marathon runs, and other public events during the year open the base to the community. Crane logs about 60,000 visitors each year from around the world.

Continuing to build upon its heritage, Crane approaches the twenty-first century as a dedicated defender of the nation and a vigorous contributor to the development of Bloomington and Indiana. ⚓

Crane's unique Hydroacoustic Test Facility is capable of simulating ocean depths of more than a mile with a wide range of temperatures.

A night-time pyrotechnic test makes a spectacular light show.

Griner Engineering, Inc.

Griner Engineering, Inc. has a history of overcoming challenges and using each new challenge as a springboard to pull its people up to the next level of achievement. This "pulling up by your bootstraps" philosophy was derived from the company's history and the attitude its people take towards turning challenges into opportunities.

The story began when John Griner founded the company in the 1970s after graduating from Bloomington High School South Vocational Program. John went to work for an Indianapolis company who made fabricated parts for the aircraft industry. With a vision to create a great machine shop in Bloomington, John convinced his employer that he and his father could weld and machine specialty parts at home.

Griner Engineering produces quality small metal parts. Photo by Kendall Reeves.

Three years of commuting to Indianapolis to work 50 hours and returning home to work another 40 hours a week finally paid big dividends in late August 1978. John quit his job in Indianapolis and continued to produce parts for his former employer in Bloomington. Meeting this challenge positioned the company on its first level of existence and turned John's dream into reality.

John wanted to grow his company, and a decision was made to purchase automatic screw machines and computer controlled lathes. These processes allowed Griner to become a supplier to many Bloomington industries and provided a solid technical product niche to expand the business.

Good news travels fast, and Ford Motor Company soon discovered the little shop in Bloomington. Ford determined that Griner's location and product niche would be of value to their Indiana plants. Griner determined that doing business with Ford could give the company unlimited opportunities for growth and provided a way to evolve the company into a cost-competitive, high-volume automotive parts supplier. Over time, Ford became Griner's main customer and began challenging Griner to drastically cut costs while increasing production. This challenge was met with the introduction of the Hydromat Rotary Transfer Machine. Once the Rotary Transfer Process was started, it became possible for the company to move into the very price-sensitive and quality-conscious production machining business. The Hydromat allowed Griner to make parts five times faster and at half the cost of their other processes.

Griner Engineering employees are known for the attitude they take towards turning challenges into opportunities. Photo by Kendall Reeves.

The next growth challenge Griner faced was a huge order from General Motors for antilock braking components, which tripled Griner's sales. Because money and skilled people were in short supply, Griner's existing people had to pull out "all the stops" and push the Rotary Transfer Process and new hires to unheard of limits. The eventual success of this project provided multiple rewards for the company and its people.

And people are what Griner is all about; people who have an interest in machinery, fixing problems, making things better; people thriving on challenge, change, opportunity; people who are committed to hard work, doing things right, and serving customer needs.

Many of these people have worked their way up through the ranks within the company. Executive Vice President and General Manager Brian Campbell, Vice President of Marketing Brian Hughes, and New Development Manager Jim Byrum joined the firm in entry level positions.

And people who have already fully developed their careers outside the firm are hired, including Vice President of Finance Jerry Taylor, Human Resources Manager Bruce Smith, and Quality Assurance Manager Howard Cross.

Griner's people are always looking for new challenges. A current challenge is to develop a new process called "cold forging" to use in conjunction with Griner's current high-precision machining process. This process, similar to the way pioneer blacksmiths forged their products, is hundreds of times faster and uses no heat. These higher-quality, lower-cost preformed parts will then be given their final precision shaping using Griner's current technology and are just another step in an ongoing process of utilizing skilled people and advanced technology to transform today's challenges into tomorrow's opportunities.

From the power-steering fluid reservoir on Toyota vehicles to the vegetable bins in General Electric refrigerators, TASUS products have proven their value at home and on the road.

Founded in 1986 by Tsuchiya Co., Ltd., TASUS has blended the best of its Japanese and American heritage to create a company that values its employees and prides itself on creating high-quality products. TASUS production capability ranges from simple plastic parts to high-quality, fully assembled, and tested ports.

TASUS's quality, precision, and molding capabilities have won contracts from the world's leading manufacturers in the automotive industry, as well as appliance and other industries. In the automotive market, where tough standards allow very little tolerance, TASUS has shown its worth by gracing many of today's most sought-after automobiles. Toyota Motor Manufacturing of N.A., Brother Industries, and Honda of America are just a few major companies to have honored TASUS with quality awards.

So how did such a worldwide operation end up in the Indiana community of Bloomington? The answer is simple—TASUS wanted a location central to its primary customers and a place that featured a high quality of life for its employees. The site provides a close proximity to Toyota in Kentucky, Honda in Ohio, and Mitsubishi in Illinois.

With Indiana University and a wealth of arts and recreation offerings, plus the natural beauty of the area's lakes, forests, and hills, Bloomington proved a good match for TASUS.

Since starting production in 1990 at its 45,000-square-foot facility on the city's west side, TASUS has grown rapidly with a 50 percent increase in sales each year. TASUS employs about 80 skilled team members working with state-of-the art computerized equipment. The team philosophy runs throughout the company, encouraging employees to contribute to the company's continuous improvement in manufacturing processes and customer service. The hallmark of TASUS is a partnership of customers, employees, suppliers, and the community working to meet challenges and achieve success through a foundation of mutual trust and respect.

Efficient assembly manufacturing cells reduce costs while enhancing quality and production.

As corporation President Melanie Hart's rapid climb to the top of the company illustrates, TASUS offers unlimited opportunities for its Bloomington employees.

In a short time, TASUS also has gained a reputation as a good neighbor. The company's commitment to community involvement is sincere and significant, ranging from social services to economic development. As top official, Melanie Hart leads the way by being particularly active in the Greater Bloomington Chamber of Commerce, having served as chairwoman of the board. During its swift rise in the marketplace, TASUS has made an important mark on Bloomington and on the nation. ⚠

The TASUS production area is spotless, organized, and efficient.

ABB Power T&D Company Inc.

While most people aren't familiar with ABB, they are served by its products whenever they flip a light switch.

ABB Power T&D Company Inc. in Bloomington is part of the ABB Group, a $35-billion global engineering leader. The group serves customers in electric power generation; transmission and distribution; industrial and building systems; and transportation. ABB customers include electrical companies and co-ops.

ABB offers customers worldwide financial and technological resources to provide expert solutions. Products, services, and technologies are engineered to meet the demand for clean, reliable power, and industrial efficiencies—in the United States and around the world.

A map in the Bloomington office shows customers on nearly every continent, with South America and Africa sporting the newest assortment of locator pushpins. ABB comprises more than 1,000 companies, operating in 140 countries with 215,000 employees.

Of the group's total sales, 57 percent are in Europe, 18 percent in the Americas, and 25 percent in Asia, Australia, and Africa. Income before taxes in 1996 was $2 billion and net income was $1.2 billion.

ABB Power T&D Company is the leading United States supplier of electric transmission and distribution equipment, systems, and services to utilities and industrial users. The Bloomington facility manufactures vacuum breakers, surge arresters, oil instrument transformers, and circuit reclosers for electrical distribution. It employs about 250 people.

Why did such an international company choose to open a Power T&D Company in a Hoosier community? An experienced workforce already in place, an existing facility that would serve its needs, the employee training ground of Indiana University and Ivy Tech State College, and a high quality of life offered by the area helped attract ABB to open its Bloomington facility in 1989.

ABB Power T&D Company has been fortunate over the years to have a solid workforce with very low turnover, if any. The company has two very active retiree groups, one in Bloomington and one in Bedford, that meet once a month for various social activities.

When it came to Bloomington, ABB partnered with the existing company union, IBEW Local 2031. Company and union officials work together to build teamwork and keep communication lines open.

The electrical equipment manufacturer continues to strive for efficiency, and look for new global markets and new product lines. Priorities include serving ABB customers with quality products and mining areas of the world for new customers. The customer-focused company is ISO 9000 certified, an internationally recognized quality certification that allows ABB to be a global competitor.

Personnel at the Bloomington plant are active participants in many civic organizations and community initiatives. As a sponsor of softball, bowling, and golf teams, ABB Power T&D Company is a familiar name in the local athletic field.

Like other manufacturers in the community, ABB's personnel are trying to network with schools, the Chamber of Commerce, and other entities to alert prospective employees of their future needs.

With its eye on the future, ABB is a company that is consistently working toward its vision of an even brighter world of tomorrow. ⚡

Vacuum breaker circuits, like these produced in Bloomington, are used to protect distribution feeder circuits in electric utility substations. Photo by McGuire Photography.

Power voltage transformers (left) are used for metering and relaying applications by electric utilities and large industrial users. Surge arresters (right) are used for protection of electric transmission lines and equipment.

Technology Service Corporation

From humble beginnings in a Hoosier log cabin, Technology Service Corporation (TSC) Indiana has grown to occupy the top two floors of a historic downtown Bloomington building—along with a premier place in the world's high-tech business.

Technology Service Corporation designs, develops, tests, and evaluates systems and advanced sensors for military and commercial customers. The company has approximately 200 employees in four principal operations and five satellite offices. Founded in 1966, the company has been 100 percent employee-owned since 1993.

TSC also has major facilities located in Los Angeles, California, Silver Spring, Maryland, and Trumbull, Connecticut. The Washington operations were established in 1970, the Connecticut operations in 1978, and the Indiana operations in 1980.

How was the small Midwest mecca of Bloomington able to compete with such heavy hitters in the field of advanced technology and highly skilled labor force as those other well-known cities?

TSC officials view the Indiana community of Bloomington as an ideal spot for recruiting high-tech employees. Concerns such as the high cost of real estate in other locations, as well as a deteriorating quality of life for many employees and their families made Bloomington a logical choice.

"We need to be able to attract and retain top engineers and scientists," explains Operations Manager Jim Shelton. "As a company where success is based on our skilled and talented workforce, we need to provide an environment offering a high quality of life and a good place to raise a family."

Easy access to Indianapolis for business seminars and papers presentations; to Indiana University with its highly skilled labor force, particularly in the area of computer science; and to Crane Naval Surface Warfare Center, where TSC has an office, are important criteria for the decision to choose Bloomington as a base.

Crane is the AEGIS Microwave Tube In-service Engineering Agent and the primary customer of TSC's Indiana operations. In 1996, TSC received a five-year, $33.4-million contract to support Crane's microwave tube/transmitter efforts.

This, together with the skilled staff within the Indiana operations, has allowed TSC to start two commercial businesses—Computer Software Services and Cultural Databases. Computer Software Services is a commercial business aimed at providing software services to companies within the proximity of Bloomington.

TSC provides software support, such as database applications, primarily to manufacturing companies. TSC also helps companies with their UNIX system problems and helps them gain access to the Internet.

The Cultural Database facility is designed to create three-dimensional databases of cultural objects, such as buildings, from stereoscopic photography. The databases are typically for either a 10-nautical mile radius circular area around a major airport for siting airport surveillance radars or for the area of the airport itself to allow siting of airport surface detection equipment.

As partners in the community, TSC employees are active in local organizations, such as the YMCA, Partners in Education, the Greater Bloomington Chamber of Commerce, and various schools and churches. The company also is a major backer in the annual Tech Connection, showcasing advanced technological solutions to meet business, education, and instructional needs in Indiana and beyond.

Always with an eye toward the future, Technology Service Corporation is a prominent and welcome player in the Bloomington economy. ⚓

Founded in 1966, Technology Service Corporation has approximately 200 employees in four principal operations and five satellite offices.

Technology Service Corporation designs, develops, tests, and evaluates systems and advanced sensors for military and commercial customers.

Textillery Weavers

A combination of commitment to dedication and hand-crafted quality, and design with an eye to the newest trends in fashion makes Textillery a unique resource in the marketplace.

The throws, woven in luxurious yarns in over 500 styles and colors, are popular in specialty gift shops and upscale department stores.

From a table

loom in the dining room of a log cabin to a 30,000-square-foot studio with a staff of 50, Textillery Weavers has been weaving warmth into homes around the world since 1976.

It started when John Rose bought his wife, Judith, a table loom for her birthday. Judith began weaving as a hobby. Her natural gift for design and vibrant, innovative use of colors coupled with John's talent for business soon made Textillery Weavers the leading producer of handwoven throws and decorative accessories in the United States.

"We do it the old-fashioned way—made by hand," says John Rose. "We have found our niche. People who buy our throws want the quality, the softness."

It is this combination of commitment to dedication and hand-crafted quality, while designing with an eye to the newest trends in fashion, that makes Textillery a unique resource in the marketplace. As appreciation for their work grows, the company has prospered, with sales tripling in the past three years.

The throws, woven in luxurious yarns in over 500 styles and colors, are popular in specialty gift shops and upscale department stores, such as Neiman Marcus, Saks Fifth Avenue, Bloomingdale's, Nordstroms, Crate and Barrell, Marshall Fields, Macy's, and Ethan Allen. Textillery Weavers also exports to Australia, New Zealand, Hong Kong, France, the United Kingdom, Germany, Mexico, Brazil, and Sweden.

"Many of the customers that started buying from us in the late 1970s and early '80s are still with us because we fill a need for beautiful woven accessories that work in every room in the house. They know that our throws are consistently strong sellers." Judith Rose says.

From a gross of $25,000 the first year, Textillery now grosses more than $3 million. The company has also been recognized for outstanding achievements by its peers and its community. In 1996, Textillery won the first ever "ARTY" award from the Accessory Resource Team for creating the most innovative product in the home furnishing industry. That same year, Textillery also won the "Small Business of the Year" award from the Bloomington Chamber of Commerce. Reviewed by business centers across the state, Textillery was judged on growth within the previous three years, "staying" power, ability to overcome adversity, and product innovation.

The Bloomington facility serves a global marketplace, yet Textillery's employees enjoy a small-city lifestyle. The company prides itself on hiring unskilled labor—often people with no job history—and teaches them to be craftspeople. Textillery trains its employees to take on management responsibilities and works with them to increase their skill levels, become more efficient, and, consequently, to increase their wages.

Textillery is committed to being an economic, intellectual, and social asset to Bloomington. That means contributing in a variety of ways—but without fanfare. For example, Textillery supports local softball teams, the Waldron Arts Center, the Wonderlab children's museum, Middle Way House for battered women and children, Bloomington Parks and Recreation's summer concerts, and "A Moment in Science" on WFIU.

John and Judith Rose take pride in the way their company has grown, as well as being proud of their employees and their community. What they are most proud of at Textillery, however, is "that we can make something beautiful, make it affordable, and can compete anywhere in the world—and that we can be true to ourselves while we do it." ⚑

Sabin Corporation

A woman carefully threads two wires into a piece of plastic tubing. In another room, a man monitors room temperature and humidity on a computer. Down the hall, a laboratory technician checks the quality of translucent plastic.

At the Sabin Corporation, employees work as though a life depends on their labors. And it often does. One of the world's premier medical plastics processing facilities, Sabin manufactures parts for use with devices such as coronary stents and catheters. Part of the Cook Group, the Sabin Corporation was established in 1967 when Cook Incorporated needed plastics for its products.

Cook Incorporated, the first Cook Group company, was founded in 1963 to manufacture and distribute wire guides, needles, and catheters. Cook Incorporated is the largest private producer of cardiovascular catheters in the world. Used in such procedures as diagnosing and treating problems in the heart and blood vessels, Cook devices are crafted under the highest possible standards.

"Everything has to be perfect when it leaves here," says Sabin President Robert Lendman. "We tell our employees to make each piece of equipment like you would if you knew it was going to be used on your mother."

Sabin began with one man and one piece of equipment in the back of a Cook warehouse. It has grown to a state-of-the-art, 183,505-square-foot facility with 160 employees, including plastics engineers who design the manufacturing processes used to make the custom products.

"Our products are in every hospital in the world," Lendman says. "Most are custom-made for our clients. Because we have so many products and each is different, it's hard to automate any part of the manufacture."

Although the vast majority of Sabin's business is supplying Cook Group companies, the firm also serves as a supplier to businesses in computer and electronics industries.

What distinguishes Sabin from other plastic manufacturers is the company's reliance upon many different manufacturing technologies. Sabin's production capabilities with all types of plastics include extrusion, injection molding, insert molding, thermoforming, and custom compounding. Unlike other companies, Sabin does it all—offering technical support, laboratories, engineering, and delivery.

Ultimately, the true business of Sabin Corporation is the pursuit of perfection. It has to be. Sabin has to get it right the first time, every time. Decades of experience working under extreme quality control guidelines have fostered an extraordinarily strong work ethic and a strict attention to detail.

"The facility is probably cleaner than most hospital emergency rooms," Lendman says. "We go to great extremes to keep it that way."

Temperature and humidity are regulated for the maximum benefit of each product. Static electricity and particulates are eliminated in the work environment. Uniforms and lab coats for employees are cleaned with special products that don't leave a residue.

Sabin has remained an innovative company by developing or acquiring the new plastic technologies necessary to support the growing needs of customers in the plastic medical components industry. The company administers an extensive preventive maintenance program to keep all machinery in peak condition, along with never-ending investments in the latest materials and processes.

Whatever the industry, whoever the customer, and whatever the project, Sabin employees never lose sight of their responsibility to provide the best product possible. They live by that commitment, as witnessed by the Sabin motto worn close to employees' hearts on company uniforms and lab coats: "Success Starts With Quality." ⚠

Sabin, one of the world's premier medical plastics processing facilities, manufactures parts for use with devices such as coronary stents and catheters.

Sabin has grown to a state-of-the-art, 183,505-square-foot facility with 160 employees, including plastics engineers who design the manufacturing processes used to make the custom products.

Cook Imaging Corp.

If necessity is the mother of invention, then Cook Imaging Corp. is one of her most interesting offspring. Back in the early 1980s, Dr. Charles Dotter gave a disturbing presentation. A later nominee for the Nobel Prize in medicine, Dotter played a recording of patients getting injections of ionic contrast media for X-rays.

As the contrast media sent a burning pain through their vessels, the patients moaned and screamed in misery. Complications after the treatment were also common. Dotter challenged Cook to develop a contrast medium that would alleviate suffering at an affordable cost to the patient.

Cook Group took the challenge. After millions of dollars and many years of research and development, Cook found what it was seeking—a radiographic non-ionic contrast medium that was less painful than the traditional ionics, didn't have the side effects, and was affordable. In August 1985, a new non-ionic, iodinated contrast compound with low toxicity was given the chemical name Ioxilan. In 1987, a new Cook company, Cook Imaging, was established to develop and produce Ioxilan.

As with most Cook products, the contrast medium was developed to provide a means for an accurate diagnosis. Once the research and development was nearly complete, it was necessary to find a clinical supply manufacturer for the medium that would be marketed and sold with the brand name of Oxilan®.

Cook wanted the plant in Bloomington after analyzing the efficiencies, quality control, and potential costs of other locations. For this reason, the decision was made in 1990 to break ground for a 44,000-square-foot, state-of-the-art, sterile manufacturing facility. From the outside, Cook Imaging looks like any modern, upscale office building, but once inside you will find a highly sophisticated and technologically innovative manufacturing facility.

The plant has 7,000 square feet of controlled environment "clean rooms," in which air is filtered through HEPA filters. Oxilan® is formulated, filtered, filled into glass vials, and sterilized at the Cook Imaging facility. Many quality control procedures are used to ensure that each lot is closely examined before its release to the market.

In a short time, Cook Imaging has begun to burst at the seams and will be branching out into other Cook facilities. The Pharmaceutical Solutions division, which specializes in sterile product filling for other companies, has rapidly expanded because of its reputation for customer service, cleanliness, and flexibility.

Cook Imaging prides itself on operating in a clean and efficient environment. Prior to each manufacturing operation, sterile areas are prepared meticulously.

Why the emphasis on going the extra mile to have a plant that not only meets but exceeds FDA requirements? "The philosophy we live by is that we are producing a product the way we want it made as if it were used on ourselves or a member of the family," says company president, Jerry Arthur.

Cook Imaging has evolved from filling serum vials to filling ophthalmic containers, syringes, and single-use tubes. However, Cook Imaging is committed to providing customers with more than just a product in a container. Its experience in all phases of manufacturing is an added assurance that any project is in good hands.

"We have a fantastic workforce," Jerry Arthur says. "There is a spirit of cooperation here that Cook encourages. We are all part of a team." ⚏

Cook Imaging has evolved from filling serum vials to filling ophthalmic containers, syringes, and single-use tubes. Committed to providing customers with more than just a product in a container, Cook's experience in all phases of manufacturing is an added assurance that any project is in good hands.

Oxilan® is formulated, filtered, filled into glass vials, and sterilized at the Cook Imaging facility. Many quality control procedures are used to ensure that each lot is closely examined before its release to the market.

People who work at Cook Urological Incorporated have given their product the highest possible compliment—whenever they have needed such a medical device for their own health care, they have insisted upon Cook Urological equipment.

That is confidence. And the employees at Cook Urological are confident that their products adhere to the strictest standards. They have to. Those products could make a difference between life and death.

Cook Urological was started in 1978 in order to offer Cook technology to urologists, who welcomed the types of devices and methods already proven useful to radiologists. From this beginning, research and development, stimulated through close cooperation with leading physicians, have resulted in a broad line of products designed to reduce trauma by circumventing major surgery in urological procedures such as biopsy, kidney stone removal, and ureteral and urethral repair.

A rapidly growing Cook Group company, Cook Urological also has two divisions, VPI and Cook Ob/Gyn. VPI manufactures and distributes a unique line of ostomy appliances, drainage pouches, and devices to relieve the problems of incontinence. In 1984 Cook Ob/Gyn brought Cook medical device technology to the practice of obstetrics and gynecology. By working with innovative physicians, Cook Ob/Gyn has created a broad line of products in the area of infertility, urogynecology, laparoscopic and hysteroscopic surgery, maternal-fetal medicine, and gynecologic oncology. Many gynecological problems can now be diagnosed and corrected through small incisions, instead of more invasive techniques, using Cook Ob/Gyn products.

Earning a worldwide reputation for outstanding quality products, Cook Urological employees are skilled at handcrafting the delicate instruments one at a time. Cook Urological products are not manufactured on an assembly line. The sharp eyes, steady hands, and dedication of the employees cannot be duplicated by a machine. Cook employees know that only the best products can leave their plant; quality is the most important issue at Cook Urological.

Products are delivered from Cook Urological's main plant in Spencer through a network of exclusive distributors and representatives throughout the world. Nothing has been spared to make the air-filtered, climate-controlled Spencer facility as clean as possible.

Cook Group chose to locate Cook Urological in the Owen County community of Spencer because of the solid Midwestern work ethic of the residents. Today, the 320 employees at the state-of-the-art facility are the backbone of the company's success.

A walk through Cook Urological shows a close-knit team. Adding to the friendly atmosphere is a shaded picnic area where employees can relax and enjoy lunch amid the first daffodils of the year. Inside the plant is the brightly decorated Cook Diner cafeteria, with its neon diner sign and popular menu featuring everything from soups, salads, and yogurts to good Hoosier cooking. Surprisingly low prices reflect the company's interest in providing nutritious and delicious meals as a service for valued employees, not as a money-making venture. Each year, employees are honored at special awards banquets, as well as having their ideas instituted through a See Your Idea at Work program. The people who work with the product are often the ones who can see ways in which to make improvements to the process, company president Chuck Franz believes.

Employees realize that Cook Urological customers are the most important people in their working lives. Not only do employees earn a livelihood for a job well done, but they also get the immeasurable satisfaction of knowing they are helping make life better for someone every day. ⚓

Cook chose to locate Cook Urological in the Owen County community of Spencer because of the solid Midwestern work ethic of the residents. Today, the 320 employees at the state-of-the-art facility are the backbone of the company's success.

Cook Urological was started in 1978 in order to offer Cook technology to urologists, who welcomed the types of devices and methods already proven useful to radiologists.

Transmetering Technologies Inc.

Transmetering Technologies uses a wide range of metering and data collection equipment. Photo by Kendall Reeves.

Transmetering's systems help conserve energy in commercial buildings, manufactured housing communities, and apartment buildings.

When Peter Dvorak

would drive past his rental property in the middle of winter and see the windows wide open, he would become frustrated at the waste of resources and money. But there was little Dvorak could do. In most older apartment buildings, there was no way to measure the utility consumption in each individual apartment.

Not content to give up, Dvorak developed a groundbreaking system to measure and monitor utility usage and record the date for each individual unit. The bottom line was that residents began to conserve energy when they were able to control and pay for their own actual usage. On average, consumption declined 30 percent when an apartment building was "transmetered." It did not take long for other property owners to realize the potential benefits of this new system. Thus, Transmetering Technologies was born.

Transmetering's system utilizes accurate sensor devices, which are installed in each apartment for any of four possible utilities—gas, electricity, water, and hot-water baseboard heat. Information from the sensor is electronically read by control hardware. Transmetering then converts the usage information to dollars and cents for each utility being monitored.

Each month, the data on usage and cost is collected, and Transmetering's service department sends out bills to each tenant and provides a toll-free customer service number for billing inquiries. Payments are collected from each customer, and the property owner then receives a monthly report, along with a reimbursement check for the resident-paid utilities.

As Dvorak puts it, "The situation is win-win for the resident and owner. The resident conserves energy, controls his costs, and generally benefits from the lower commercial utility rates the property owner passes through. The owner benefits by reducing his operating expenses significantly, which increases net operating income and the property's value."

In an industry that is fragmented and sees new competition entering daily, Transmetering is uniquely positioned to become a dominant national player. As the submetering of all utilities, and most recently water, becomes mainstream, having the ability to install systems and serve customers in all geographic regions will become imperative.

In addition, by the year 2000, the utility industry as a whole will be deregulated, eventually allowing consumers the ability to choose their provider of electricity or gas with the same ease as choosing a long-distance company.

"From its headquarters in Bloomington, Transmetering will operate branch offices in 5 regions and 38 states, and will be knocking on the Canadian border," Dvorak predicts. "We have positioned ourselves to provide efficient reading, billing, and collections services not only to our own customers, but also to the big utility companies looking to outsource and cut costs. We will also become a dominant player in the field of utility brokering. We will represent enough individual customers, businesses, and property owners to negotiate substantial savings for all of our clients in a deregulated environment."

Dvorak goes on to say, "Our business is changing on a daily basis, and we must adapt to keep pace with market demands and technological innovations. The bottom line is, we are not a technology company; we are a service business. The technology we employ is only a means to an end. Our ultimate product is a service that reduces costs and encourages conservation of our precious resources." ⚤

Dillman Farm is a Hoosier success story. From its small-town beginnings in a cook shed to its new 12,000-square-foot facility, the local company has grown into a nationwide business.

Dillman Farm has mail order customers in every state. Its popular home-style products also are sold at the Dillman Farm retail store in Bloomington, as well as several food outlets, such as Krogers, Mr. D's, Bloomingfoods, and the Dogwood Shoppe.

It started back in 1970, when Carl and Sue Dillman began making apple butter in a restaurant's small kitchen. Carl Dillman and the restaurant owner thought it would be a nice touch to offer homemade apple butter and bread to their patrons.

The idea worked. Before long, the Dillmans had added strawberry and peach preserves to serve an ever-expanding customer base. The next Dillman generation, son Cary, joined the business, and today the company offers over 60 products, with butters, preserves, and jellies all made at the Dillman Cookhouse. The Dillmans have built a full-fledged business on a reputation of creating the highest quality and best taste using only natural ingredients with no preservatives or additives.

Maintaining that commitment, Dillman Farm uses local suppliers for its fresh ingredients, whenever possible. The wine used to make the Dillman Farm Soft Red Wine Jelly comes from one of Indiana's oldest wineries, the Oliver Winery.

Dillman Farm's persimmon pulp comes from local trees; its sorghum is made by the Amish in southern Indiana; and its Indiana Select Popcorn with plump, robust kernels comes from fertile Hoosier fields.

Dillman Farm corn meal and whole wheat flour

come in two-pound cloth bags. The corn is grown and stone ground at the farm. On the back side of the corn meal is a recipe for corn bread made by the real Grandma Dillman. Served with tomato or other fruit preserves, this makes an easy and delicious old-time meal.

The home-cooked taste of sweet summer fruit can be enjoyed in Dillman Farm pumpkin butter, strawberry-rhubarb preserves, apple cinnamon jelly, orange marmalade, tomato preserves, and amaretto-peach preserves. Other tasty Dillman Farm products include peanut butter marshmallow cream, barbecue sauce, Sue's sugar cream pie, peach cider, jalapeno jelly, and chocolate amaretto with cherries and pecans dessert topping.

Packed in a white decorator metal pail and bedecked with a gingham and logo ribbon bow, the Dillman Farm Signature Pail makes a striking presence with its gift of food. Containing popular Dillman Farm flavors, the pail clearly reflects the clean and crisp simplicity that personifies Dillman Farm—no trendy decorator statement, just classic good taste.

The Dillmans traditional old-fashioned values and neighborly support extend into the community. Dillman Farm gift baskets have raised revenue for local organizations as prizes and raffle items. The Hoosier Hills Food Bank has received a wealth of delicious Dillman Farm products that aren't "quite perfect enough" to be sold. Small defects such as crooked labels or dented lids mean low-income and homeless people will enjoy flavorful Dillman Farm treats donated to the food bank.

Dillman Farm is strongly rooted in the past. It stands firm on old-fashioned values and pride at being part of the Bloomington community and the home of delicious food just like Grandma used to make. ⚑

Indiana fresh apples cooked down to butter just like in the old days, whole fruit preserves that taste as good as Grandma's—cooked in small batches, sweetened with pure cane sugar, and never any preservatives added—these qualities make Dillman Farm products a favorite for any occasion. Photo by Kendall Reeves.

Select, whole fruit, picked and frozen at its peak, ensures fresh fruit taste in every Dillman Farm jar. Photo by Kendall Reeves.

Independent Packaging

When Jack Culver and Chuck Romanski suddenly found themselves out of a job in 1994, they knew it would be hard to start at the bottom of the corporate ladder again.

With more than 68 combined years of industry experience between them, the two senior managers started a brand new company—Independent Packaging. With Romanski as president and Culver as vice president of manufacturing, the duo picked Bloomington as their base because it had one of their most important requirements—a skilled and dedicated workforce suddenly jobless from a packaging company shutdown. They assembled 105 employees, including Jim Bast, plant manager and one of the three founding members of Independent.

On June 29, 1994, Independent Packaging officially was funded. On July 1, 1994, work crews started demolition on a vacant building, gutting the entire structure with the goal of putting together a state-of-the-art, 40,000-square-foot manufacturing facility. New German printing presses were installed. The new company would be dedicated to making one product for one market: flexible packaging for wholesale bakeries.

The push was on to meet a September 19 deadline. Independent Packaging had contractually committed to its customers to ship bags on that date. A little more than a half-hour before deadline, the first roll came off the press. Independent Packaging was in business and has been going full-scale ever since.

The entire company hit the ground running. From the beginning, Independent Packaging has been determined to be the service leader in the bakery packaging industry. Customer service is without question the company's hallmark. From its Dallas headquarters, the 14-person management team, sales staff, and customer service team focus on the customer. The team is supported by a computer network that's tied into the manufacturing plant in Bloomington to provide on-line, real-time tracking of order status and other key data.

"Because we're a small independent, we try to be more innovative," says Bast. "Customers approached us and asked if we could make a square-bottom bag or the zip lock bag. Our reply was, 'Why not?' Because of the lack of bureaucracy, our decision-making chain is pretty short—one phone call."

The employee relationship strategy at Independent Packaging is simple: Everyone is part of the team, and like a true team, the success of the organization is dependent on everyone working together.

"We want everyone to know this is their company," Culver says. "One of the reasons it took three times as long to get the financing was that we insisted everyone be part of a company-wide profit sharing plan. If Independent Packaging makes a profit in any given quarter, all employees get a quarterly profit sharing check."

"When we were thinking of starting this business, I told Jack that I don't ever want to cut or eliminate jobs again," Romanski says. "I want to dedicate the rest of my business life to creating jobs."

The company makes 4 million bread bags a day, running 24 hours a day, 7 days a week. The bags are marketed to 49 states for use by the nation's top bakeries.

Culver says there is one additional secret ingredient to the mix that makes Independent Packaging a success: Hoosier pride—a set of values and a work ethic that just won't tolerate being second best. ⚹

With customer service as the company's hallmark, Independent Packaging is determined to be the service leader in the bakery packaging industry.

 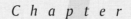

Business and Finance

Bloomington, Indiana, is located in a region where the traditional craft of patchwork quilting is still practiced and celebrated today. Meticulously stitched together from pieces of fabric, handcrafted quilts are prized for both their utility and beauty. Often the quilts are handmade by several quilters working together. Each quilt is carefully planned, the individual blocks are created and then pieced together.

The process of creating a quilt serves as a fine analogy for the cooperative efforts of the people and organizations that come together to make Bloomington what it is. Just like the creation of a quilt, the efforts of many have effectively integrated disparate community elements into a cohesive whole. The result is an extraordinary community that is both artful and utilitarian.

In many regards, Bloomington is like most communities: businesses are devoted to increasing profits and servicing customers; social service agencies address human needs; and governments provide services that must be addressed collectively.

But, different from some communities, in Bloomington each of these segments comes together to form a synergistic whole. The Greater Bloomington Chamber of Commerce, working with many partners in business, government, and the nonprofit sector, is proud of the role it has played in helping to create a utilitarian, integrated, and robust community "quilt." Strength is derived from each component, but the whole is more than just a sum of the parts because of the relationships between the elements. The Chamber works hard to create and maintain those linkages.

Everything the Chamber does is in response to one of the three parts of its mission, says President Steve Howard. The first, "We Advocate For Business," is the basis for Chamber activities to improve infrastructure, education, efficiency of government, and other factors that are necessary for economic growth. For instance, because a skilled and work-ready workforce is so critical to the success of its members and the community, the Chamber works to improve the area's school systems. It devotes major resources to the Franklin Initiative, Monroe County's School-to-Career initiative. The program provides an important link between the business community and area schools.

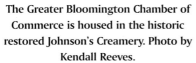

The staff of the Greater Bloomington Chamber of Commerce facilitates action on behalf of members. Photo by Kendall Reeves.

The Greater Bloomington Chamber of Commerce is housed in the historic restored Johnson's Creamery. Photo by Kendall Reeves.

To help implement its role as a business advocate, the Chamber publishes a monthly newsmagazine, *Business Network*. With circulation of 11,000, its timely articles are an informative resource to businesses, government leaders, and individuals in the region. The publication represents the Chamber's perspectives and also stimulates dialogue within the community about critical issues.

In fulfilling the first part of its mission, the Chamber also connects businesses to government. The Chamber advocates on behalf of business in legislative matters. Beyond making direct contacts with government officials on behalf of its membership, the Chamber also facilitates communication with lawmakers by hosting programs that address community issues and by cosponsoring a televised legislative forum.

One of the Chamber's most important efforts has been the creation of the *Business Agenda,* a compilation of the issues and activities that the Chamber believes are key to business and the community. This continuously evolving document focuses the Chamber's activities and is a tool to facilitate dialogue with community leaders. As a result of the *Business Agenda's* comprehensive approach to community issues, the Chamber has built new partnerships and collaborations in recent years. A notable example is the increased number of nonprofit organizations that have joined the Chamber. These agencies see their membership as a way to increase their visibility, form relationships with businesses, and learn business skills. They also take advantage of the opportunity to inform the business community about their missions.

The second mission element, "We Serve Our Members," is implemented by providing discount

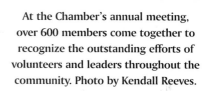

programs, forums for networking, expositions, professional development programs, and other activities. Some Chamber projects have become community traditions. Business Expo, for example, attracts more than 125 exhibitors and 5,000 attendees from throughout the region. Also, at the Chamber's annual meeting, over 600 members come together to recognize the outstanding efforts of volunteers and leaders in the community.

A newer Chamber initiative, Tech Connection, is also designed to provide service to members and the community. The event offers an opportunity for the region's growing number of technology-based firms to share information and demonstrate products, services, and innovations. One major outcome of Tech Connection is helping the community become aware that technology is an increasingly important part of its economic base.

The Chamber has many initiatives devoted to assisting small businesses. For instance, the Business at Breakfast seminars offer topics tailored to small businesses at a time that is convenient to those who must also "mind the store." Held monthly, the sessions address subjects such as technology, human resource management, advertising, sales, and competing with mass merchants.

Of special note, the Chamber hosts the Small Business Development Center and is a partner in the Bloomington Business Incubator. These co-located facilities provide small businesses with expert assistance and a supportive environment during the crucial start-up phase. The Chamber also hosts the Manufacturing Assistance Service, which provides support for small- and medium-sized manufacturers.

"The first two elements of our mission are straightforward and fit the model of what Chambers of Commerce usually do," Howard says. "The third, 'We Promote Our Community,' is sometimes misunderstood. This element goes well beyond just singing the praises of Bloomington, although that is an important part of it."

People are sometimes surprised to learn that, in response to the third element of its mission, the Chamber commits resources to child care, health care, diversity, youth, housing, and other community issues. The reason, Howard says, springs from the economic relationship between businesses and the communities in which they are located. "That's why the Chamber invests in social service programs," he says. "They are an important part of the equation for providing an environment that attracts world-class employers that can thrive and invest in our community."

In addressing important social service issues, the Chamber is a catalyst for coordinated action.

Special effort is made to identify key issues, make sure they are fully appreciated, and to facilitate linkages between the various interested parties from government, business, and nonprofit organizations.

Despite a rapidly changing environment, the Chamber will continue to hold true to the elements of its mission. It will remain a business-driven community leadership organization. In that role, the Chamber will address broad community issues, and it will help develop linkages between those involved to seek collaborative strategies.

The Chamber's successes are fueled by the energies of its volunteers. Its more than 1,000 members are the hardworking men and women from business, government, and the nonprofit sector who build the economic base that supports the entire region. The Chamber's leaders come together from diverse backgrounds to work on common issues, to make the most of shared assets, and to ensure the community's continued success.

Each year when more than 2,500 visitors attend the Indiana Heritage Quilt Show in Bloomington, they can do more than just appreciate many high-quality, handcrafted quilts. They can also, as those who live here do, appreciate Bloomington and its many pieces that come together like a fine quilt. The Greater Bloomington Chamber of Commerce is proud to have contributed to the community's success and to be a part of that patchwork. ⚠

At the Chamber's annual meeting, over 600 members come together to recognize the outstanding efforts of volunteers and leaders throughout the community. Photo by Kendall Reeves.

Lloyd Olcott, Chamber Gold member, greets IU Chancellor Herman B Wells at the Chamber's annual meeting. Photo by Kendall Reeves.

Cook Group Incorporated

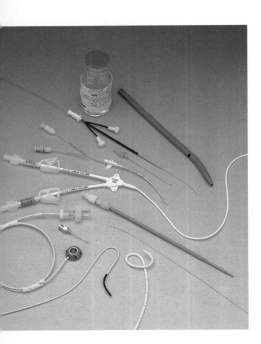

Cook Group Incorporated is a multinational group of companies that offers speciality products and services to customers around the world. Cook listens to the needs of its physician customers, and works with them to create innovative products that can ultimately benefit millions of people.

The restored Cochran House serves as the headquarters of Cook Group Incorporated.

The foundation of what is today Cook Group Incorporated began in 1963 as the dream of William A. Cook and his wife Gayle. Today, instead of one company there is a multinational group of companies that offers speciality products and services to customers around the world. Cook listens to the needs of its physician customers, and works with them to create innovative products that can ultimately benefit millions of people.

In 1963, Bill and Gayle Cook moved to Bloomington from Chicago in their old Corvair. Using the second bedroom of their Bart Villa apartment in Bloomington, the Cooks fabricated catheters, wire guides, and needles—products necessary to practice the Seldinger percutaneous entry technique. The Seldinger technique allows access to the cardiovascular system via the circulatory system through a simple puncture site rather than a surgical incision. The procedure had been developed in Sweden a decade before but had been slow to be adopted in America. Part of the problem was that there was no single established source of supply for products used in the technique. That's where Cook came in. Cook Incorporated became the first company to meet the needs of early angiographers in the United States.

Eager to test the market for his new devices, Bill Cook signed up at the last minute for a small booth at the 1963 conference of the Radiological Society of North America. No booth space was left at the most important annual meeting of physicians involved in radiology. However, Cook was told he could set up a folding table by the Coca Cola vendor. Fortune smiled on Cook in two ways. First, the day was so hot that attendees constantly walked by Bill's table for cold drinks. Second, Bill attracted the interest of Dr. Charles Dotter, credited as being the father of modern interventional radiology.

After watching Cook at work fashioning catheters, Dr. Dotter asked if he could borrow the equipment overnight. Cook entrusted much of his scarce investment to a stranger. The next morning, Dotter returned with a batch of catheters he had created in his hotel room. A lasting relationship was born between a physician with an idea and a man who could turn it into medical technology.

That first year, the Cooks were the only employees in their home business. When wire guide and catheter fabrication began to spread to the kitchen and living room, the company needed more space. In 1964, the first of many moves was made. After relocating to a house in 1968, Cook was quoted in a newspaper article at the time as hoping that the company's 20 employees might even grow to 100 in 10 years' time. Cook has accomplished that goal many times over.

As applications using the Seldinger procedure expanded into new areas, the market for Cook products increased. The Cook Group began to grow beyond the manufacture of wire guides, catheters, and needles; in 1969, when Cook Incorporated needed a source of plastic tubing, Sabin Corporation was created. William Cook Europe A/S was established in Denmark to manufacture devices which met the requirements of the European radiology market. European sales and marketing subsidiaries were established in Spain, the United Kingdom, Germany, Italy, France, Sweden, Switzerland, Belgium, and the Netherlands. As additional needs developed, companies were formed for the manufacture of devices for other medical disciplines, real estate and historic preservation, retail management, communications technology, transportation, and travel.

Each Cook Group company is responsible for its own physical resources, personnel, and financial performance. At the same time, the subsidiaries support one another through mutual distribution of products and through shared technologies. Cook Group companies have developed high-quality products to meet new and diverse needs.

Medical manufacturing subsidiaries of Cook Group Incorporated include Cook Incorporated and its five divisions: Cook Radiology, Cook Cardiology, Cook Critical Care, Cook Endovascular, and Cook Surgical; Cook Biotech Incorporated; Cook Imaging Corporation and its division Cook Pharmaceutical Solutions; Cook Vascular Incorporated; K-Tube Corporation; Laser ArmorTech Corporation; Sabin Corporation; Cook Urological Incorporated and its divisions Cook Ob/Gyn Incorporated and VPI Ostomy; Wilson-Cook Medical Inc.; Cook (Canada) Inc.; William A. Cook Australia Pty. Ltd. and its divisions Cook Veterinary Products and Cook IVF (*in vitro*

fertilization technology); William Cook Europe A/S; and Cook Ireland Ltd. Non-manufacturing subsidiaries include Cook Aviation; Grant Street Inn; Bloomington Antique Mall Inc.; Fountain Fabrics; CFC, Inc.; Star Travel Services Inc.; Cook Family Health Center Inc.; Med Institute; and a professional basketball team in England, the Manchester Giants.

Cook companies have remained privately owned, retaining a family-run atmosphere where the customers, not shareholders, drive the business. This affords the organization a better perspective on how medical manufacturers can influence the development of new products to improve the public health. "Cook stands for innovation and quality," says Steve Ferguson, chief operating officer of Cook Group Incorporated. "Our future will depend on how well we do with both."

Many Hoosiers remain unaware of the worldwide scope of business conducted from the firm's Bloomington headquarters. Yet no place knows the influence of the Cook Group of companies better than its hometown. Throughout the years, its corporate "good neighbor" policy has played a leading role in the evolution of Bloomington and Monroe County.

Cook has benefited the community in so many ways it is hard to conceive of Bloomington without that invaluable influence. Downtown Bloomington revitalization efforts were spearheaded by Cook through CFC, Inc., its real estate arm. The landmark Graham Plaza anchoring the downtown and Fountain Square Mall are among CFC renovation projects, as was the restoration of the Cochran House, now the headquarters of Cook Group Incorporated. The Cook Group boosted fundraising efforts for the Monroe County Historical Museum expansion with a major pledge. The popular Star of Indiana Brass and Percussion Corps is sponsored by Cook, as is its transportation arm, Star of Indiana Charter Service, both based in Monroe County.

The beautiful YMCA Fitness Center on the south edge of town is there only because a Cook Incorporated grant provided a significant part of the $2.2 million dollars needed to construct the facility. Why the emphasis on providing the Bloomington community with such a top-notch YMCA facility? Growing up in Illinois as the son of a grain elevator operator, Bill Cook didn't have much money. His own YMCA membership was made available by scholarship. He hasn't forgotten the influence of the YMCA on his life.

In West Baden, about an hour and a half drive south, a unique project is taking place through a partnership between Historic Landmarks Foundation of Indiana and CFC, Inc. The two organizations have joined forces to renovate and market the 1902 hotel once billed as the Eighth Wonder of the World. The West Baden Springs Hotel had been ranked among the most endangered National Historic Landmarks. Featuring a six-story domed atrium (the largest clear-span dome in the world when built), 700 rooms, and natural mineral springs used for bathing and drinking, the resort drew celebrities from all around the country. CFC, Inc. is supporting a multimillion-dollar partial restoration to save this landmark and make the 600-acre property marketable.

Higher education in Indiana also has benefited from the Cook Group. Steve Ferguson serves on the Indiana State Higher Education Commission. Bill and Gayle Cook have given substantial gifts to the Indiana University School of Medicine, School of Education, and School of Music, and they provided funds for the library at the School of Music which now bears their name. In addition Bill gives of his own time by serving as a member of the IU Board of Trustees, and Gayle is a member of the IU Foundation Board. In 1997, Cook Group Incorporated established the Reverend Ernest D. Butler humanitarian scholarship for IU undergraduate students. Named after a local civil rights leader and pastor at the Second Baptist Church, the scholarship will provide educational and living expenses for a full-time student on the Bloomington campus, with preference given to minority applicants.

Millions of dollars have been provided by Cook Group Incorporated to private and public medical research and to The Charles Dotter Institute of Diagnostic and Interventional Radiology, an interdisciplinary medical facility at Oregon Health Services University. In Bloomington, a Cook Group donation established and equipped Bloomington Hospital's first cardiovascular catheterization laboratory.

Cook company employees themselves volunteer thousands of hours of their own time each year to various non-profit organizations and events, making them one of the city's largest employee volunteer corps. The whole Cook organization effects a personal difference in countless lives.

During its swift rise, the Cook Group has made and continues to make long-lasting contributions in the area of health care and to the quality of life worldwide. ⚘

The Cardiac Rehab Heart Team from the Monroe County YMCA Family Fitness Center benefit from a top-notch YMCA facility thanks to a Cook Incorporated grant that provided a significant part of the $2.2 million dollars needed to construct the center.

The Historic Landmarks Foundation of Indiana and CFC, Inc. have joined forces to renovate and market the West Baden Springs Hotel, ranked among the most endangered National Historic Landmarks. CFC, Inc. is supporting a multimillion-dollar partial restoration to save this landmark and make the property marketable.

Monroe County Bank

Monroe County Bank is the area's last independently owned bank headquartered in Bloomington. Since its founding in 1892, Monroe County Bank has been committed to providing quality financial products and outstanding customer service while staying attuned to the needs of Bloomington.

With local management and a local board of directors, Monroe County Bank is in a unique position to make decisions that are tailored to fit the financial needs of area customers. All decisions about loans, rates, and fees are made locally.

This dedication to the needs of local customers has enabled Monroe County Bank to grow into a $300-million company that offers the latest innovations in banking to residents of southeastern Indiana. Despite its success and expansion beyond Bloomington, residents still refer to Monroe County Bank as their "hometown banker."

Monroe County Bank's new banking center, located south of College Mall, is designed to accommodate the bank's growing staff and to meet the needs of the twenty-first century customers. The banking center will house the new Mall Road branch office and be home to the bank's Trust, Controllers, Brokerage, and Human Resources Departments.

Key to Monroe County Bank's success is its personnel. The bank is an important employer with a 1997 payroll of nearly $4 million. The philosophy is to train employees to focus on the needs of customers. As a result, Monroe County Bank is known for its friendly, professional people who take the time to know customers' names and wants.

The special needs of Monroe County's growing senior citizen population are met with Prime Time Banking, which is open to anyone over 50. Special events, such as ice cream socials, give members and bank associates the chance to interact.

Monroe County Bank is committed to providing quality financial products and outstanding customer service while staying attuned to the needs of Bloomington. Photo by Kendall Reeves.

The relationships between Monroe County Bank, its customers, and the community have resulted in unique product offerings, particularly for senior citizens and women.

The special needs of Monroe County's growing senior citizen population are met with Prime Time Banking, which was created in 1989. The program, which is open to anyone over 50, sponsors educational programs, social events, and trips, including memorable treks to Paris, the Panama Canal, and Alaska.

Women can learn more about a wide array of financial issues by attending Monroe County Bank's educational seminars. These free lunch-hour gatherings provide women with the information they need to accomplish financial goals for themselves and their families.

Providing quality services to customers is just part of Monroe County Bank's philosophy. The bank also believes in the importance of service to the community. It has been a long-standing policy to endorse and encourage the community service and philanthropic activities of employees.

Monroe County Bank took this philosophy to the next level during its 100th anniversary in 1992. Deciding to forego the usual trappings of a business anniversary, Monroe County Bank instead concentrated on community service projects. Employees volunteered at the Bloomington Boys and Girls Clubs, served as museum docents, and built a Habitat for Humanity House.

These types of activities personify Monroe County Bank's approach to banking—looking for the needs of others, taking time to smile, helping out those who need help, and putting people first. The commitment of Monroe County Bank hasn't changed much since cashier Sam Dodds opened the doors in 1893. As Bloomington's "hometown banker," Monroe County Bank will continue to serve the special needs of its customers and community well into the next century. ♠

Nestled in the rolling hills of southern Indiana, Bloomington is a beautiful city with a heart that beats ever stronger in its thriving downtown. But it wasn't too long ago that Bloomington seemed headed for the ranks of other cities throughout the nation. Suburban malls and neighborhood shopping centers drained many downtown shops in once bustling cities, leaving boarded-up buildings and empty streets.

The turning point for Bloomington came when local businessman Bill Cook and his wife, Gayle initiated the renovation of the Graham Hotel on the northwest corner of the square in the late 1970s, and the city built the Regester parking garage next door. The old hotel was transformed into the Graham Plaza by CFC Inc., a subsidiary of the Cook Group.

In the years since, over 120 buildings have undergone either complete renovation or some type of improvement. "I think the Cook organization proved that it could be done, and that gave other people the confidence to try it," says Talisha Coppock, executive director of the Commission for Bloomington Downtown.

Formed in 1984 as part of the National Main Street program, the commission has a 22-member board representing most aspects of downtown— property owners, historic preservation, retail, local government, Indiana University, financial institutions, industry, Convention and Visitor's Bureau, Chamber of Commerce, and service businesses.

Banks and churches joined the effort and made commitments to stay downtown. Suggestions to demolish the Monroe County Courthouse or shift county offices to the city's east side were dismissed. The City of Bloomington made public improvements, such as lighting, landscaping, parking facilities, and street paving.

The center of the downtown is now anchored by the beautifully restored County Courthouse. Scores of shops, restaurants, commercial offices, and residences branch out for several blocks in four directions.

The historic Showers Center to the northwest houses City Hall, Indiana University Research Park, and a variety of private businesses. The Convention Center to the southwest and the adjacent Courtyard by Marriott Hotel provide a meeting place for local, regional, and national groups.

To the south, the Waldron Arts Center offers a popular venue for theater, music, dance, and art. To the east, Kirkwood Avenue is the link and entrance to the IU campus through the Sample Gates. Along the street are financial institutions, shops, restaurants, and the Monroe County Public Library. Farther east is the Carmichael Center, with its mix of retail, office, and residential space.

"Drawing people downtown to live and celebrate is a crucial part of revitalization moving forward," Coppock says. "Special events do just that. The downtown hosts over 30 special events a year by groups throughout the community."

Bloomington's outdoor music festival, Hoosierfest, acquaints Indiana University students with the joys of downtown. The Lotus Music Festival promotes world music in seven different downtown venues. The Star of Indiana Grand Prix Mini Race thrills spectators of all ages and draws people downtown from surrounding communities. An Easter egg hunt attracts parents and small children for fun on the courthouse lawn. The Taste of Bloomington features over 30 of the city's top restaurants and tempts appetites with local specialties. The Fourth Street Arts Festival exhibits work from over 100 artists.

No matter what the season, activity is buzzing in downtown Bloomington. Dedicated volunteers from all walks of life have rolled up their sleeves to help invigorate the crown jewel of Bloomington— its charming downtown. ⚐

The center of the downtown Bloomington is anchored by the beautifully restored County Courthouse. Scores of shops, restaurants, commercial offices, and residences branch out for several blocks in four directions. Photo by Kendall Reeves.

The renovated Showers Brothers Furniture factory provides 300,000 square feet of prime downtown office space. The Showers Plaza is a popular gathering place for special events. The fountain was the result of a One Percent for the Arts Program by the City of Bloomington and private sponsors.

ONB

ONB unites the resources and financial strength of a banking powerhouse with a legacy that is pure Indiana. This full-service banking institution uses its good business sense and friendly determination to make life better for those it serves.

In 1885, a few Bloomington businessmen joined forces to start Workingmens Building Loan Fund & Savings Association in the back of a jewelry store on the south side of the downtown square.

Even with its humble Hoosier beginnings, the aim of the organization was apparent—to provide the greatest confidence and return to the saver, and the best possible terms to the borrower.

The association showed steady growth through the years and weathered the Depression without loss to a single customer. Workingmens developed into one of the most highly capitalized savings institutions in the United States and became a sought-after commodity in the banking world.

As Bloomington's oldest independent business, Workingmens merged with Old National Bancorp of Evansville in 1996. The unification allowed it to retain banking decision-making in Bloomington, while being able to increase its number of locations and offer a broader array of products and services to its customers.

Old National Bancorp brought an equally impressive background to the merger. Old National Bancorp was recently recognized as one of the country's 10 safest in *U.S. Banker's* annual ranking of the 100 largest U.S. bank holding companies.

Today, ONB is a full-service financial institution offering a complete line of retail and commercial services for families and businesses. Along with its downtown office, ONB has banking centers at College Mall, Whitehall Plaza, and in Ellettsville.

With its wealth of financial services, ONB can help its customers plan for their financial futures and deal with today's financial needs.

But the best indication of ONB's success comes from the trust of its customers and the long-time commitment of its employees. For decades, loyal customers have turned to ONB for financial services—many of them using the same financial institution their parents and grandparents used.

And there at the offices to serve them have been ONB employees, some of whose careers extend to more than a quarter of a century each.

ONB staff members also work hard to make a difference in their communities. They can be found volunteering for local organizations and activities, serving the community's youth, seniors, and non-profit agencies. The staff is also dedicated to housing issues, since ONB is committed to assisting builders with their projects and helping individual families finance their own homes.

The management at ONB is proactive in business issues and is involved in such professional groups as the Chamber of Commerce and Bloomington Economic Development Corporation. These volunteer activities are aimed at promoting a higher quality of life in Bloomington and the Monroe County area.

Moving toward the twenty-first century, ONB continues to build on its heritage as an outstanding financial resource and a true community partner.

As "Your Bank for Life," ONB is dedicated to providing all the financial services its customers need on their journeys through life. ⚏

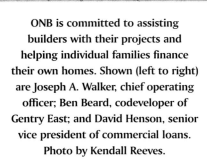

ONB is committed to assisting builders with their projects and helping individual families finance their own homes. Shown (left to right) are Joseph A. Walker, chief operating officer; Ben Beard, codeveloper of Gentry East; and David Henson, senior vice president of commercial loans. Photo by Kendall Reeves.

The best indication of ONB's success comes from the trust of its customers and the long-time commitment of its employees. Pictured (left to right) are Jerry Hays, senior vice president of retail lending; Janet Burks, Ellettsville branch sales manager; Dan L. Doan, president and CEO; and Ken Ritchie, senior vice president of retail banking. Photo by Kendall Reeves.

Bloomington/Monroe County
Convention & Visitors Bureau, Inc.

The fresh awakening of spring, the warmth of a summer day, the crisp colors of fall, the snowy tingle of winter. No matter what the season, Monroe County's year-round getaways are bound to appeal.

But it takes more than natural beauty and a wealth of activities to draw visitors. It takes a talented and knowledgeable convention and visitors bureau to spread the message with style and marketing savvy. That's the important role played by the Bloomington/Monroe County Convention & Visitors Bureau, Inc.

"We have all the elements to attract people—arts, culture, festivals, sports, outdoor activities, good restaurants, natural beauty, Indiana University, and a safe community. We work very hard to promote everything this area offers," says Executive Director Valerie Peña.

Incorporated as a private, not-for-profit corporation in 1977, the Bloomington/Monroe County Convention & Visitors Bureau is funded through a three-percent hotel/motel tax. Located in the newly built Visitors Center, the bureau has seven full-time and eight part-time employees. It is governed by a 19-member board of directors composed of representatives from the local hospitality, industry, and civic areas of the community.

Behind the scenes, the bureau participates in community activities, such as the annual Indiana Heritage Quilt Show and the Lotus World Music and Arts Festival. The bureau prints 115,000 visitors guides a year. "And we go through every single one of them," Peña notes.

But camera-laden tourists, IU sports fans, and antique store browsers aren't the only folks the Convention & Visitors Bureau is luring to town. Bureau workers are busily promoting Monroe County as a convention and meeting spot, too.

The results to the community are significant. The convention and tourism industry in Monroe County generates more than $155 million in tourist expenditures, as well as over 4,400 jobs for local residents. It is estimated that local government revenues produce over $8 million from local tourism and convention efforts, and the overall resident income generated is in excess of $73 million.

About 1.5 million visitors come to Monroe County each year. The average number of dollars spent per party per day when visiting and staying overnight is $214. Tourism is the third largest industry in Monroe County, and Monroe County is ranked eighth in the state for the most visitors.

Cited by magazines as a great place to retire or a good bicycling town, and in books which list good retirement spots, healthy places to live, and stress-free locales, the area has won national attention.

When the film *Breaking Away* caught the hearts of moviegoers in 1979, the bureau found a natural theme—Breakaway to Bloomington. Centered on the annual Little 500 bicycle race, *Breaking Away* promoted the area's beauty, warm hospitality, and reputation as a mecca for bicyclists. The "Come Out and Play" invitation with its festive "jumping figure" was later added and has become the Convention & Visitors Bureau's trademark slogan.

Bloomington and Monroe County also have benefited in recent years from a national trend toward shorter vacations. Being located within a day's drive from over half the population of the United States is a handle the bureau has successfully used to attract visitors.

"Our largest percentage of visitors is repeat business," Peña said. "There's no better salesperson than someone who has had a good time here and seen the beauty for themselves. Once we get someone here once, they tend to tell their friends and become return visitors themselves." ⚐

Visitors to Bloomington and Monroe County are greeted by the friendly and helpful staff of the Bloomington/Monroe County Convention & Visitors Bureau. Photo by Kendall Reeves, courtesy of the Bloomington/Monroe County Convention & Visitors Bureau.

The Bloomington/Monroe County Convention & Visitors Bureau plays an important role in drawing visitors to the natural beauty and wealth of activities available in the area. Photo by Kendall Reeves, courtesy of the Bloomington/Monroe County Convention & Visitors Bureau.

Citizens Bank of Central Indiana

Being known as the "friendliest bank in town" is a difficult reputation to maintain. But Citizens Bank has been working on it since around the turn of the century.

Through several different name changes, Citizens Bank has always tried to keep that goal in mind. Citizens' slogan, "Leading the Way," is exemplified by the approach it takes in serving its customers, its most important asset.

It all started back in 1906 when two brothers laid the foundation for the original bank. Monroe County is known nationwide for the high quality of stone found around Bloomington. Two enterprising brothers, Ben F. Adams Jr. and William H. Adams, owned and operated one of the many area quarries.

Because of the investment potential, the two brothers sold Adams Quarry and organized The Bloomington National Bank by depositing $50,000 worth of bonds with the Comptroller of the Currency. Eight directors were appointed, and stock was purchased by highly respected people of different professions, including housewives.

In October 1906, the brothers opened their doors, and the first loan was made to Central Oolitic Stone Company for $8,800. Since that modest beginning, Citizens Bank has garnered a reputation in the Bloomington-area small business community as the lending institution most likely to be in tune to the needs of small business. Citizens Bank has served as a launching point for a wide range of successful small businesses.

The bank was mostly family owned and often referred to as the "Adams Bank." Three generations of Adamses served as bank presidents—founder William H., his son William B., and his grandson William R. The bank was sold to a Nashville businessman in 1980, became part of Indiana Bancshares in 1988, and Bloomington Bank & Trust in 1989. In 1993, it combined with the Bargersville State Bank and became Citizens Bank of Central Indiana.

Always looking to stay ahead of customers' needs, the bank opened the area's first drive-up banking facility in 1960. The popular service offered the newest and most efficient devices for banking from automobiles.

Today, Citizens Bank offers a full line of banking services with four regional offices—three in Bloomington and one in Nashville. President James Rusie says many of the bank's customers have been with it for more than half a century, and the bank has many long-time employees.

"We are committed to the community by offering full-service banking and building rewarding relationships with our customers," Rusie says. "Our customers are not just numbers to us. They are the reason we are here, and we treat them with the kind of personal service they deserve."

As befits its long-standing partnership with the community, Citizens Bank has made significant contributions to the area's special quality of life. Ranging from United Way, Habitat for Humanity, the Chamber of Commerce, and Bloomington Economic Development Corporation to the Boys Club and Little League baseball, Citizens Bank has been a major benefit to the place it calls home. ⚓

Citizens Bank is committed to the community and works to build rewarding relationships with its customers. Photo by Kendall Reeves.

Citizens' slogan, "Leading the Way," is exemplified by the approach its staff takes in serving customers. Photo by Kendall Reeves.

Conseco Risk Management (CRM) is in business to protect its clients, and all that matters to them, against the risk of unforeseen economic loss. CRM solves its clients' risk management problems through an extensive selection of competitively priced products and over-the-top service. CRM offers commercial property and casualty insurance, personal risk management, employee benefit programs, claims service, and loss prevention and control.

As an independent organization drawing upon the products and resources of a wide array of insurance companies, CRM affords its professional staff the flexibility to design fully individualized risk management programs. If a client has a need that can't be met by what is currently available, CRM will create something new.

Conseco Risk Management is a subsidiary of Conseco, Inc., a Fortune 500 financial services company based in Carmel, Indiana. Conseco leads the market in the sale of retirement annuities and universal life insurance and is one of the nation's leading providers of supplemental health insurance. Conseco is dedicated to leading the process of change in the financial services industry by setting the standard of performance in every market it serves.

CRM was formed in 1989 to serve as Conseco's property and casualty agency. As it grew—adding personal, commercial, industrial risk management and association clients—the agency came to be recognized for its superior service and innovative programs. Today CRM is one of the nation's largest and fastest-growing independent insurance agencies. The company serves clients throughout the United States and beyond, and has become the leading agency for several of its insurance providers.

Certainly the key to Conseco Risk Management's success is the caliber of its workforce. Because of its size and reputation, CRM has been able to attract experienced professionals with in-depth knowledge of the industry. Many of CRM's executives are former agency owners or insurance company managers who bring decades of experience and diverse backgrounds to the task of providing superior risk management.

In 1996, CRM acquired Wells & Company, a fifth-generation family business, and its subsidiary affiliates, Joe Dial Insurance and the Evansville Insurance Group. Wells' history of innovation, rapid growth, and expertise in the agency-brokerage segment of the insurance industry was a perfect fit with CRM's financial strength and management ability.

Conseco Risk Management's Bloomington location is that of its subsidiary, formerly known as Joe Dial Insurance. The Bloomington staff remains committed to its neighbors—the people who enabled the agency to grow from a small hometown business into one of the largest property and casualty insurers in southern Indiana.

From its origin in 1973, Joe Dial Insurance took seriously its responsibility to the Bloomington community. Over the years, both of the companies that acquired Dial—first Wells, then CRM—have heartily supported the agency's tradition. Today, Conseco Risk Management continues to lend a helping hand to Bloomington-area organizations concerned with education, culture, housing, youth, the elderly, health care, and other human services.

Specifically, CRM supports the YMCA, the Monroe County Historical Society, the Indiana University Foundation, the John Waldron Art Center, the Boys and Girls Clubs, local youth groups and nonprofit youth sports organizations, the United Way, and others. ⚓

Conseco Risk Management's Bloomington location is that of its subsidiary, formerly known as Joe Dial Insurance. The Bloomington staff is committed to the people who enabled the agency to grow from a small hometown business into one of the largest property and casualty insurers in southern Indiana.

NBD Bank

Going the "extra mile" for customers is a way of life at NBD. The Bloomington bank adheres to the philosophy that it's the extra services, the sincere smiles, the attention to detail, and the drive to meet customer needs that make it such a successful community institution.

With corporate ties to a large regional holding company, NBD offers the best of both worlds. NBD was founded in 1834 as Indiana National Bank. AS NBD, it declared its first dividend in 1934 and has never missed paying one.

On the local level, NBD prides itself on being flexible enough to work with its customers, whatever their banking needs. NBD offers a full range of banking services, all designed to make banking easier for busy customers.

The management of NBD makes banking personal and friendly, convenient, and uncomplicated. All branches—four in Bloomington and two in nearby Bedford—are situated with an eye towards convenience and the potential for growth. NBD realizes that convenience is important for busy people today. The bank offers a wide variety of flexible, timesaving financial products and services that help simplify banking and make time for other important things in life.

The main office of NBD is located on the first floor of the renovated Fountain Square in downtown Bloomington, one of the city's best-known landmarks on the courthouse square. As part of that extra touch—led by company bank President Ron Walters, Corporate Service Manager Chuck Rudman, and Retail Bank Manager Scot Davidson— NBD offers the area's best banking hours. Doors open at 8:30 A.M. and close at 5:30 P.M. But customers will find NBD greeting the banking day with open doors at least five minutes earlier than the scheduled opening and holding the closing time at least five minutes later.

The needs of every sort of customer can be met at NBD. The bank offers a variety of checking accounts and such services as banking by phone or by computer, trust and investment services, installment loans, home mortgages, student loans, and major

credit cards. NBD features 24-hour convenience with ATMs and telephone banking.

NBD listens and responds to customers' needs. When customers said they would appreciate a downtown drive-up location, NBD opened such a facility. Equipped with three teller windows that can accommodate business transactions and change orders in addition to personal banking transactions, the new service has proven a welcome addition for banking customers, as well as for those doing personal business.

NBD has established a tradition that supports economic growth and quality of life in Monroe County. The bank's officers and employees serve as volunteers for the area's many charities and in leadership roles in organizations.

All these activities relate to NBD's mission of going the extra mile for both its customers and the community it calls home. Today, as it has been throughout the history of NBD, the company is consistently focused in its aim to be the premier financial institution in the area. Assisting customers with their financial needs is what the bank is all about—living up to its goal as a bank that prides itself on "giving 110 percent." ▲

NBD offers a full range of banking services, all designed to make banking easier for busy customers.

NBD prides itself on being flexible enough to work with its customers, whatever their banking needs.

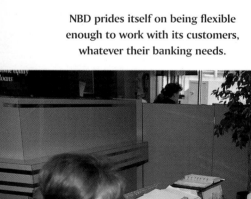

Rogers Group Investments

When Ralph Rogers started his roadside crushing operation in Bloomington nearly a century ago, it was the beginning of a long, prosperous love affair between his family and the city he called home. Today, Rogers Group Investments and quality real estate development are synonymous. For over 50 years, four generations of the Rogers/Rechter family have selected and developed projects that are bringing families together and jobs to the community.

Standing in the front yard of the High Street home where Rogers once lived, one can practically survey the hundreds of acres that stood before him and witness, firsthand, what an impact he and his company have had on the community. Among the developments in Rogers' "front yard" are the string of churches on Second and Third Streets, the Rogers and Binford Elementary Schools, the first phase of College Mall, Eastland Plaza, the Windemere and Covenanter neighborhoods, the Auto Mall Road commercial area, Jackson Creek Shopping Center, and the new Rogers Farm neighborhood.

Rogers Group Investments develops land through the careful selection of business partners who have a keen eye on responsible stewardship. Many of the developments intertwine the concepts of preservation, ecology, and thorough planning. The projects are engineered to achieve the optimum use of the land while maintaining the high quality of life that makes Bloomington special.

Many Rogers Group Investments initiatives reap multiple dividends. For instance, a 1994 Property Improvement Award from the Greater Bloomington Chamber of Commerce was not the goal when Rogers Group Investments decided to fill in an old quarry site on the near west side. While the recognition was a pleasant affirmation, the reward was the resulting Landmark Business Center and the newly constructed EuDaly, Inc. buildings, which include the Indiana Workforce Development Center and Transcom. The Workforce Development Center, a model for other such centers statewide, is a place where people can go to find jobs and receive training. Transcom joined the ranks of Bloomington employers as well, bringing 200 new jobs to the community.

On the northeast side, Rogers Group Investments creatively reclaimed a piece of property formerly used as a dump site and then partnered with a Florida firm to secure tax credits and build low-cost housing.

On the east side of Bloomington, Rogers Group Investments brought together four other partners and a design to bring diverse segments of Bloomington together. The concept of intergenerational living development will be realized as a result of a student housing complex built by Capstone Development Corp., upscale apartment living in the "The Fields" by Abodes, Inc., single-family residential homes developed by Richland Construction, and a retirement living complex by Holiday Retirement Group, all located on the 120-acre Rogers Farm. "The Fields" partnership was forged with an eye on preservation—an existing pond and grove of trees remain on the site, as does an 1800s-era cabin. Additionally, Abodes, Inc. turned the old Rogers Farm cattle barn into "The Fields" clubhouse, a restoration project that landed the company the Chamber's 1997 Property Improvement Award.

Since its inception, Rogers Group Investments has maintained a focus of stewardship in planning. The company will continue to build relationships that result in innovation and preservation of land in order to maintain the quality of life in Bloomington for decades to come.

For over 50 years, four generations of the Rogers/Rechter family have selected and developed projects that are bringing families together and jobs to the community.

Rogers Group Investments develops land through the careful selection of business partners who have a keen eye on responsible stewardship. Many of the developments intertwine the concepts of preservation, ecology, and thorough planning.

Indiana University Credit Union

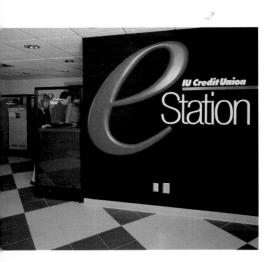

The e-Station is an all electronic branch located at the Indiana Memorial Union in Bloomington. Photo by Kendall Reeves.

Seven Indiana University employees each pooled $5 of their own money to form a credit union in 1956. More than four decades later, the Indiana University Employees Federal Credit Union has nearly $300 million in assets and serves 57,000 people.

Today, IU Credit Union offers a complete line of financial services and electronic conveniences at 10 branches located throughout Indiana—plus 3 drive-ups and 14 automated teller machines. An ever growing variety of 24-hour electronic services keeps members in touch with tomorrow, today. These innovations include the Home Teller computer linkup, EXPRESS bank-by-phone, AnyHour loan-by-phone service, and the e-Station, an all electronic branch located at the Indiana Memorial Union in Bloomington.

Credit unions are financial cooperatives with no outside shareholders to please or to pay. When someone joins the cooperative, he or she becomes an owner. This distinction benefits members, as credit union resources are focused on providing affordable financial products and services. Sixty-eight million American adults are members of some credit union. They find ownership denotes lower loan rates, higher savings rates, and generally fewer and lower fees for services than they get at other financial institutions.

Regulated by the National Credit Union Administration (NCUA), the IU Credit Union is examined annually, required to follow federal rules and regulations, and is federally insured by NCUA for deposits up to $100,000. The sixth largest credit union in Indiana, the IU Credit Union's field of membership is comprised of more than 160 companies and organizations, including IU faculty, staff, and students. Employees of these companies/organizations and their family members are eligible for membership. Credit union membership can be a lifetime benefit. Even if a member changes employers, retires, or relocates, the member can remain an IU Credit Union member by simply keeping $25 on deposit, which is equal to one ownership share.

IU Credit Union owners count on an extra dose of personal service and benefits which may not be dispensed elsewhere. When it comes to service, the IU Credit Union treats its members like they own the place, because they do. Members elect the volunteer board of directors they want to run the credit union.

People who work at the IU Credit Union apply a philosophy of excellence by serving as strong citizens of their own community. Employees care, and their attitude comes through with every transaction and every community activity. IU Credit Union is dedicated to putting into action on all levels its guiding philosophy of "people helping people." ▲

IU Credit Union offers a complete line of financial services and electronic conveniences at 10 branches located throughout Indiana—plus 3 drive-ups and 14 automated teller machines. Photo by Kendall Reeves.

Public Investment Corporation

Don Seader had the skills, the experience, and the loyal customers to open his own automotive repair shop. However, Seader didn't have a place for his new business, nor did he have the start-up money to finance such a facility.

Instead, he turned to Public Investment Corporation (PIC). Now Seader is the owner of a thriving business, World Wide Automotive Service, in the PIC industrial park.

Started in May 1995, World Wide Automotive Service provides employment for several top-notch automotive specialists and was honored in 1997 with the local Chamber of Commerce Environmental Award.

But Seader's success story is not an isolated case. Such tales are repeated throughout the PIC industrial park on the southwest side of Bloomington. PIC has invested more than $8 million in the site where 32 buildings offer plenty of space for entrepreneurial or distribution businesses needing 4,500 to 20,000 square feet. The site is now home to a variety of businesses providing about 500 jobs for the area economy.

"The park provides a place for entrepreneurs to get started," says PIC Vice President Charles "Pete" Dunn Jr. "Sometimes, people have a good idea for a business but they might have trouble getting financing. We rent the buildings so a new business owner won't have money tied up in a building."

Circle-Prosco, a chemical company, was the first to move into the PIC industrial park in the 1970s. Other businesses include Lee Supply, Reynolds Farm Equipment, Hertz Penske, Maaco, Federal Express, Pegasus Communications, Auto Parks Warehouse, Norandex Vinyl Siding, and Penny Lane Child Care Center. Providing child care in the industrial park seemed a natural since so many parents work in the area.

A development company with deep Bloomington business roots, PIC has 146 stockholders and is led by President Richard Schmalz and board members Frank Hrisomalos, James Ferguson, Ted Ferguson, Walter Roll, George Yost, and Charles "Pete" Dunn Jr.

Over the years, PIC also has helped numerous people realize the American Dream of home ownership. By financing house sales, PIC has enabled people who didn't have a large down payment to buy a home. Among PIC's major accomplishments was the extension of sewer service to the west side of town, a feat the city of Bloomington couldn't afford to do on its own. The lack of sewage lines was a huge deterrent to development on the west side. Since then, the city's west side has blossomed with housing, commercial, industrial, and service construction.

One of the largest and most promising PIC projects is 140 acres of undeveloped land at the northeast corner of Tapp Road and Indiana Highway 37, across from the Southern Indiana Medical Park. The land is being developed for tenants who are interested in medical offices, general offices, and combination warehouse-office businesses.

Since the late 1950s, PIC has been helping people fulfill their dreams—whether it has been in starting a business, buying a home, or finding a convenient, affordable, and dependable child care facility. Long a treasure in the community, Public Investment Corporation continues to build a strong future on a proud tradition of giving people a chance to develop their potentials. ⚠

Public Investment Corporation has invested more than $8 million in the site where 32 buildings offer plenty of space for entrepreneurial or distribution businesses needing 4,500 to 20,000 square feet such as Federal Express. Photo by Kendall Reeves.

Maaco is another satisfied Public Investment Corporation client. Photo by Kendall Reeves.

Bank One, Indiana, N.A.

Setting a goal is easy. The hard part is achieving it. By all measures, Bank One, Indiana is reaching what it had set out to do—"Aim for the 'impossible.' Exceed the expected."

In its pursuit to settle for nothing less than being a national leader in providing financial services, Bank One has an all-encompassing motto, "One to One," and a can-do attitude that drives the organization.

Bank One has a rich history in the community. Started as the First National Bank of Bloomington, it opened on September 14, 1871, with only $100,000 in assets. The bank's doors remained open through three major depressions and the panics of 1910, 1921, and 1931.

Over the years, mergers enabled the bank to grow and prosper. In 1987, First National Bank affiliated with BANC ONE CORPORATION and became Bank One, Bloomington, NA. On September 1, 1992, the Bedford National Bank joined Bank One and created dominance in both markets with approximately $500 million in total assets.

A pioneer in Indiana's banking history, Bank One's roots were established more than 150 years ago. Throughout its existence, Bank One has maintained its position as number one. Bank One was the first in Indiana to offer its customers bank credit cards, common trust funds, and bank ATM machines.

The consistency of the banking experience at Bank One is one of the primary benefits customers enjoy. Bank One's employees care, and that attitude comes through with every transaction.

The needs of every customer can be met at Bank One. The bank offers a variety of checking accounts and services such as trust, business banking, investments, and financial planning. Business and personal lines of credit, installment loans, home mortgages, student loans, and major credit cards offered by Bank One help consumers fulfill their dreams. Bank One has been the bank of choice, shown by the people in the community, making it the largest financial institution in Monroe County.

Bank One offers 24-hour convenience banking with ATMs, computer home on-line banking, and telephone banking. In addition, Bloomington is home to one of Bank One's first fully automated banking centers that enable customers to apply for and receive an installment loan from $1,000 to $10,000 in about 10 minutes.

The banking center also has a phone center where customers can access account information or apply for larger loans. Business customers making deposits are able to use the Bank One Depomatic Deposit machine. The device enables customers to make a deposit and receive an instant receipt. A coin and currency counter/dispenser also is available at the branch.

As more and more customers use technology to conduct their banking, Bank One is committed to cutting-edge innovations to make banking easier.

Bank One has established a tradition that supports economic growth and quality of life in its community. The bank's employees serve as volunteers for the area's many charities and in leadership roles in organizations. An annual list of employee participation and financial support reads like a "Who's Who" of local organizations, emphasizing activities that benefit children and senior citizens.

The standards of service and community involvement set over a century ago are high standards, and the challenge of meeting them is great. But that's the way Bank One likes it. After all, setting high goals and overcoming challenges is what being a great bank is all about. ▲

Bank One has established a tradition that supports economic growth and quality of life in its community. Photo by McGuire Photography.

In its pursuit to settle for nothing less than being a national leader in providing financial services, Bank One has an all-encompassing motto, "One to One," and a can-do attitude that drives the organization. Photo by McGuire Photography.

Chapter

13

Professions

Andrews, Harrell, Mann, Chapman & Coyne

"Comprehensive legal services to businesses and individuals" is the philosophy which guides the Bloomington law firm of Andrews, Harrell, Mann, Chapman & Coyne. A desire to blend skills and experience motivated the firm's partners in 1994 to merge what were then two established practices to form a new firm.

The move was a strategic one, principally intended to broaden the scope of legal services the firm could provide. The merger brought together a dozen attorneys with more than 250 years of combined experience in a variety of practice areas. This diversity of expertise would establish Andrews, Harrell, Mann, Chapman & Coyne as a full-service legal firm, one well-positioned to assist the rapidly growing business and industrial base in south central Indiana.

"Business and industry in this area is not only expanding, but operating in an increasingly complicated regulatory environment," said William H. Andrews, partner. "Our clients need sound information to stay competitive, and they need it from legal advisors who can draw on multiple resources and perspectives."

Since 1994, the firm's expanded services for business, industry, and institutions have attracted a steady stream of new clients, including those who previously sought specialized legal representation outside the region. Services provided by the firm include business planning and formation, employment law, contracts, mediation, real estate zoning, corporate law, probate and estate planning, and assistance for Bloomington's hundreds of family-owned businesses, including such services as family business succession planning.

As a result, Andrews, Harrell, Mann, Chapman & Coyne now represents an extensive list of business and commercial clients in industries ranging from insurance, banking, and real estate to construction, retail sales, and the media. Clients are confident in the firm's legal expertise and value the firm's high community profile in helping them establish important business contacts in the community.

Andrews, Harrell, Mann, Chapman & Coyne advises new entrepreneurs and also acts as local counsel to national companies who desire representation in matters requiring expertise in litigation, acquisitions, and local real estate and zoning.

In addition to business clients, the firm represents individuals and families in the Bloomington area. Some want assistance on matters such as landlord/tenant disputes. Others are seeking planning advice, particularly in the areas of contractual agreements and estate planning. Many individuals contact the firm seeking recourse in civil trials, and still others need representation on a criminal matter.

Litigators and other attorneys at the firm are supported by a staff of skilled paralegals, researchers, and legal assistants. They can utilize the resources in the firm's extensive law library for research. They can also quickly access comprehensive and current case law, statutes, and regulations through a sophisticated computer research system.

In addition, Andrews, Harrell, Mann, Chapman & Coyne employs accountants, legal secretaries, couriers, and a title searcher. Such in-house services offer efficiencies that ultimately translate into cost savings for the client.

The firm is careful not to let a wealth of resources overshadow personal attention. A compassionate and professional relationship with all clients was a priority for three decades before the 1994 merger and remains so today.

Andrews, Harrell, Mann, Chapman & Coyne is a full-service legal firm, well-positioned to assist the rapidly growing business and industrial base in south central Indiana.

Services provided by the firm include business planning and formation, employment law, contracts, mediation, real estate zoning, corporate law, probate and estate planning, and assistance for Bloomington's hundreds of family-owned businesses, including such services as family business succession planning.

Senior partners at Andrews, Harrell, Mann, Chapman & Coyne are directly involved in representing clients while managing the steady growth of the firm to keep pace with manpower and other resources.

The building housing the law firm has become a community landmark. The firm's investment in the building mirrors its investment in the community and is a symbolic connection between the firm and the city in which it prospers. The link is more than symbolic, however. Andrews, Harrell, Mann, Chapman & Coyne is committed to providing leadership as well as behind-the-scenes assistance to important causes and projects in the Bloomington area.

Attorneys at Andrews, Harrell, Mann, Chapman & Coyne contribute significant time to pro-bono legal assistance, supporting the firm's fundamental belief that legal counsel should not be denied to individuals on the basis of finances. Besides professional services, the firm provides support and manpower for numerous not-for-profit organizations. Attorneys can be found chairing a Chamber of Commerce committee, serving as directors for dozens of community organizations, running a booth for a church fund-raiser, donating money to the United Way, or providing one-on-one tutoring for area youngsters.

Located in the shadow of the state's flagship university, Indiana University, the firm is a sought-after source of guest speakers who can provide knowledge as well as perspective. Attorneys are regularly asked to work with students in the various colleges at IU and students enrolled in the School of Law.

As a longtime member of the Bloomington Area Chamber of Commerce, the firm is dedicated to promoting the south central Indiana region and investment in its future economic health. To that end, Andrews, Harrell, Mann, Chapman & Coyne has taken active roles in several community milestones, such as the creation and formation of local economic development entities. The Bloomington Community Foundation and the Bloomington Advancement Corporation are two examples of organizations created to stimulate economic growth and contribute to a healthy economy that benefits the community as a whole.

The Bloomington high schools have also taken advantage of the firm's legal expertise in the area of public governance. Andrews, Harrell, Mann, Chapman & Coyne provided the legal work necessary to form foundations for the city's two high schools. The Panthers For Better Education and The Cougars For Better Education organizations act as fund-raising arms for the schools, decreasing the schools' dependence on outside aid and providing the economic means to increase opportunities for students.

Andrews, Harrell, Mann, Chapman & Coyne is inextricably tied to Bloomington and south central Indiana by a strong sense of loyalty and a firm commitment to the area's well-being. Its legacy is still unfolding, but will undoubtedly be defined by the many important relationships the firm has forged with the local governments, the schools, area businesses, and countless individuals. The community is poised to enter the twenty-first century and Andrews, Harrell, Mann, Chapman & Coyne will be an integral part of the journey. ⚑

Bunger & Robertson

The heritage of Bunger & Robertson dates back to 1949, when the firm became Bloomington's first true partnership of lawyers. Before that, most of the city's attorneys were sole practitioners or in family practices.

Over the years, the firm has grown in size and in the variety of legal services offered. With a team of talented attorneys concentrating in specific practice areas, Bunger & Robertson is poised today to meet the challenges of the twenty-first century with a commitment to technology, innovation, and excellence.

The law firm has kept pace with the growth of Bloomington. As the economy of the Hoosier city has become more sophisticated, so has the breadth and scope of legal services delivered by the firm. The firm's clients include small businesses and individuals, as well as publicly held corporations. It represents banks and other lenders, local government entities, and health care providers.

Members of the firm take a responsive approach to their relationships with clients. Emphasis is placed on personal attention and open communication. Bunger & Robertson's long list of clients vouches for the popularity of its methods as well as the diversity of its practice. The list includes some of the region's best-known businesses and organizations, such as Bloomington Hospital, the Monroe County Community Schools, B. G. Hoadley

Quarries, Owens, Bryan and Reed Realtors, national insurance companies such as Auto Owners and State Farm, and many local and statewide businesses, as well as individual clients.

The firm also stands high in the eyes of its peers in the legal community. This respect was evidenced when firm attorney Joseph D. O'Conner was elected to serve as president of the Indiana State Bar Association, its youngest president in its 100-year history, as well as being a delegate to the American Bar Association. That legacy of respect goes back a long way to when founder Len E. Bunger served as city judge from 1951-53 and prosecuting attorney in 1953-55.

Because they understand the process so well, Bunger & Robertson attorneys always search for solutions that will avoid a trip to court. The firm remains committed and dedicated to lalternative dispute resolution as a means to avoid costly litigation. When an alternative resolution is not possible, members of Bunger & Robertson work to win. They do so with the personnel and experience to get the job done efficiently and economically.

The Bunger & Robertson philosophy of merging quality legal services with personal concern carries over to the area of business and commercial law. The firm's business lawyers understand the needs of business people. They offer representation that keeps the client's business goals in mind. That means avoiding troublesome situations whenever possible. Experienced attorneys cover the areas of probate and estate planning, insurance law, civil litigation, real estate, business organizations, health care law, school law, family law, nonprofit and

Because they understand the process so well, Bunger & Robertson attorneys always search for solutions that will avoid a trip to court. Photo by Kendall Reeves.

charitable organizations, mediation, and other alternative dispute resolution services.

Clients also benefit from Bunger & Robertson's strong ties and stable relations with local units of government, the state legislature, and state and federal agencies. These are grounded in the attorneys' diverse experience in the public as well as the private sector.

Adhering to the Bunger & Robertson philosophy of being committed to "quality, service, professionalism, and, most importantly, our clients," are attorneys Don M. Robertson, Thomas Bunger, Joseph D. O'Connor, James L. Whitlatch, Samuel R. Ardery, Margaret M. Frisbie, John W. Richards, William J. Beggs, Holly M. Harvey, and Stephen G. Miller.

While excellent legal advice gives clients an advantage in achieving their objectives, Bunger & Robertson recognizes that client satisfaction extends far beyond technical competence. Clients benefit from the firm's strong commitment to the concept of client service teams, tailoring their representation to the objectives of each client.

In addition to the firm's dedication to its clients, the members of Bunger & Robertson share a commitment to the legal profession. The firm supports its profession's highest ethical standards through its involvement in the Indiana State Bar Association and Foundation, the American Bar Association and Foundation, Indiana Equal Justice Fund, and Legal Services Organization. Attorneys in the firm are encouraged to provide pro bono representation to those unable to pay for services. So diligent has Bunger & Robertson been in providing those free services that the firm has been honored with the State Bar Association Pro Bono Award two times in the 1990s.

Bunger & Robertson also strongly continues its founders' commitment to "put back into the community from which we make our living." As a result, the firm's volunteers are actively involved in supporting organizations such as the Bloomington Hospital Foundation, Western Golf Association, Evans Scholar Foundation, United Way of Monroe County, Bloomington Chamber of Commerce, Monroe County United Ministries, Abilities Unlimited, various churches, youth sports, and the Bloomington Boys and Girls Club. The firm also is involved with Indiana University through teaching positions and support of university activities, such as the Auditorium Series and support of public radio and television.

Bunger & Robertson is proud of its strengths— a strong foundation, an outstanding portfolio of clients, top quality service, involvement in the community, and dedicated people. ⚖

Bunger & Robertson is proud of its strengths—a strong foundation, an outstanding portfolio of clients, top quality service, involvement in the community, and dedicated people. Photo by Kendall Reeves.

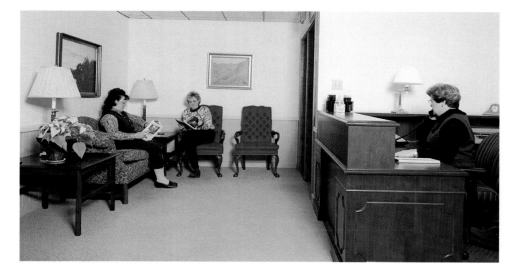

Olive LLP

With an emphasis on service excellence, technology, training, and people, Olive LLP restructured the firm to develop specialized services for the manufacturing, construction, health care, nonprofit, and financial service industries. Shown are (left to right) Susan C. Bradford, Manager; Carroll W. Moore, President of Cardon & Associates, Inc.; C. Larry Davis, Member of the Firm; and Lisa M. Fulkerson, Manager. Photo by Sheldon.

With an 80-year history, Olive LLP is the 15th largest accounting and consulting firm in the United States. Pictured are (front row, left to right) Kent N. Rodgers, Associate Member; Dennis K. McGuire, Chief Operating Officer; (back row, left to right) C. Larry Davis, Member of the Firm; and Mary A. Horn, Member of the Firm. Photo by Sheldon.

Olive LLP's **dynamic** plan to meet changing client needs is working. With an 80-year history, offices throughout Indiana, Illinois, and Ohio, a worldwide network of affiliate CPA firms, and more than 600 personnel, the 15th largest United States CPA firm is achieving its goals for the future.

Olive began to reshape its vision for client service nearly 10 years ago. With an emphasis on service excellence, technology, training, and people, Olive restructured the firm to develop specialized services for the manufacturing, construction, health care, nonprofit, and financial service industries.

"Olive has been responsive to the specialized tax, financial, and consulting needs in Bloomington and surrounding areas," says Dennis McGuire, Chief Operating Officer of Olive's Bloomington office. "We work closely with our clients and offer over 100 value-added services."

"Manufacturing companies are challenged by competition, industry regulations, plant requirements, and financial resource issues," says Mary Horn, Bloomington's Manufacturing Industry Team Leader. " Olive consultants help manufacturers by streamlining operations to achieve a greater efficiency for a sharper competitive edge and improved profit margins."

"Profitability and cash flow are the keys to a contractor's success," says Dave Conner, Bloomington's Construction Industry Team Leader (not pictured). "We help clients build and maintain a profitable business through margin aggression, automation, and management of the regulatory and contractual risk environments."

"The health care arena is changing rapidly," says Bloomington's Health Care Industry Team Leader, Larry Davis. "Our team works with today's health care providers in the areas of cost containment, mergers and acquisitions, cost reporting, and creative financing."

"Nonprofit organizations need experts in board development, strategic planning, and identification of alternative funding sources," states Kent Rodgers, Bloomington's Nonprofit Industry Team Leader. "Olive works with nonprofit clients as an active business partner to expand organizational capabilities, enhance operational structure, and increase financial stability."

"Olive's Management Consulting Services (MCS) team provides clients with state-of-the-art computer systems consulting, including strategic systems planning and implementation, software evaluation and selection, and systems training and support," says McGuire. "Other MCS services include employee benefits consulting, strategic business planning, ISO and QS 9000, and business process improvement."

"Olive's industry focus benefits both its clients and the firm," says McGuire. "We work in partnership with our clients, allowing them to seize opportunities and position their organizations to confront changing demands. Their success is our success." ⚠

Employment Plus, Inc. has earned a top-notch reputation as a temporary and permanent job placement agency that emphasizes "putting the plus in your business."

Locally owned and operated by Debbie Hamilton and Mike Ross, the agency offers guaranteed satisfaction as testimony of the confidence Employment Plus has in its applicants.

That total commitment policy must be working. While other employment service companies have started up and quickly folded, Employment Plus is rapidly growing. Now located out of four offices—Bloomington, Bedford, New Albany, and Corydon—Employment Plus services more than 500 businesses in nine south central Indiana counties.

And those businesses are singing the praises of Employment Plus. "Employment Plus has been a valuable asset for our recruiting needs," says John Behne, plant superintendent for Contech Construction Products, Inc. in Mitchell.

"The quality of their employees continues to exceed those of the competing agencies in our area," Behne says. "Their service, in dealing with our emergency needs, has allowed our plant to operate efficiently."

Employment Plus has a list of over 1,500 employees to refer for temporary positions, and that number continues to grow as employees learn that the agency provides pleasant and profitable work assignments. By using performance testing, Employment Plus carefully matches an assignment with an employee's skill level.

From the client's perspective, the program works. "Employment Plus has always responded immediately to our needs and follows requirements exactly in sending qualified applicants," says Sandra Packman, human resources manager for Boston Scientific Corporation in Spencer.

"The biggest complaint most businesses have about employment agencies is not receiving what they asked for. Employment Plus will not send an applicant that doesn't meet your requirements," Packman says.

Over the years, Hamilton and Ross say they have noticed a major change in employment services. Many companies are now using employment agencies to help screen for full-time employees. "A company will now hire a temporary employee for approximately six to nine weeks so they can evaluate an employee prior to making a permanent hiring decision," Ross says.

At Employment Plus, standards are high and clients recognize that. The agency is dedicated to providing clients with the best possible help—employees who will meet assignments enthusiastically and complete them with competence and on time.

Since she was born and grew up in Bloomington, Hamilton says that gives the service run by her and Mike Ross an extra edge over other employment agencies. "I worked in the personnel field approximately 10 years and already had the foundation and reputation before I started Employment Plus," Hamilton says. "They appreciate that we are a locally-owned business offering personalized friendly service." ⏶

Locally owned and operated by (left to right) Debbie Hamilton and Mike Ross, Employment Plus offers guaranteed satisfaction as testimony of the confidence it has in its applicants. Photo by Kendall Reeves.

L.A. Merry & Associates, PC

Since its founding in 1982, L.A. Merry & Associates, PC has focused on a strategy of client-centered dedication to excellence.

Since its founding in 1982, L.A. Merry & Associates, PC has focused on a strategy of client-centered dedication to excellence. In a world of continuously changing regulations and economic conditions, such a strategy is sometimes tough to maintain. But the firm has experienced continuous growth and is looking forward to meeting the challenges in the years to come. L.A. Merry & Associates is large enough to provide clients with the level of expertise required to deal with complex assurance, tax, and management challenges. But it is also small enough to offer special attention and be sensitive to each client's specific needs.

The firm understands that many individuals and businesses feel overwhelmed by the increasingly complex world of finance, where each day a new crop of circumstances seems to spring forth with uncertain promises. "It's more than just being a typical accountant," founder L.A. Merry says. "It's helping people and business owners interpret the numbers to develop and implement a strategy. Whether it's accounting, taxes, or a general business matter, we're a key member of their team."

As the economy and world around it change, L.A. Merry & Associates is evolving to better serve its clients with a continuing emphasis on personalized professional services. In addition to the traditional financial reporting and tax returns, the firm emphasizes business consulting, computer and network consulting, along with other specialized areas such as business valuations, real estate development, and "controller-for-hire" services.

The firm's dedication to its clients has earned the company recognition with the highest of all compliments—client loyalty and referrals. "I think it shows in your work and relationships with your clients when you really care about what you're doing. Your clients recognize that with their trust and loyalty. When you get a referral you know you've done a good job, and it's an incentive to keep up the hard work," Merry says. It is client loyalty and referrals that give the firm clients all over the United States, Europe, and Asia. According to Merry, "People come to Bloomington for work with the university or one of the industries. We do consulting work for them while they're here. Often they will continue to use us as their CPA after their Bloomington connection has ended. Technology makes it easy to communicate, but you still have to do a good job to generate that loyalty."

The firm, and particularly its founder, is proud of Bloomington. That sense of pride was a big factor in their commitment to the renovation project of the former Hicks House on North Walnut Street, which is now the firm's office. Located in one of Bloomington's historic districts, the house is listed on the inventory of historic landmarks. With a longstanding interest in historic renovation, it had always been a goal of L.A. Merry to find a permanent home for the business in such a location. Built in 1896, the building had fallen on hard times. Now beautifully refinished and decorated by Merry, the office is a welcome addition to downtown Bloomington.

For the future, L.A. Merry & Associates is committed to remaining on the leading edge of financial, tax, and management services. With a qualified staff of certified public accountants ready to guide their clients into the twenty-first century, they plan to manage their growth in a way to continue to meet that number one goal of client-centered dedication to excellence. ⚏

L.A. Merry & Associates' commitment to Bloomington is evidenced in the renovation of the former Hicks House on North Walnut Street, which is now the firm's office.

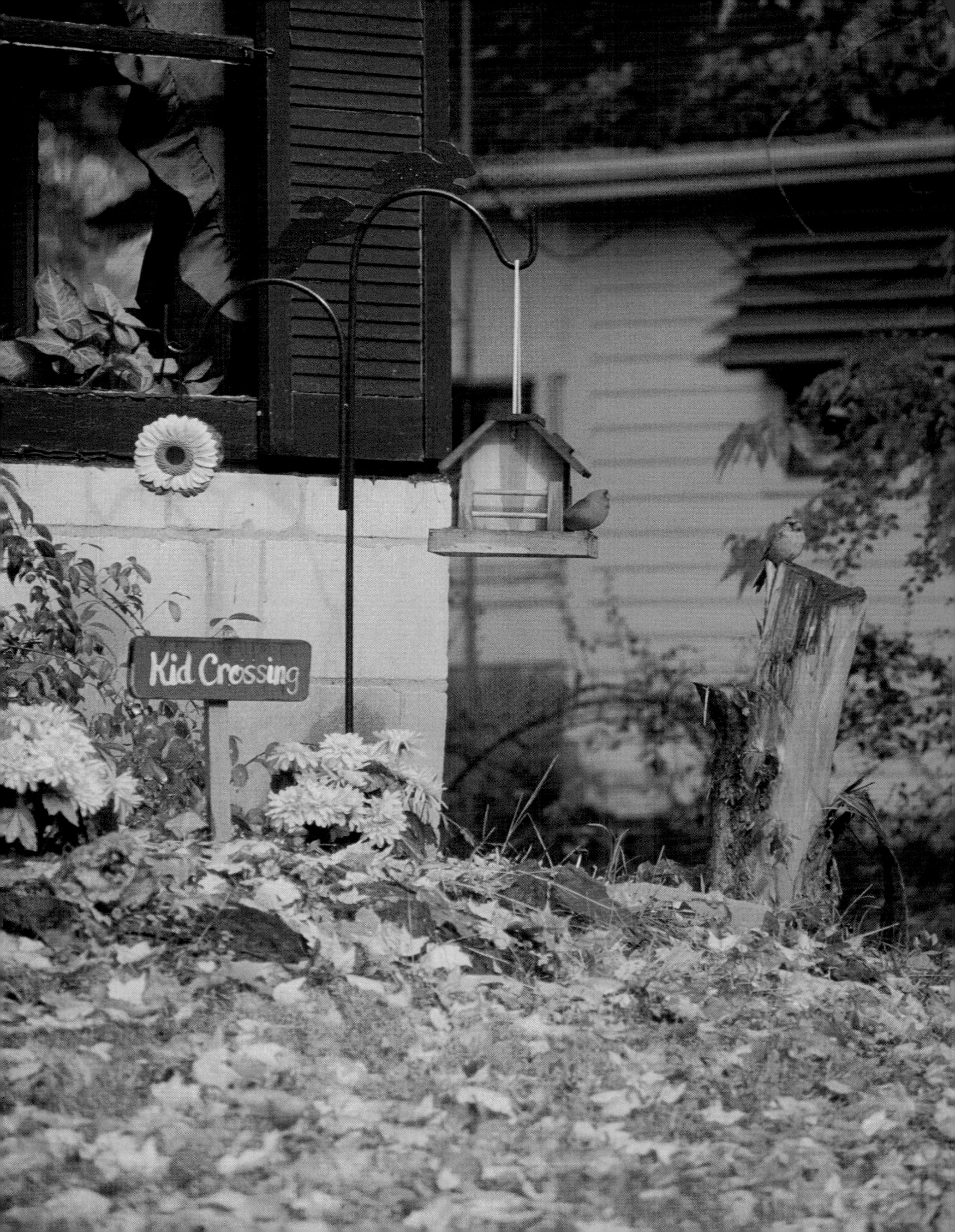
Kid Crossing

Indiana Limestone Company, Inc.

For over seven decades, the Indiana Limestone Company has been helping build America, the world, and even its own state in Indiana limestone. The Indiana State Office Building One is a fine example of the company's craftmanship.

The Indiana Limestone Company, Inc. (ILCI) is building a monumental legacy one project at a time. Memorials carved from Indiana limestone grace most town squares and courthouses around America. The nation's capitol boasts an impressive array of distinguished monuments, virtually all of them formed from Indiana limestone.

Limestone landmarks have helped create a worldwide architectural attraction in Washington, D.C. The Pentagon—the largest government project ever constructed—was built of ILCI's Indiana limestone, as were the Federal Triangle Buildings, Internal Revenue Building, National Cathedral, the Department of Commerce, the National Archives Building, Franklin Square, the Welcome Center at Arlington National Cemetery, and the Capitol Reflecting Pool.

The Empire State Building in New York is made of Indiana limestone, as are the headquarters for the General Motors Corporation in Detroit, the Chicago Merchant Mart, the Atlantic City Convention Hall, the Chicago Tribune Tower, the Nebraska Capitol in Lincoln, the Mellon Institute in Pittsburgh, Butler University in Indianapolis, Proctor & Gamble offices in Cincinnati, the Crescent in Dallas, and the Indiana War Memorial in Indianapolis.

When the biggest federal government

project since the Pentagon was visualized, the creators knew exactly what was needed—Indiana limestone. And they knew where to head—to the Hoosier company that is the largest fabricator and quarrier of dimensional limestone in the United States.

For two years, the Bedford company cut 400,000 cubic feet of limestone in the geologic basement of Monroe and Lawrence Counties for the Ronald Reagan Building and International Trade Center. Then it custom-sawed almost 245,000 cubic feet. The Reagan Building required about 50,000 more cubic feet of Indiana limestone than the Empire State Building. That is around 18,000 tons of limestone—enough to fill 750 semi-trailer flatbeds, which carried the finished stone from Indiana to Washington.

Though the stone came from five different ILCI quarries, the company used computers to arrange different stones according to color and texture in a way that would allow it to blend with the weathered Federal Triangle Buildings constructed in the Depression era. Working from drawings of the building, the company cut smaller panels of about 300 pounds each. Masons bolted the panels to the steel structure of the building—17,000 on one wall alone. The Indiana stones arrived perfectly sequenced and color-coordinated.

The new Reagan Building, referred to in 1987 congressional debate as "the missing tooth in the smile of Pennsylvania Avenue," now presides over the Washington landscape with its permanent limestone image. Constructed of 240,000 cubic feet of finished Indiana limestone, the building completes the Federal Triangle Complex, which was started in the 1920s.

The structure of Indiana limestone is unique, and

ILCI's Joyner Mill facility in Oolitic, Indiana, is an automated, high-volume facility for fabricating dimensional cut-stone in a variety of finishes. Adjacent to Joyner Mill is ILCI's Central Block Storage Yard, where most of ILCI's raw block inventory is stored. ILCI's current inventory includes 10,000 limestone blocks with an average size of 100 cubic feet each.

Indiana limestone is effectively used in interior and exterior walls, and in flooring applications in commercial buildings of all types, including banks such as the Union Planters National Bank in Memphis, Tennessee.

the Indiana Limestone Company offers architects and builders a versatility that is unmatched by any other supplier of limestone.

The Indiana Limestone Company began in 1926. But its story goes back to the earliest days of the infant limestone industry.

The deposits are found in Indiana's Monroe and Lawrence Counties, the remnants of sandbars formed about 330 million years ago when the Midwest was a vast, shallow, tropical sea. The known deposits are large enough that the usable stone will last in excess of 100 years, says company manager George James. "We will not run out of stone. It will last beyond any future that we can foresee."

Because Indiana limestone is so pure and the microscopic fossils are so evenly distributed, it is easy to carve in ornate, flowing architectural styles. The 30- to 90-foot deep deposits are unusual in that the stone they yield is devoid of geological imperfections. Quarriers often can go through the full, 90-foot depth of a deposit recovering stone from the bottom that has the same color and consistency as the top. That is important to architects who want to construct a skyscraper in stone but want an absolute continuity of color and texture from bottom to top.

In 1860 Nathan Hall built a small mill in Bedford and began the first commercial quarrying effort of Indiana limestone. At that time, men quarried by blasting a year's supply of limestone in one crashing heap, hand sawing the stone, and hauling it from quarry to mill by horse and oxen. In 1866,

the first steam-powered saws were purchased, which revolutionized the industry.

The first commercial shipment out of Bedford was consigned to John Rawle of Chicago. This was a shipment that would be of great importance to the Indiana limestone industry. When the embers had burned down in the Great Chicago Fire of 1871, Chicagoans noticed among the ruins that some buildings fared better than others. Indiana limestone buildings survived particularly well. The first large building scheduled to go up in the city's reconstruction was a new city hall. Architects selected Indiana limestone as the building material. The magnificence of the new city hall and the attention it attracted from famed architects was a big boost for the Indiana limestone industry.

The Indiana Limestone Company, Inc. was formed on June 1, 1926, to help pull together the various small limestone companies which dotted the region. Twenty-four limestone companies were involved in the merger, which included 21 quarries, 36 mills, and over 6,000 acres of land. The companies represented 90 percent of the area stone industry.

In 1927, Indiana Limestone Company quarried a million tons of limestone and was running its mills 24 hours a day. As the rest of the country saw the high quality results, the popularity of limestone quickly spread. During 1928 and 1929, production topped 14 million cubic feet for both years, which was thought to be an all-time high.

In the mid '30s, the depression hit hard. Times were especially difficult for the limestone industry

The Ronald Reagan Building and International Trade Center is the largest government building project since the Pentagon. Indiana Limestone Company, Inc. is proud that its stone was selected for both the Pentagon and the latest Federal Triangle building. Delivery of the limestone for this project required 750 semi-truckloads from facilities in Indiana to Washington, D.C., over a 24-month period. ILCI supplied the limestone cladding for most of the historic Washington, D.C., buildings, including the limestone used in constructing all six buildings that comprise the Federal Triangle complex.

and its communities. In 1920, it was estimated that 67 percent of all building stone shipped nationwide was from Lawrence and Monroe Counties in southern Indiana. By 1935, that figure was down to 41 percent. Since over half of all public construction during the period of 1933-38 was being done by the federal government, federal contracts were essential. In 1940, Congress agreed to use Indiana limestone for the new Pentagon building.

A new source of income also came from the increased use of waste blocks as "breakwater" in the Great Lakes. One project alone used 4,700,000 cubic feet of block. Indiana limestone and other natural stones began to receive more attention from leading architects during the '80s. Popularity of the natural building stone had risen dramatically by the end of the decade.

However, according to company President Brian Moore, the first and foremost thing Indiana Limestone builds into each job doesn't have anything to do with stone. Indiana Limestone is dedicated to building customers' trust. For over seven decades, the Indiana Limestone Company has been helping build America and the world in Indiana limestone. The company's premier status as a leader in the stone industry has been derived from its quality, engineering, and service the company gives to each of its customers in every phase of a project.

The Indiana Limestone Company engineering staff uses a blend of today's technology and "hands-on" experience to support its customers from the beginning to the end of their projects. The use of computer-aided drafting to provide accurate drawings is just a part of the technology. The company also helps in the design and construction stages by trying new ideas in panelization by reducing lifts and utilizing structural capacities of the stone. This value-engineering service can result in drastic reductions in setting costs and assembly requirements. Providing technical information such as thermal performance, wind load calculations, attachments to steel, and other areas is an important part of the company's engineering support. The skills and experience of its professional staff are value-added benefits to Indiana Limestone clients that are unmatched elsewhere in the industry.

The Indiana Limestone Company owns 2,300 acres in Lawrence and Monroe Counties. Its Joyner Mill site in Oolitic is used for high-volume, dimensional-cut stone fabrication. The facility produces semifinished stone or finished product in a variety of finishes. The dedicated staff of skilled craftsmen at Indiana Limestone provides clients with the quality for any project and a promise to deliver on time to meet tight building schedules.

Indiana Limestone can apply a variety of finishes, including smooth honed, abrasive, four-cut tooling, and bush hammered to create any desired design effect. Stone options for Indiana Limestone include the following:

Buff Indiana Limestone—The well-known and widely used buff color range is available in uniform colors ranging from a brown tinted buff to a light cream shade. Buff limestone features a fine to coarse grain texture with distinctive limestone characteristics.

Crown™ Buff Indiana Limestone—Crown™ Buff Indiana Limestone is an extremely fine-grained select grade limestone from the Crown™ Quarry. It is very white with a slight cream tint.

Gray Indiana Limestone—This beautiful gray stone is very uniform in color and can range in shade from light silver to a distinctive blue-gray. The texture is fine to medium grain, featuring many limestone characteristics. The stone is normally available in large sizes, making it well suited for floor-to-floor panels.

Variegated Indiana Limestone—For a unique appearance, Variegated Indiana Limestone adds an element of interest. The blend of gray and buff ranges from all gray to all buff to a variety of intermediate combinations. Variegated Indiana Limestone features the characteristics of natural limestone and fine to coarse grain texture. Some of the largest projects completed recently have used Variegated Indiana Limestone.

Crown Silver Buff™—Crown Silver Buff™ is a very fine-grained select grade limestone from the Crown™ Quarry. It is very light colored with a neutral to gray tone.

Indiana Limestone provides designers with the ideal solution for a building material that offers elegant beauty, durability, and fireproof properties. Indiana limestone offers superior integrity and will outlast most of the other components of the structure. The limestone is resistant to weathering, making it suitable for any climate condition throughout the United States. In addition, it is extremely dense for excellent heat loss/heat gain properties. Indiana limestone is effectively used in interior and exterior walls, and in flooring applications in commercial buildings of all types, including office buildings, federal facilities, banks, and hospitals. Indiana Limestone is also commonly used in residential construction.

With its legendary success and reputation, it would have been easy for the Indiana Limestone Company to rest on its past accomplishments and continue with business as usual. But that's not the company's style. Instead, Executive Vice President Carol Blackwell says, "Indiana Limestone is constantly searching for a better way. The company is seeking for ways to become more efficient and responsive." By combining advanced technology and common sense, Indiana Limestone has created new ways to extract more stone in less time with less harm to the environment.

Indiana Limestone continually searches for a better way to create value. Applying innovative mining and fabrication techniques, the company is able to offer superior quality limestone at a surprisingly affordable price. The versatility and durability of its products are what had initially attracted architects and contractors to the Indiana Limestone Company. What keeps them coming back time and again is the company's unique blend of custom handscraftsmanship, technical expertise, and engineering support.

The multifaceted company understands that people are its greatest resource. That resource is readily shared. Indiana Limestone encourages all employees to be responsible stewards of their community. Employees pursue diverse community interests, from supporting both the Bloomington and Bedford Chambers of Commerce to teaching Sunday School classes, coaching sports teams, donating money to local police departments, delivering holiday food baskets and gifts to needy families, and volunteering as tutors to at-risk students.

In particular, the Indiana Limestone Company promotes an emphasis on education. The firm holds that good students make good citizens and great future employees. That's one reason the company supports a stone-cutting curriculum at Bedford High School, uses work/study students from Indiana University, and participates in a half-day program for high school drafting students.

The Indiana Limestone Company is a popular spot for tours from local school and civic groups. It also provides countless pieces of Indiana limestone for arts programs at local schools, churches, and arts centers.

Today, the Indiana Limestone Company stands on a firm foundation of tremendous natural resources, modern technology combined with traditional handcraftsmanship, and a reputation unparalleled in the industry. Heading into the twenty-first century, the Indiana Limestone Company continues to play a vital part in changing the face of the nation. ⚒

Indiana Limestone landmarks have helped create a worldwide architectural attraction in Washington, D.C., including the National Archives Building.

Weddle Bros. Construction Co., Inc.

Some high-profile Weddle Bros. Construction Co. projects include the General Electric plant (shown here), the Monroe County Public Library, the John Mellencamp Indoor Practice Facility at Indiana University, and office buildings for the Unity Physicians Group.

Weddle Bros.' projects, such as the Monroe County Public Library, dot the landscape of Bloomington and Monroe County.

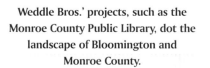

For almost half a century, Weddle Bros. Construction Co., Inc. has set the standard for construction throughout the Midwest and Southeast. If you want to see the quality workmanship and the vast capabilities of this company, all you have to do is look around, as Weddle Bros.' projects dot the landscape of Bloomington and Monroe County. Weddle Bros.' employees are dedicated to providing projects of lasting value for their clients and for the communities in which they live and work.

Established and incorporated in 1952, Weddle Bros.' reputation for excellence extends to commercial, industrial, historic renovation and restoration, highway, bridge, and general construction projects. In addition to a diverse client base, Weddle Bros.' experience encompasses just as wide a range of project delivery methods. These project delivery methods include lump sum bid, the all inclusive Design/Build method, build-to-suit (with leaseback available), construction management services, and negotiated contracts with a guaranteed maximum price. Through teaming and partnering, Weddle Bros. works in partnership with its clients to determine the best method of project delivery to meet the clients' needs.

Almost every contractor claims to deliver quality projects, built on time and on budget. Weddle Bros. not only has a proven track record to back up its claims, but it also has received national recognition and awards for quality in its projects. This demonstrates that quality is more than just a good-sounding promise. In 1995, Weddle Bros. was the National Quality Initiative (NQI) Award runner-up, and in November 1997, Weddle Bros. received the National Quality Award for the best quality project in the United States. The NQI Award is given to the construction project team that has shown superior results through teamwork, innovation, value, and customer satisfaction. The NQI Award is judged by a panel of representatives from 10 national construction associations and organizations, including the Associated General Contractors of America, the American Consulting Engineers Council, and the American Public Works Association.

Weddle Bros. believes the best testimonials for the company, though, are the projects it has completed. Some high-profile local projects include the General Electric plant, the Columbia House Membership Center, the John Mellencamp Indoor Practice Facility at Indiana University, the Monroe County Public Library, many projects at the Bloomington Hospital, and at Morgan County Memorial Hospital. Also included in this prestigious list are office buildings for the Unity Physicians Group, corporate offices for the General Acceptance Corporation, restoration and renovation projects such as the Johnson Creamery Business Center, Rawles, Swain, and Wylie Halls at Indiana University, and governmental buildings such as the Monroe County Criminal Justice Facility and the Morgan County and Greene County jails.

Weddle Bros. takes both pride and satisfaction from the fact that it not only delivers quality projects for its customers and community, but also the fact that it has developed long-lasting and mutually beneficial business relationships. Even during periods of significant growth in the company, over 80 percent of Weddle Bros.' construction projects are with customers for whom it has previously worked. This demonstrates an impressive record of continuing business relationships because of the company's integrity, customer responsiveness, and ability to bring value to its clients.

Weddle Bros. has grown to include 110 full-time employees and as many as 200 additional field construction workers during peak construction times. Weddle Bros.' team professionals know the industry inside and out. They are big-picture people, able to keep the final goal in mind from the earliest stage of the project. Their expert abilities at preparing conceptual estimates are a tremendous asset to their clients and design team.

Beyond its building work, Weddle Bros. is known for its bridge and other highway work. Numerous bridges over the Wabash and White

Rivers and on every interstate highway in Indiana and most major thoroughfares throughout the state have major structures built with Weddle Bros.' quality. Weddle Bros.' quality is also in many of the community's schools—including the recent Bloomington High School South addition and renovation, Edgewood High School, Jackson Creek, Batchelor, and Tri-North Middle Schools, and the new Grandview Elementary School—as well as many buildings on the Indiana University campus.

Weddle Bros.' corporate headquarters are located in Bloomington, Indiana. The company has three operating divisions—the Building Division and the Highway Division are both headquartered in Bloomington, and the Southeast Division is located in Orlando, Florida. The company also has an office in Evansville, Indiana, and facilities in Bloomfield, Indiana. At the helm of the company is President Lee E. Carmichael, Executive Vice President Gary R. Walton, Vice President and Building Division Manager Donald L. Turner, Vice President and Highway Division Manager Scott A. Sieboldt, and Vice President Robert L. Carter.

Many high-profile projects have also been completed by Weddle Bros.' Southeast Division, including many throughout all the Walt Disney World properties. This impressive list of projects includes all the hardscape for the Disney MGM Studio's theme park, the Disney Indy 200 Race Track, the Disney World Wedding Pavilion, the Magic Kingdom Parade route renovation, Pleasure Island, the Fantasia Golf Spectacular, and also countless behind-the-scenes projects for support facilities needed to produce the Disney magic.

In addition, Weddle Bros. has also completed many projects for Sea World of Florida. Included are exhibits such as the Wild Arctic, a major addition to Shamu Stadium, the Penguin Encounter, the Games and Arcade Area, and the massive Children's Play Area. Among the many other projects of note completed by Weddle Bros. is work at the Kennedy Space Center, where it constructed a 40,000-square-foot superflat slab for the Solid Rocket Booster Facility. This slab, which had to be within an eighth-inch tolerance over the entire 40,000 square feet, enables NASA to use air pallets to move the solid rocket boosters used for the space shuttle missions around this facility.

While Weddle Bros. is justifiably proud of all its many high-profile projects, each and every project, no matter the scope or size, is very important to the company. Each project receives the same attention to detail and quality. The management and employees of Weddle Bros. truly believe and understand that client satisfaction is the bottom line. The company offers its clients the services they need from start to finish, turning first-time clients into long-term friends.

Weddle Bros. is also dedicated to doing all it can to serve the communities in which its employees live and work. As good corporate citizens, the company supports a multitude of civic activities from economic development to sponsoring youth sports and other worthwhile youth activities, to providing donations and volunteers for local charities.

Weddle Bros. takes pride in its profession and is committed to its clients, employees, and community. Its goal is to have each project meet or exceed the clients' expectations—first time, on time, every time. With this mission in mind, Weddle Bros. is helping build cities—including its hometown of Bloomington—one landmark at a time. ♠

Weddle Bros. believes the best testimonials for the company, are the projects it has completed, including the John Mellencamp Indoor Practice Facility at Indiana University.

Weddle Bros. works in partnership with its clients to determine the best method of project delivery to meet the clients' needs. A fine example of this philosophy is the Unity Physicians Group office building.

CFC, Inc.

The heart of any city is its downtown. And Bloomington has a very good heart with a beat that seems to be growing ever stronger. A major force behind the city's vitality is CFC, Inc.

It wasn't too long ago that Bloomington seemed headed for the ranks of other small cities throughout the nation. Suburban malls and neighborhood shopping centers drained many downtown shops in once thriving cities, leaving boarded-up buildings and empty streets. Perhaps no single project contributed more to turning downtown Bloomington into what it is today than Fountain Square Mall on the south side of the square. In 1985, CFC, Inc. purchased 11 deteriorating buildings across from the Monroe County Courthouse. The buildings were an unsafe eyesore that detracted from the downtown's beautiful limestone courthouse. Paying strict attention to historic detail, CFC turned the dilapidated strip into an exciting 130,000-square-foot complex housing 57 professional offices, community rooms, and retail establishments.

Opened in 1989, Fountain Square Mall helped reestablish the historic look of downtown. The exterior has the turn-of-the-century feel, but the interiors are modern and up-to-date, combining the warmth and beauty of tile walkways, gleaming oak trim and doorways, a softly rippling waterfall, and a dramatic glassed-in elevator in the central atrium. Fountain Square Mall helped bring activity back to the Courthouse Square and spurred other developers to believe in downtown.

Quality workmanship is a facet of everything CFC does. Jim Murphy, president of CFC, says much of the company's success comes from paying attention to detail. "When we lease space, we make a commitment to quality service—ground and facility maintenance and 'customer services,' " Murphy says. "It would be very easy to ignore some of those things. But we don't."

A Cook Group company, CFC, Inc. was founded in 1973 with a different mission. Its original purpose was to finance loans to Cook employees. CFC evolved into a real estate management and development company, with investments in apartments, commercial buildings, and renovated historic and architecturally significant structures. CFC had demonstrated that older structures can be renovated and reused in ways that preserve the past, enhance the character of the community, and succeed financially.

Ask Jim Murphy about the

company and he enthusiastically lists its projects. It takes both hands. Some highlights include: 1976— CFC restores the James Cochran House built in 1850. Amid warnings that "it can't be done," CFC strips away years of neglect to uncover a community gem. 1979—CFC renovates the Graham Plaza (Graham Hotel) at Seventh Street and College Avenue, converting an old hotel to prime office and retail space and the City of Bloomington constructs the Regester Parking Garage next to the Graham Plaza. 1980—CFC converts the old Curry Building at 214 West Seventh Street into a 16-office building. 1982—CFC renovates the 1928 Washington Terrace Apartments, once used as a communal dormitory, and returns them to apartment use. 1983— CFC converts the Illinois Central Freight Depot, built in 1906, at Sixth and Morton Streets, to office space. 1984—CFC buys the Tom Taylor Food Building at 311 West Seventh Street, eventually turning it into the Bloomington Antique Mall, home to about 100 antique dealers. 1985—CFC renovates a portion of the east side of the square, naming it Uptown Plaza. 1987—CFC purchases and relocates the 1883 Zeigler House. Now restored to its original beauty and connected by an enclosed breezeway to the historic Gilstrap House, the home has become the popular Grant Street Inn. 1996—CFC, as part of the Cook Group, forms a partnership with Historic Landmarks Foundation of Indiana to renovate and market the long-neglected West Baden Springs Hotel. Built in 1902, the unique and massive Orange County structure once attracted guests from across the country because of the supposed curative powers of the nearby natural springs. CFC contracted Pritchett Brothers Construction Inc. to head the renovation process, the largest project CFC or Pritchett Brothers had taken on.

But that's not all. There's the Johnson Hardware Building with its limestone sills and headers, interesting brickwork, and extension of the existing limestone sidewalk. The CFC project won the 1996 Historic Rehabilitation Project Award from the Commission for Bloomington Downtown. CFC created the Madison Park and Lincoln Place Condominiums, putting more residents in the central city. CFC also was instrumental in establishing the Convention Center of Monroe County, on a prime downtown spot. A Marriott Courtyard Hotel later was added to the Convention Center to provide a major draw for the Bloomington area.

The saw-toothed roof of the old Showers building lights much of the downtown Bloomington skyline and represents one of the city's most successful cooperative efforts. Built in 1910 as the Showers Brothers Furniture Company, the crumbling structure was renovated into a sparkling $24-million facility through a unique partnership of the City of Bloomington, Indiana University, and CFC. The three entities struck a deal in 1993 to save the landmark and turn it into a city hall, research park, and new office space. The 65,000-square-foot CFC section, about a third of the entire Showers building, sports two atria that show off the original architecture and skylights. Large factory windows and archival photos of the old furniture company are featured in the main south entrance atrium. Merging of the old and new has been integral to CFC's numerous projects around downtown Bloomington. "People here like that idea of blending business with history," Murphy says.

In 1996 CFC made headlines nationwide with its groundbreaking Bicycle Apartments in Bloomington. The 76 units are a way to attract people who want to live and work in the downtown area and don't want to own a car. Each apartment comes with a bicycle. In fact, having a car is a violation of the lease. The CFC project is one creative way to help make affordable housing available in the central area. The Bicycle Apartments won the Adaptive Reuse Project Award in 1996 from the Commission for Bloomington Downtown.

CFC's dedication to quality and service is matched by its commitment to the community. The company is a civic benefactor in many ways, and the annual Canopy of Lights is just one of them. The twinkling of 200,000 lights (100 miles' worth), carefully wrapped around each branch of every tree on the Courthouse Square, is a fantastic holiday gift from CFC. CFC is active in a number of groups that touch local citizens, such as Habitat for Humanity and youth organizations.

The spirit of giving to the community involves all employees, who volunteer for a host of non-profit and service organizations. Their efforts are supported by a company that cares. The bottom line is the benefit to others. CFC generosity, as in all things, reflects a pursuit of excellence and is a legacy as enduring as its brick-and-mortar projects. ⚐

In 1996 CFC made headlines nationwide with its groundbreaking Bicycle Apartments in Bloomington. The apartments won the Adaptive Reuse Project Award in 1996 from the Commission for Bloomington Downtown.

CFC created Lincoln Place Condominiums, putting more residents in the central city.

Pinnacle Properties Management Group, LLC

Peter Dvorak had a dream and the ambition to build a business that would leave its mark in the commercial and residential real estate market for years to come. His belief that Pinnacle Properties would be founded on a reputation of quality construction and superior service is the foundation upon which Dvorak has created a rapidly expanding company.

"Our main focus is on older and historic buildings," Dvorak says. "Our general philosophy is that it's better to recycle—to restore and renovate existing buildings instead of tearing them down to build new projects."

From its first basement office where visitors had to duck to avoid hitting furnace ducts to its current headquarters in one of Bloomington's most beautiful landmarks, Pinnacle Properties has built an excellent reputation as a major developer of older properties.

"I like to take old properties that have been neglected or mismanaged and fix them up," Dvorak says. "It's satisfying to find the hidden beauty in a building and help reestablish the community pride that goes with restoring the character and usefulness to a neighborhood structure."

Dvorak had no idea where his interest in real estate would eventually take him. He bought a small single-family house and fixed it up. Then came another and another. "The second home I moved into and renovated myself to get hands-on experience," he says. "I sanded floors, peeled wallpaper, stripped woodwork, and painted. I wanted to know exactly what went into such a project."

The Allen Building in downtown Bloomington was one of Pinnacle's largest projects. The 1904 landmark had fallen into disrepair, and was in danger of condemnation. Only after 54 new steel beams were erected to shore up the structure could the massive facelift begin. Decades of dirt, paint, and filth were removed, original details were restored, and eventually the building glowed with new life as 22 apartments and 5 commercial spaces emerged from the dust.

Since then, Pinnacle Properties has branched out to other markets in south central Indiana, Indianapolis, and southwest Florida. Pinnacle is now one of the largest privately held landlords in Indianapolis. At the end of 1996, the company controlled over 1,400 apartments. Acquisitions are on a pace for the company to exceed 3,000 units by the year 2000.

Headquartered in Bloomington, Pinnacle Properties now has two full-service offices in Indianapolis, along with 15 satellite offices. With 60 employees, the company's size has multiplied twenty-fold over the past six years. Its emphasis now is on concentrating on properties with more than 100 units.

Pinnacle's Bloomington offices are located in the historic Buskirk-Showers house, built circa 1890. Extensively renovated by Pinnacle in 1995, the building was recognized in 1915 by the local paper as "the most beautiful home in Bloomington." Ghost stories about the 100-year-old house have flourished for generations, and many locals are convinced the building is haunted.

Pinnacle Properties' contributions to the community are equally impressive. A strong supporter of downtown growth and revitalization, the company is an active member of the Commission for Bloomington Downtown and the Chamber of Commerce.

Pinnacle is also involved in assisting the homeless population in Monroe County. The company has started a holiday tradition in which Pinnacle Properties donates one night of shelter for the homeless in each of their tenants' names, in addition to providing support throughout the year. Big Brothers/Big Sisters of Monroe County is also an important organization to Pinnacle's employees, who participate as "bigs" as well as in fund-raising activities.

The company and its employees are also strong patrons of the arts, and are involved with the Bloomington Symphony Orchestra and Bloomington Area Arts Council. A member of the BSO board of directors, Dvorak says, "I think the arts are a very important part of our community, and I try to support their activities every way I can." ⚘

Pinnacle Properties' headquarters are located in downtown Bloomington on North Walnut Street. Photo by Kendall Reeves.

The Allen Building, located at Kirkwood and Walnut Streets in downtown Bloomington was one of Pinnacle's largest projects. The 1904 landmark had fallen into disrepair, and was in danger of condemnation. The building now boasts 22 apartments and 5 commercial spaces. Photo by Kendall Reeves.

Rogers Group, Inc.

There are few companies in Bloomington that can match the rich tradition of Rogers Group, Inc. Started as a small roadside crushing operation in 1908 by 19-year-old Ralph Rogers, the company has become one of the largest privately held crushed stone producers in the central and southeastern United States.

Today, quarries producing crushed stone are still the backbone of the company. Asphalt, road construction, sand and gravel, and building materials also play integral parts in the company's profile.

Rogers started Bloomington Crushed Stone in the late 1920s, and his first quarry operation was on South Adams Street, where the current Rogers Group complex stands. The quarry operation moved to the area south of Cascades Park in 1939 and to its present location on Oard Road in 1954.

In the 1920s and '30s, federal legislation initiating highway construction increased the demand for crushed stone, and Ralph Rogers opened his first quarry to supply it. At that same time he also began operations in asphalt and paving. During the next 20 years, Rogers became one of the first subcontractors on the construction of the atomic bomb plant at Oak Ridge, Tennessee, and later built and supplied crushed stone for all the roads at the Crane Naval Weapons Support Center in Martin County, Indiana. Federal legislation created the nation's interstate highway system in the 1950s, and Rogers continued to grow by providing crushed stone and building roads.

Nearly everything in Bloomington has a touch of Rogers to it—whether it is from the aggregate used everyday in home building and paving streets, to the larger, more visible projects such as Bloomington Hospital, the Monroe County Airport, Indiana University's Memorial Stadium, or a long stretch of Highway 37.

Producing quality construction aggregates in harmony with neighboring communities and the environment is a top priority of Rogers Group. An annual recipient of beautification, safety, and environmental awards from the National Stone Association, Rogers Group won more 1997 awards per site than any other company in the industry.

Rogers Group is known throughout the communities it serves as a good corporate partner. Individual employees and the company as a whole support a wide variety of organizations through volunteer hours, sponsorships, and donations. It's not unusual to find a Rogers Group employee at a Leukemia Society planning meeting, mentoring a high school student, speaking to a prospective new business, or offering a quarry tour to a group of fourth graders. Their involvement spreads across a broad spectrum of initiatives, including support of local chambers of commerce and economic development groups, the United Way, Junior Achievement, and Boys and Girls Clubs.

Rogers Group stays competitive in the crushed stone industry with the implementation of state-of-the-art equipment and innovative product offerings. The development and marketing of ProStone, a premium golf course bunker material made of crushed limestone, is an example of such innovation.

With corporation headquarters in Nashville, Tennessee, Rogers Group employs 1,500 people in seven states. More than 300 are employed in southern Indiana. ⚐

Rogers Group's annual Rock the Quarry provides people of all ages an opportunity to tour the quarry, enjoy live entertainment, and share in good food and games. It is one of the many community activities sponsored by Rogers Group.

Rogers Group, Inc. was started as a small roadside crushing operation in 1908. Today, the company is one of the largest privately held crushed stone producers in the central and southeastern United States.

Superior Lumber & Building Co.

One high-profile project that reflects the Superior pride in workmanship is the historic Showers Factory, which was renovated for use as a city hall. Photo by Kendall Reeves.

Shortly after World War II, three local men involved in the construction industry decided to start their own company. Wayne Morris, John Hudelson, and Wade Whaley joined forces to create what they envisioned would be the area's premier general contractor and building supplier.

Along these lines, the partners chose to call their venture Superior Lumber & Building Co., Inc. Instead of using their names, the men wanted to choose a word that described what they intended to be—Superior. Since 1948, this vision has been coming true.

Two of the founders' sons, Jim Morris and Ed Hudelson, began working for the company during school vacations, learning the business from the ground up. Morris and Hudelson joined their fathers and eventually took over the operation of the company. In 1984, Morris and his wife, Donetta, became the sole owners.

Over the years, Superior phased out its lumber and building supplies, choosing to serve as a general contractor specializing in commercial, industrial, and educational buildings.

Morris now has two associates—Roger Richardson, who joined the firm in 1986, and Frank Young. Janice Spriggs, office manager since 1987, has helped round out the efficient office team.

Morris inherited the old-fashioned virtues upon which Superior Lumber & Building was founded. "Our reputation is our most important asset," Morris says. "People know that we value our word."

That reputation has stood them in good stead. Superior has left its mark of excellence throughout the community. High profile projects graced by the Superior touch include Greene School District, Saint Paul's Catholic Center, South Central Community Mental Health Center, and many other buildings.

As a true test of quality work and satisfied clients, Superior Lumber & Building Co. numbers many repeat customers among its business list.

One recent high-profile project that reflects the Superior pride in workmanship is the

historic Showers Factory, which was renovated for use as a city hall. Superior Lumber & Building was the successful bidder for the interior renovation. "We had a short time to do the work," Morris recalls. "We started the work in April and they had an open house set for November."

The project was completed on time, and scores of people paraded through to see the beautiful new facility. Even today, Morris enjoys visiting the Showers complex and seeing how the transformation was made from a warehouse to a beautiful public building. Morris finds it appropriate that his father, who died in 1979, once worked in the old furniture factory as a teenager—the place he helped to enjoy a rebirth by the company he founded.

With such a solid and respected business, Morris knows it would be possible to pull out of Bloomington and move to a larger city. But that won't ever happen, he says. "This has been a great place to live, work, and raise a family. The community has been good to us, and we have supported the community in many ways."

Hearkening back to the company's origin and guiding principles, Morris says he has found another reason why the name chosen so long ago is an appropriate title. Over the years, the local and dependable employees who have helped guide Superior Lumber & Building Co. to the forefront of the construction industry have earned recognition for being the best in their field—in a word, for being Superior. ▲

Under the guidance of (left to right) James T. Morris, Frank A. Young, and Roger Richardson, Superior Lumber & Building has earned the reputation for being one of the best in its field. Photo by Kendall Reeves.

Steele-Beard Electric Company, Inc.

Since its founding in 1950, Steele-Beard Electric Company, Inc. has been providing its customers with quality electrical installations. There is no mystery to how Steele-Beard Electric has become one of the leading electrical contracting firms in Indiana. It takes an unrelenting commitment to excellence to maintain the consistent quality for which Steele-Beard is known. No advertising or front-office hype is necessary—a solid history of performance draws customers back and attracts new projects through word-of-mouth testimonials.

The story of Steele-Beard begins almost half a century ago when two electricians looking for work decided to start their own business. Working out of a truck and then from a tiny office in back of a building, David L. Beard and James R. Steele earned the respect of clients. Starting out doing residential work, Steele-Beard expanded into commercial, industrial, and institutional electrical contracting.

While some things have changed since that time—for example, the company now has a fleet of vehicles and its own office building—the goal has remained the same: to provide quality workmanship on projects that are completed on time and within budget.

Steele-Beard's experience in a variety of markets has attuned the firm to the specific challenges each type of project brings. In recognition of the time constraints that govern many industrial and commercial projects, for example, the firm can provide its customers with custom design and installation on a fast-track basis. Likewise, Steele-Beard is equipped to perform the varied electrical work

necessary in schools and colleges, from large auditoriums and cafeterias to small classrooms and computer labs.

Quality workmanship is a facet of everything Steele-Beard does. The firm encourages all employees to attend seminars and workshops to help them remain at the top of their field of expertise.

With about 150 employees at the height of the work season, Steele-Beard can handle electrical contracting projects of all sizes, no matter how sophisticated the systems. Steele-Beard has successfully completed major electrical construction projects in Illinois, Tennessee, North Carolina, Wisconsin, and Ohio, as well as throughout the state of Indiana. These projects include schools, hospitals, university buildings, manufacturing plants, and correctional facilities.

Some of the biggest projects in the area carry the Steele-Beard trademark of excellence—including Indiana University, Bloomington Hospital, Monroe County Justice Facility, Monroe County Community Schools, General Electric, Woodbridge Post Office, and Independent Packaging.

Steele-Beard also offers expertise in areas such as design and build, motor controls, fire alarm systems, telecommunications wiring, temperature control wiring, and computer power systems.

A true family business, Steele-Beard is now into its third generation. However, the Steele-Beard family extends well beyond the bloodlines. All of its employees have helped create a company with an outstanding reputation.

In a sense, it's all part of the company's broad-based "good neighbor" policy. At every level, Steele-Beard strives to be a positive presence in the community and a good corporate neighbor. Locally, Steele-Beard supports a range of local charitable organizations and efforts.

Steele-Beard's success is living proof that its two founders identified a need in the community and filled it with an overall commitment to excellence. Steele-Beard Electric Company, Inc. is proud of its old-fashioned values and equally proud to be a part of the Bloomington community. ⚘

Steele-Beard Electric has become one of the leading electrical contracting firms in Indiana. Photo by Kendall Reeves.

The story of Steele-Beard begins almost half a century ago when two electricians looking for work decided to start their own business. Working out of a truck and then from a tiny office in back of a building, they earned the respect of their clients. Photo by Kendall Reeves.

Education
and
Quality of Life

Indiana University

Ernie Pyle was a Pulitzer Prize-winning journalist who brought the immediacy of World War II to millions of Americans through his newspaper columns about soldiers' lives. Hoagy Carmichael composed his popular songs "Star Dust" and "Georgia on My Mind" on a battered piano in a college student hangout. Isiah Thomas became one of the National Basketball Association's most sparkling players, finishing his criminal justice degree during the off-season. Dr. James Watson was the youngest Nobel Prize winner ever for his discoveries concerning the molecular structure of nucleic acid. Michael Uslan served as executive producer of the hit *Batman* films. Theodore Dreiser became one of America's most important novelists, writing *An American Tragedy* and *Sister Carrie*.

Students find a haven in the South Lounge of the Indiana Memorial Union, the nation's largest student union.

All are alumni of Indiana University. As their varied career paths illustrate, Indiana University offers the diverse capabilities of a dynamic school on the move.

Indiana University is expert at making the most of opportunities and challenges. It's been that way since the beginning. On January 20, 1820, Indiana Governor Jonathan Jennings signed a bill from the Indiana General Assembly, creating the State Seminary. On January 24, 1828, the State Seminary became Indiana College by act of the General Assembly. It became Indiana University on February 15, 1838.

Today, the 1,860-acre campus in the rolling hills of southern Indiana is considered one of the five most beautiful campuses in the nation, as cited in Thomas Gaines' book *The Campus as a Work of Art*. A stroll around the campus and the Bloomington community shows why Indiana University is repeatedly singled out for its beautiful setting. The university features a wealth of trees, flowers, lush green spaces, and distinctive limestone buildings.

One of the university's greatest attractions lies just beyond the gates of the campus—the city of Bloomington itself. A small city of 65,000, Bloomington has been chosen as one of the top 10 college towns in America for its "rich mixture of atmospherics and academia" by Edward B. Fiske, former education editor for the *New York Times*. Also, Rand McNally has selected Bloomington as one of the eight most desirable places to live in the nation based on economy, personal safety, climate, housing services, and leisure activities.

Bloomington is sometimes referred to as a paradox. While it offers many big city attributes, it does so within the atmosphere of a small town. Over the years, many people have described its overall charm. In his later years, Hoagy Carmichael spoke of Bloomington "calling out" to him and said that wherever he went in life, he always missed Bloomington. Local resident and rock star John Mellencamp paid homage with his classic hit "Small Town." Pulitzer Prize-winning author and IU Professor of Computer Science Douglas Hofstadter dedicated one of his books, *Metamagical Themas,* to the city: "For Bloomington—and all the times we've shared."

The Sample Gates provide a dramatic entrance to the campus.

Dunn Meadow, shown with the Indiana Memorial Union in the background, provides a popular gathering place for IU students.

Superlatives fit many aspects of Indiana University. The Indiana Memorial Union is the nation's largest student union. Because of its international prominence, IU offers speakers and cultural opportunities from throughout the world. In fact, Bloomington is a magnet for scholars, musicians, artists, and speakers who regularly visit and bring their special talents to supplement outstanding campus programs. Students have the cultural advantages of a large metropolitan area in the friendly, small college town of Bloomington.

Indiana University draws talent from around the world. Students come from all 50 states and more than 130 foreign countries. With about 26,200 undergraduates and 6,800 graduate students, Indiana University works hard to meet the diverse needs of its expanding population. It strives to enhance the quality of existing programs while developing innovations to meet new needs.

In a move to address the changing climate in higher education, IU President Myles Brand proposed the university's "Strategic Directions Charter: Becoming America's New Public University." Eight university-wide task forces, made up of 250 faculty, staff, students, alumni, and community leaders, acting on President Brand's idea, created the planning document, which received unanimous endorsement by the Trustees of Indiana University and charts the course for the future of IU.

"It is my firm conviction that for Indiana University to be successful in the future, we must become not more private, but more public. I am convinced that the most successful public universities of the future—Indiana University foremost—will be those that strengthen their ties to the state while simultaneously accommodating fiscal realities and renewed calls for accountability."

Brand has said that IU's Strategic Directions Charter is akin to a business plan, designed to change the way the university operates. "In reshaping the university," he says, "we are building on, not abandoning, past successes, enhancing our state

role, enhancing our partnerships with the corporate sector, enhancing our cooperative and collaborative relationships with other constituencies. We will become a national leader in responding to the challenges we face by exemplifying the best traditions of public higher education, reconfigured appropriately for the contemporary environment."

What sets the Strategic Directions Charter apart from other long-range planning documents is that Indiana University has put its money where its planning is and specifically allocated resources to achieve the goals set forth in the

Kurt Masur, New York Philharmonic music director, was recently a guest conductor of the Indiana University Philharmonic Orchestra.

charter. Some of those goals reinforce IU's core purposes, such as placing "student learning, intellectual exploration, persistence, and attainment at the center of the university's missions." Others make Indiana University even stronger and more responsive in meeting its public obligations, such as strengthening partnerships with the community, ensuring that IU reflects the diversity of American society, and guaranteeing that the university operates in the most efficient, effective, and accountable manner possible.

The university is now moving ahead to meet those goals. It has already created an Advanced Research and Technology Institute; begun the implementation of a university-wide associate of arts degree program; and launched an intense marketing campaign—all of which were specified in the charter. Brand called upon the university community to submit proposals that would advance the goals set forth in the charter. Hundreds of initiatives were submitted, and more than 100 have been

The School of Law Library, with more than 570,000 volumes, is one of the 20 largest law libraries in the country and the largest in Indiana.

The New Testament of the Gutenberg Bible is one of the many treasures of IU's Lilly Library.

funded thus far, including strategic investments in areas of excellence deemed important for preserving the university's national reputation. Before the process is complete, IU will have invested more than $20 million in seed money for projects inspired by the Strategic Directions Charter.

Indiana University offers more than 5,000 courses in more than 100 degree programs. Through the core curriculum, the university seeks to produce well-rounded students able to think and act productively on the many interwoven issues that characterize contemporary life. Because of IU's broad liberal arts foundation, a choice of major can be deferred until the end of the sophomore year. Students have the flexibility and time to choose the appropriate academic program for their personal and professional goals.

Undergirding all its activities is the university's threefold mission of teaching, research, and service. A concern for high-quality teaching and learning is foremost. The award-winning faculty strive to use the latest knowledge and technology to make the classroom experience an invigorating and lasting one. As a public institution, IU is able to offer an excellent education at a reasonable price. In addition, IU participates in every federal loan, grant, and employment program for undergraduate students (including federal direct lending), as well as its own programs. The majority of IU undergraduates receive one or more types of financial assistance, for a total of almost $70 million annually.

Indiana University is home to one of the largest research library systems in the United States; IU's library system contains 7 million bound volumes and 27 million other items. The libraries on the Bloomington campus consist of the Main Library, which houses the research collections, government publications, and the undergraduate library; 15 departmental libraries; 12 libraries in the Halls of Residence; 3 extra-system libraries; and the Lilly Library, which houses a major collection of rare books and manuscripts. More than 5.5 million books and journals and 12 million other items, including audio, video, and microform materials, are available at the campus.

Some of the university's other facilities include a variable-energy cyclotron, two observatories, around-the-clock computing facilities, modern multimedia broadcasting and journalism facilities, extensive archaeology and geology laboratories, museums, excellent art studios and printmaking facilities, a nationally respected art museum and

library, and Bradford Woods, which is a 2,300-acre outdoor education facility.

New IU students are often overwhelmed by the sheer quantity of extracurricular activities available. Involvement in these activities provides students with the opportunity to establish friendships, develop interpersonal skills, and further education outside of the classroom. IU also has one of the most respected student opera companies in the Western Hemisphere; it's the only university opera company to have performed on the stage of New York's Metropolitan Opera.

Basketball and Indiana go together. Cheering the Hoosiers on is a way of life for thousands of people. Indiana University has a multitude of sporting events and dedicated fans, whatever the season. IU is a member of the Big Ten athletics conference, and Hoosier teams have won 20 national titles, including six consecutive titles in swimming/diving; five titles in basketball; three each in cross-country and soccer; and one each in outdoor track/field, wrestling, and women's tennis. In addition, IU athletes have won 125 NCAA individual championship titles, and 113 have been Olympic athletes. The annual Little 500 bike race is a popular attraction, recounting the glories of competitive biking, as captured in the movie *Breaking Away*.

For home games, IU's student-athletes compete in some of the nation's finest facilities, including the 52,000-seat Memorial Stadium, the multipurpose 17,500-seat Assembly Hall, the Billy Hayes all-weather 10-lane track, Sembower Field for baseball, and the 9,000-seat Bill Armstrong Stadium, home to the Little 500 and the nationally ranked soccer team. Other facilities include the spectacular Counsilman Aquatic Center and Billingsley Diving Center, indoor and outdoor tennis courts, an outdoor 50-meter pool, and a golf complex with an 18-hole championship course, a par-3 course, and a 25-tee driving range.

Since the beginning, Indiana University has forged a strong bond with the community. The partnership is a two-way street—whatever is good for Bloomington benefits the university, and whatever helps the university will carry over to the city. The university has had a major impact on the city.

Community service is a hallmark of Indiana University. There is a tangible connection between town and gown. University volunteers can be found helping youngsters through Big Brothers/Big Sisters and the Boys and Girls Club; feeding the needy at the Community Kitchen; working at the animal shelter; leading meetings for the Hospital Board of Directors; participating in the Mayor's Parking Task Force; assisting with the Bloomington Redevelopment Commission; and working with

Abilities Unlimited. Whenever a community need arises, university volunteers are there to reach out a hand and help find a solution. "Indiana University is an integral part of being a resident of Bloomington. Giving back to our community is acknowledging the many gifts received from those people and institutions influencing my life," says Sue H. Talbot, a Bloomington native who holds three degrees from Indiana University and is a former Indiana State Teacher of the Year.

The impact of Indiana University on the local area is astounding. Consider that the campus has had about $215 million worth of construction in the last 25 years and brings in about $80 million annually in private contracts and grants. More than 5,400 Bloomington residents work at IU. Their contributions to community organizations are difficult to assess, but it is clear that they contribute significantly to the quality of life in the place they call home. The Good Friends tutorial program for Monroe County public schools has 265 IU volunteers. Over 40 IU employees serve as elected or appointed officials for Bloomington and Monroe County government. More than 200 campus volunteers serve on committees for the annual United Way campaign. Also over 55 agencies have IU employees on their boards of directors. IU personnel and research expertise collaborated with the city of Bloomington in developing the Showers Project and Seminary Square, and offered transitional assistance with the Thomson Consumer Products plant closing.

According to 1993 figures, IU brought about $52 million into

Monroe County for visitor shopping, food, lodging, and recreation. Reduced fee medical services for the community include three eye examination clinics and an audiology clinic. The university also operates a community legal service clinic. IU libraries are open to all state residents. IU students and employees contribute 27 percent of the annual United Way budget with over 50 percent of the Vanguard donors ($1,000 plus) from the ranks of IU. IU contributes over $300,000 to Bloomington for salaries and fire protection. The university's annual purchasing of goods and services in Monroe County exceeds $16 million. IU contributes a payment in lieu of taxes on property each year to the Monroe County Community School Corporation to subsidize K-12 students living on IU property. IU Business School students alone contributed 4,613 volunteer hours to the Bloomington community. The School of Business has over 500 students working with its volunteer program, Business Students Involved in Community Service.

Indiana University is an exciting, unique institution that reflects its history and cherishes its traditions, even as it moves forward with a proud vision of the future. ⚹

Spirits run high at Assembly Hall, home of the IU men's and women's basketball teams. The banners commemorate men's NCAA national championships in 1940, 1953, 1981, and 1987.

Sunlight floods the atrium of the nationally respected IU Art Museum.

The green spaces and limestone buildings of Indiana University leave a lasting impression on all who spend time here.

WTIU, Channel 30

Children watched spellbound when WTIU, Channel 30, began telecasting on March 3, 1969, with a children's series, *The Friendly Giant,* This service has become an integral part of the community—Indiana University's public television station.

Fulfilling its responsibility as a public television station, WTIU offers a public affairs program that addresses local issues. A Bloomington café provides the setting for a 1997 discussion among Indiana's foster care program.

WTIU transforms its studio into a coffee house for televised performances by area musicians. WTIU distributes this and other series that promote local talents, expertise, and activities to other public television stations statewide and nationally.

Since that black-and-white program, WTIU has grown to serve more than 175,000 television households in over 20 counties within a 50-mile radius of Bloomington in west and south central Indiana. The station consistently provides intelligent, informative, culturally elevating programs, including a proud tradition of local programming. Since it signed on the air, WTIU has been a leader in broadcast service to its viewers and their community.

"On any given day, WTIU programming may not be all things to all viewers. But, on the other hand, on any given day, WTIU may be the most important source of television for many," says General Manager Don Agostino.

WTIU and public television are also changing to meet people's needs in the present-day rich media environment. Besides providing the region's best entertainment vehicle for children, WTIU broadcasts programs designed to educate, nurture wonder, instill confidence, and foster individual character. As part of its Ready-to-Learn service, WTIU includes public service messages that stimulate thought and present young viewers with valuable information they can use. It also teaches child care providers and parents how to extend the educational value of public television programs into the lives of preschoolers, so they will enter formal schooling "ready to learn."

WTIU also provides more video material for classroom use than any other source, supplementing its programming with print and World Wide Web resources for students and teachers and offering interconnection with peer learners worldwide.

The area's leading source of broadcast information for adults, WTIU offers an extensive array of choices. Viewers can enjoy the best of music and performance, learn about remodeling, discover the value of attic treasures, or create tempting dishes. And for hard news and public affairs, no other station touches the WTIU lineup that augments the national *NewsHour* broadcasts with student-produced *News Forum* and valuable business information on *The Nightly Business Report.*

The community recognizes WTIU as its definitive information source. To maintain this reputation, the station provides specialized local programming. On *Editor's Desk,* area journalists interview state news makers about local implications of statewide issues and services. The Indiana University president and faculty members discuss contemporary ideas and issues on *Pro & Con.* Community specialists exchange views on local issues on *Community Café.* And during election campaigns, WTIU broadcasts candidate forums and debates.

Each year fans count on WTIU's *Big Red Football,* the station's longest-running series, and Hoosier women's basketball and volleyball games. Viewers have also been able to see major speakers when they've visited IU, including the Dali Lama, Janet Reno, Donna Shalala, Warren Christopher, The Honorable William Rehnquist, and Tipper Gore.

WTIU's goal is to offer engaging, entertaining, thought-provoking noncommercial television. And this service is paid for in large part by Indiana University and financial support from viewers and underwriters who respond during the station's on-air fund drives. WTIU also depends heavily on volunteer support from the community, and it offers employment opportunities and professional training to hundreds of IU students.

Communication makes the difference between a true community and simply a collection of people. Since 1969, WTIU has provided cohesion through effective communication. WTIU reflects its community, honors the public service efforts of others, enhances public understanding, and dedicates itself to being a television service that viewers want to invite into their homes as a trusted teacher and companion. ⚠

WFIU Radio

For many people, tuning in to WFIU may be an important way to start the day off right. It's a seven-day-a-week ritual, offering fast-paced entertainment and information as only public radio from Indiana University can provide.

Throughout the day, WFIU is a friendly companion, sharing music, news, and information. The momentum hat WFIU enjoys today has been building since its debut in 1950, spurred by the station's growing emphasis on local community programming.

Founded as a "training ground" for students, WFIU has matured from an infant station working out of a war surplus Quonset[tm] hut to a state-of-the-art studio in the Radio/TV Center on the Indiana University campus. Starting with 37.5 hours of programming per week, WFIU has grown along with the university and now provides 24 hours of listening pleasure daily, 365 days a year.

A prime force behind WFIU's creation, former university president Herman B Wells says: "We little dreamed in 1950 that four decades later we would be listening over this station to some of the finest performances from the concert halls of the world, and beyond belief, to music from our own Indiana University School of Music, grown to enviable heights. WFIU's growth in maturing from clumsy, ill-equipped beginnings to its present sophistication of performance and presentation is almost miraculous."

Along the way, the station, at 103.7 on the FM dial in Bloomington, has witnessed and facilitated countless changes in the public radio field, including being one of the 90 charter members to carry the popular National Public Radio (NPR) news program *All Things Considered.* Branching out to audiences in Columbus, Terre Haute, and Kokomo, WFIU was also an early leader in serving its listeners with information on the World Wide Web. Now WFIU introduces the scholarship and expertise of IU to the rest of the world through the distribution of locally produced programs such as *Harmonia* and the modular mini-program *A Moment of Science* that are aired by public stations nationwide.

At any given moment, more radios in south central Indiana are tuned to WFIU than any other station. But to say WFIU is the number one radio station doesn't tell the whole story. Today, the station is not just strong in ratings; it is also strong in community involvement. As a community presence, it sponsors children's art contests and ensemble performances, and provides educational outreach in partnership with local schools, among many other activities. It is an indispensable source of information during important community events, such as city and council elections.

WFIU's performance in the community—and on the airwaves—makes it clear that the station is working to put into action the words of its mission statement: "The pursuit of excellence is the primary goal of Indiana University and, therefore, the guiding principle of its component parts. In that light, it is WFIU's mission to enrich the radio audience in south central Indiana with a broadcast service that educates, informs, entertains, and enlightens, drawing upon the resources of the university and the community." WFIU is committed to extending its legacy of excellence into the twenty-first century. ⚓

The Indiana University Radio and Television Center's 1998 addition houses the studios and offices of WFIU, public radio station, and WTIU, public television station, along with the offices and classrooms of the Department of Telecommunications and IU Multi-Campus Technology facilities, including the Virtual Indiana Classroom Project. The glass facade opens onto the Arboretum near the IU Library.

WFIU continued to originate programming during the Radio/TV Center's two-year construction project. In a temporary studio, *Herald-Times* editor Bob Zaltsberg (left) joins Bloomington's John Fernandez when he answers call-in questions on WFIU's live monthly program, with Station Manager Christina Kuzmych in the control room.

As a part of its educational outreach mission, WFIU has sponsored a contest to encourage composers to write for radio and to reward them with the broadcast of the performances of their winning works.

Ivy Tech State College

In 1997, the Bloomington campus of Ivy Tech State College broke its 2,000 enrollment mark for the first time.

Primary areas of study at Ivy Tech include accounting, administrative office technology, associate in science in nursing, business administration, computer information systems, design technology, electronics, general technical studies, industrial technology, and practical nursing.

Indiana's youngest college

was born in 1963 with a big mission—to make available to all Indiana residents college-level, job-oriented training.

Today, Ivy Tech State College is the state's third largest college with major instructional centers in 22 communities around the state offering more than 50 programs of study in many diverse fields. More importantly, all the programs are geared to manpower needs in the various regions and lead directly to employment.

Figures show that 98 percent of Ivy Tech graduates get jobs in their fields of study. And the college is still growing. At its Bloomington campus, Ivy Tech enrollment has more than tripled since 1985, when 550 students crossed its threshold. In the spring of 1997, the Bloomington campus of Ivy Tech broke its 2,000 enrollment mark for the first time. About two-thirds of Ivy Tech students are part-time and one-third are full-time.

The reasons for such phenomenal success? "Affordability, accessibility, and state-of-the-art technology," says Dr. Thomas Jordan, executive dean.

Ivy Tech tuition costs are about one-third less than its community neighbor, Indiana University. Ivy Tech also is accessible for students on varying levels of the education spectrum, from GED recipients to people with doctorates.

The Ivy Tech campus at Westbury Village is located near easy highway access to serve Monroe and Lawrence Counties, plus other contiguous counties. To help its students compete in this high-tech world, Ivy Tech is constantly updating its equipment to stay ahead of technological advances.

Ivy Tech is not only dedicated to maintaining an open-door enrollment policy, but it also wants its graduates to face open doors when they have completed their programs. A dedicated administration team is lead by Executive Dean Thomas Jordan, Director of Instruction Brenda Sands, Director of Business and Industrial Training Larry Greenwalt, and Director of Student Services Diana Jacobs.

At the Bloomington campus, faculty and staff members are ready to provide the attention and support students need to accomplish their educational goals. Classes are small and instruction is personalized by highly qualified educators who are experts in their fields.

Ivy Tech State College Bloomington campus offers technical program courses, which may be taken for two-year associate's degrees, one-year technical certificates, and career development certificates. Additionally, many courses are offered on

a continuing education basis for people not wanting to pursue a course of study leading to a degree, but wanting to enhance personal or professional skills.

Primary areas of study include accounting, administrative office technology, associate in science in nursing, business administration, computer information systems, design technology, electronics, general technical studies, industrial technology, and practical nursing. Classes are offered during the day, evening, and on weekends.

Long gone is the simple idea of a "trade school," as the state-supported college has become a place to enroll, get the training, then get the job. Lately, among the college's students have been those with degrees from traditional four-year schools who need more marketable skills.

With all this demand on resources from such a variety of students, school officials continually look for ways to meet the needs of this population. In some locations, Ivy Tech campuses are providing dual credit in local high schools to ensure that graduates can offer important skills in the workplace directly after graduation.

And it's not just "book learning" that employers are requiring. Conflict resolution, interpersonal skills, and organizational abilities also are in demand in the office or on the shop floor. Many of these "contract" classes seep into the regular curriculum, too, so that degree students or continuing studies students can benefit, as well.

Increasingly, area employers are turning to Ivy Tech to train workers for the future. Ivy Tech offers customized industrial training for business. The training programs are as varied as the businesses who request them. Some employers may send only one or two people to existing classes, while others request entire programs to teach from 30 to 100 students.

One of the more popular courses is medical office administration, which grew out of contracts with Bloomington Hospital. What was happening in the medical community meant that more people were needed who were trained in medical insurance, terminology, law, and ethics. The training is a nice reflection of Ivy Tech responding to what is needed in the community.

But all this fine-tuning of offerings is continually evaluated to be sure it's in line with accreditation guidelines. More and more, students are taking their Ivy Tech certificates and degrees and, eventually, attending other schools. School officials and students alike want to ensure that the Ivy Tech credits apply toward a four-year or advanced degree.

The Ivy Tech Bloomington campus features many services to assist students while in college. Financial aid from federal, state, and private sources is available to those who qualify. Career counseling and placement services are available to students, as well as academic and personal counseling. Peer tutoring and instructor-led tutoring is offered to students while they take classes.

Many Ivy Tech credits will transfer to local colleges, including Anderson University, Ball State University, Bethel College, Indiana State University, Indiana University, Manchester College, Purdue University, Rose-Hulman Institute of Technology, Saint Mary of the Woods College, University of Southern Indiana, and Vincennes University.

Although it is not a residential campus, Ivy Tech has worked out an arrangement so its students can live in Indiana University housing.

Ivy Tech recognizes the educational, recreational, and social values of student organizations and extracurricular activities. Students can participate in the Student Senate, special interest clubs, and as a student ambassador representing Ivy Tech at campus and local events. Ivy Tech also offers Phi Theta Kappa, a national honor fraternity providing members opportunities to develop leadership and promote scholarship, service, and fellowship. Membership to Phi Theta Kappa is based on academic standing.

Entertaining social activities are sponsored throughout the year for students and their families. A Halloween party, haunted house, Easter egg hunt, dances, movie outings, and other get-togethers help provide the friendly atmosphere enjoyed at Ivy Tech.

The college's contributions to the community are equally impressive. Students and instructors volunteer at Shelter Inc., the March of Dimes Walk-A-Thon, the holiday Shop With a Firefighter for needy children, the Red Cross Blood Drive, and Partners in Literacy, along with many other projects.

Part of an exciting future for Ivy Tech includes the construction of a new Bloomington campus. Located in Park 48, just west of Bloomington on Highway 48, the new facility will continue to feature the latest in learning technology and offer area citizens the very best in learning environments—all the reasons why Ivy Tech State College has become such a positive force in the community, in local business, and in the lives of its students. ⚘

More and more, students are taking their Ivy Tech certificates and degrees and, eventually, attending other schools.

Area employers turn to Ivy Tech to train workers for the future. The school offers customized industrial training for business.

T.I.S. Incorporated

Since its humble beginning, T.I.S. has always reached for success—not only as a financially secure business with an excellent reputation, but also as a valued community citizen with a heart. Photo by Kendall Reeves.

In 1962, Jack D. Tichenor saw a need and visualized a way to fill it. College students used many textbooks during their course of study. Why not create a local company to sell used textbooks to college bookstores around the country? Before the year ended, Raymond Tichenor joined the company, and the brothers began their business trek down the sometimes rocky road of financial pressures, growing pains, and difficult decisions.

Almost four decades later, the road has smoothed out, decisions have come more easily, and the brothers' vision has grown into a 325-employee wholesaling, manufacturing, and retailing corporation serving all aspects of the college bookstore industry.

Tichenor College Textbook Company offers an on-line computerized inventory of over 35,000 used college textbook titles. An industry-wide reputation for individualized one-to-one service has helped the wholesaler grow to supply nearly 1,000 independent and institutional college stores in all 50 states and Canada with clean, quality books.

Tichenor Publishing specializes in high-quality instructional materials for the educational marketplace as well as full-service printing and binding for area businesses and the community at large. Attention to detail and unparalleled customer service has helped gain the micropublisher stature as a regional leader in custom publishing.

Taylor Imprinted Sportswear supplies licensed sportswear to retailers throughout the Midwest and commercial sportswear to local markets, including the Indiana University Student Foundation for the annual Little 500 bicycle race.

T.I.S. College Bookstores are conveniently located on the campuses of Indiana University in Bloomington, Ball State University in Muncie, and the University of Illinois in Champaign. The bookstore in Bloomington is a mainstay for students and alumni. The eastern wall of the building features a trick-of-the-eye mural that appears to be a colossal bookshelf with huge oversized books, a ball cap, a computer, pencils, and more.

As a business deeply rooted in education, T.I.S. is a firm believer in helping others succeed by providing opportunities to learn. A substantial amount of profits are returned to the university communities where T.I.S. College Bookstores are located through several scholarships and donations. One of these includes the Jack D. Tichenor Scholarship Award, which was established after his death in recognition of his love of sports and deep respect for the athlete. The award is presented annually at Indiana University to the male and female athletes with the highest scholastic average.

A "Spirit of Service" Committee helps T.I.S. focus on ways to give back to the community, from monetary support to providing printing services to supplying volunteers for projects. T.I.S. employees are allowed to use work time to volunteer with local organizations and activities, such as the Friends Learn With Mentoring program and Habitat for Humanity.

Since its humble beginning, T.I.S. has always reached for success—not only as a financially secure business with an excellent reputation, but also as a valued community citizen with a heart. This vision continues well into the future as a second generation of the Tichenor family grows into the business alongside an extremely capable and dedicated employee team. ⚑

The T.I.S. College Bookstore in Bloomington is a mainstay for students and alumni. The eastern wall of the building features a trick-of-the-eye mural that appears to be a colossal bookshelf with huge oversized books, a ball cap, a computer, pencils, and more. Photo by Kendall Reeves.

It's high noon at the Monroe County YMCA Family Fitness Center. The air is filled with the whir of exercise bikes, thump of basketballs on hardwood floors, splash of swimmers slicing through the water, musical beat of rhythmic feet in aerobics, giggles of toddlers turning cartwheels on tumbling mats, and hellos of friends greeting each other.

One of the brightest jewels in the crown of Monroe County, the YMCA is a natural gathering spot for people from all walks of life, all ages, economic status, race, creed, sex, and ability.

From its founding more than 100 years ago at Indiana University, the local facility was built in 1981 and, after two expansions, has grown to be the largest in the state—now an 85,000-square-foot structure situated on 20 beautiful acres. The Monroe County YMCA has over 400 volunteers and close to 12,500 members, a staggering number for such a size community.

And members make good use of the YMCA. They flock to its two gyms, two pools, two whirlpools, three racquetball/wallyball courts, indoor track, outdoor fitness trail, aerobic room, mat room, dance studio, youth room, three-room child care complex, three weight rooms, outdoor day camp and nature trails, two conference rooms, two full-size basketball courts, two youth program rooms, and loft meeting area.

But it takes more than state-of-the-art facilities to make a successful YMCA. It takes caring and well-trained staff who are genuinely concerned with offering programs that build a healthy spirit, mind, and body for all.

The YMCA offers many annual special events for the Bloomington community: a Spring Run and Fall Run featuring 5K and 10K races and a fitness walk; Cardiac Rehab Golf Tournament; Brass Theater, a youth scholarship fund-raiser; Corporate Challenge; Healthy Kids Day; and a New Year's Eve Party featuring fun for all ages as they welcome in the new year in a safe, nonalcoholic environment.

Summer camps are an important part of any childhood, and the Monroe County YMCA offers an exciting array of options for local youth. Camp Arrowhood Day Camp, Camp Stem Residence Camp, many sports camps, Surf & Turf Aquatic Camp, as well as a Counselor-In-Training program provide great opportunities for children from ages 2 to 16 to make lasting memories and lifetime friendships.

The Monroe County YMCA has always been committed to the health and wellness of the community through its emphasis of prevention programs. An unusual collaboration between Bloomington Hospital and the YMCA offers new hope and health to people with coronary artery disease. The Cardiac Rehabilitation Program often takes patients from death's door to a new life of health and vigor.

Like its members, the Monroe County YMCA has dedicated itself to self-sufficiency. It is sustained by voluntary donations and membership fees. No person is turned away due to lack of funds; scholarships are given and cherished by those who need them.

Over the years, the YMCA's stated goal has remained unchanged: "To put Christian principles into practice through programs that build a healthy spirit, mind and body for all."

To that end, the Monroe County YMCA emphasizes the core values of caring, honesty, respect, and responsibility in all its programming and in daily life at the YMCA. The Monroe County YMCA helps Bloomington build strong kids, strong families, and a strong community. ⚐

The Monroe County YMCA Family Fitness Center is located in the southeast quadrant of the city.

One of two pools, this lap pool is always open for lap swimming.

Star of Indiana

Theater lights dim, the curtains open, and the stage becomes a kaleidoscope of sights and sounds. The passion, power, and precision of the world's best young professional brass musicians, percussionists, dancers, and vocalists fill the auditorium.

In dazzling costumes, Dorothy and the characters of Oz dance down the yellow brick road to find the amazing Wizard in the Emerald City. With a quick change of scenery, it's the streets of New York, where two warring gangs duel in *West Side Story.*

Welcome to Brass Theater™ featuring the Star of Indiana. Surprisingly, the talented entertainers presenting this grand showcase are young professionals between the ages of 17 and 22.

Founded in 1984 by Bloomington businessman Bill Cook, Star began its life as a drum and bugle corps competitor. Cook was so moved by the positive experience his son had during a summer with an Iowa drum corps that he became an instant drum and bugle corps devotee.

The primary objectives of the newly founded Star were to provide a challenging drum corps experience to young members, to entertain, and to be competitive. Star of Indiana certainly succeeded. In its first year of competition in Drum Corps International, Star placed 10th at the World Championships—the first corps ever to finish that high in its debut season. Star rose steadily in the ranks, eventually winning the DCI World Championship in 1991. Then Star changed directions. The group accepted an invitation to perform with the famed Canadian Brass quintet starting in the summer of 1994. They called it "Brass Theater."

"Brass Theater has elements of marching band, symphonic music, jazz, and even a bit of Broadway," explains Star executive director and president Jim Mason. "It's time that the orchestra comes out of the pit and onto the stage—the music is the centerpiece. Dance and movement interpretations are supported by lighting and a set design which also uses multimedia projection and effects to enhance the impact of the experience."

Since its inception, Star's Brass Theater has received nothing short of ecstatic praise. "Every place we go, the only word to describe the audience is 'stunned,'" Mason says.

Brass Theater set out on a 10-city tour that included a stop at a sold-out Lincoln Center. The July 1, 1994, issue of *Drum Corps World* described it as "a total mind-blower, a wonderful diversion, and as [and more] innovative as anything we've ever seen on the field. Plus—and this is a big one—it is entertaining beyond belief."

In 1997, the Star of Indiana took on another challenge. For almost a month, the Star performed in concert at The Grand Palace Theater in Branson, Missouri. The show was a musical and theatrical montage in which the musicians also exhibited acting abilities. At the end of the season, the Star of Indiana annually provides a major extravaganza fund-raiser show for the Monroe County YMCA.

The Star of Indiana shares its love of music with Monroe County fifth- and sixth-grade students. Beginner and advanced programs allow students to participate in individual, ensemble, and full band experience. The Star provides lessons, as well as instruments, for those who cannot afford them.

The Star of Indiana encourages members to develop relationships that are musical and nonmusical—relationships that last a lifetime, along with memories of audiences who enjoyed this unforgettable, spine-tingling spectacle of total family entertainment. ⚜

In its first year of competition in Drum Corps International, the Star of Indiana placed 10th at the World Championships—the first corps ever to finish that high in its debut season.

In dazzling costumes, Dorothy and the characters of Oz dance down the yellow brick road—this is Brass Theater™, featuring the Star of Indiana.

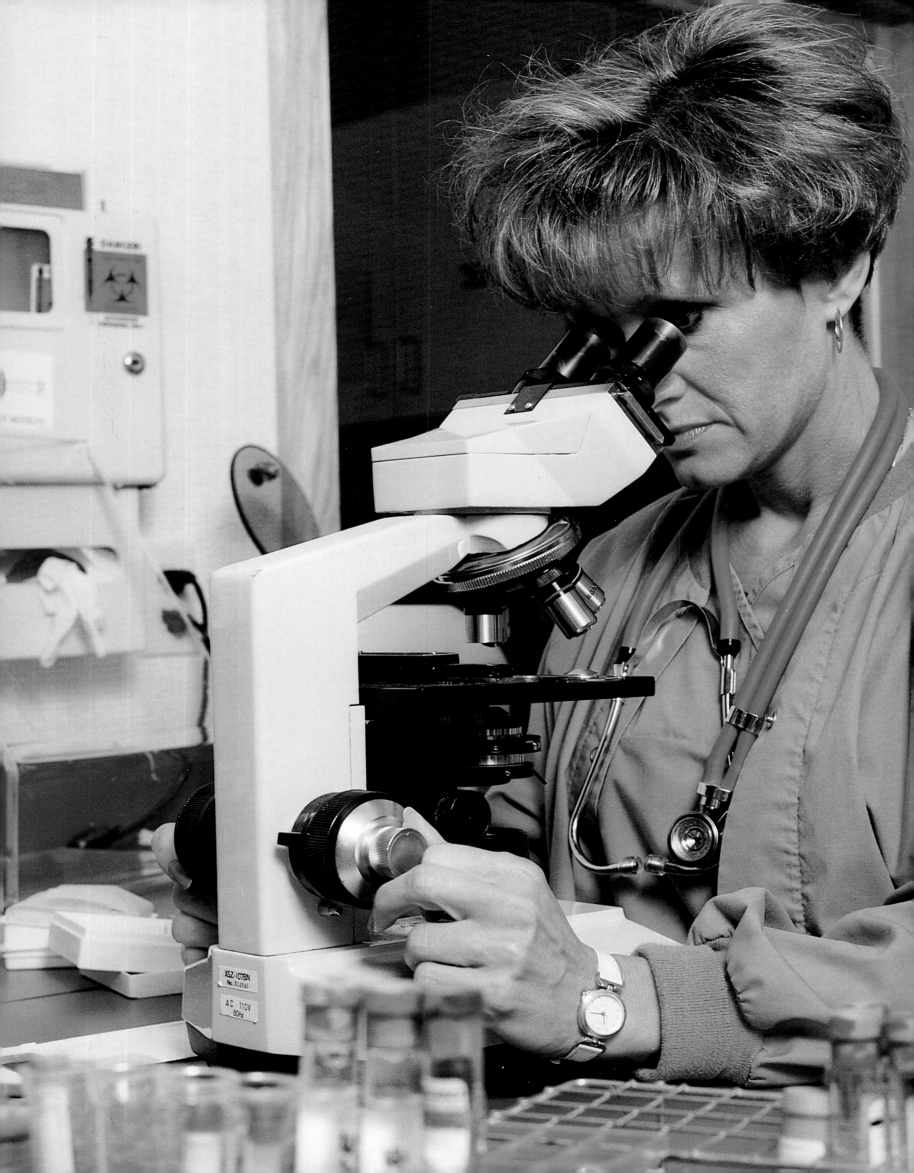

Chapter

16

Health Care

Bloomington Hospital
& Healthcare System, 238-241

Cook Family Health
Center Inc., 242

Bloomington Hospital & Healthcare System

For more than 90 years Bloomington Hospital has served the health care needs of a growing community. From its modest beginnings in a two-story brick house at Second and Rogers Streets (the result of a year-long civic campaign by the city's Local Council of Women), Bloomington Hospital has evolved into a multifacility campus, providing sophisticated inpatient and outpatient care, not only to residents of Bloomington and Monroe County, but also as a regional referral center to residents in eight surrounding counties in south central Indiana.

physicians represents over 30 different medical specialties, and its patient care staff is made up of highly trained nursing specialists, therapists, and technicians.

At Bloomington Hospital, residents of southern Indiana get expert care close to home without the inconvenience of long commutes and the stress of navigating big cities and big city hospitals. For a closer look at some of the sophisticated and highly personalized services patients find at Bloomington Hospital, five specialty areas are highlighted: its comprehensive heart and cancer centers, state-of-the-art orthopedic (bone and joint) services, and family-oriented maternity and psychiatric programs.

Maternal and Child Services

Childbirth is a family affair at Bloomington Hospital. The comfort and convenience of mothers and their families were key considerations in the design of private maternity suites. Labor, delivery and recovery all occur in one place, and if they wish, expectant parents may choose to include other family members in the experience.

Tender loving care, skilled nursing services, and modern technology make even a difficult birth less stressful. Delivery by cesarean section is conveniently accomplished in obstetrical surgery suites located in the Labor and Delivery Area. The hospital's commitment to continuity of care ensures that the same nurses will care for a patient during labor, delivery, and postoperative recovery.

Bloomington Hospital's obstetric nurses, many of whom have worked in the Labor and Delivery Area for years, take great pride in giving the highest quality of care and individual attention to new mothers and babies, no matter how brief their hospital stay. The privilege of participating in the arrival of a new life is never taken for granted by the dedicated staff of the hospital's Maternal and Child Services.

Mom and Dad proudly show off their son, just minutes after giving birth in Bloomington Hospital's beautiful Labor & Delivery room. Over 1,800 babies are delivered at Bloomington Hospital every year.

Bloomington Hospital–Big City Services, Hometown Atmosphere

As the regional referral center for south central Indiana, Bloomington Hospital provides a full range of services, from general maternity and emergency services to very specialized procedures including neurosurgery, open-heart surgery, and complex joint replacement surgery. The hospital offers all the high-tech diagnostic, treatment, and rehabilitation services found in large metropolitan centers with one distinct advantage: a level of personalized care that can only be found in a hospital where the staff knows it is often taking care of neighbors. Its medical staff of more than 250

Comprehensive Heart Services

Bloomington Hospital is the only hospital between Indianapolis and the southern corners of the state to offer a comprehensive range of heart services, including open-heart surgery, cardiac catheterization, balloon angioplasty, and stent placement. With heart disease the leading cause of death and disability in the country and this community, immediate access to the most current treatment, rehabilitation, and prevention options is an asset and proven lifesaver for southern Indiana residents.

Not everyone who experiences a heart attack or who has cardiovascular disease needs open-heart

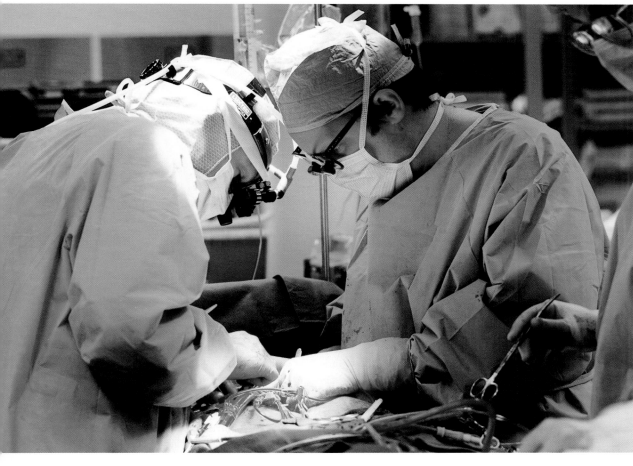

Each year, Bloomington Hospital performs over 200 open-heart surgeries and valve replacements in the newly built Cardiovascular Services wing. Stents, balloon angioplasties and catheterizations are performed daily in the two state-of-the-art cardiac cath labs.

surgery. In the hospital's Cardiac Catheterization Labs, cardiologists take a picture of the heart to determine what treatment is needed. Many people can benefit from balloon angioplasty, a nonsurgical procedure which opens up clogged arteries, and is also performed in the lab.

Bloomington Hospital's unique 14-bed Cardiovascular Recovery Area allows cardiac patients to spend their time from admittance to discharge in the same unit, with the same nursing staff. This recovery area, unique among hospitals, is very popular with patients and their families.

Psychiatric Services

Bloomington Hospital has the largest and most complete inpatient psychiatric program in south central Indiana, including the only short-term adolescent psychiatric unit in the area. Treatments for stress, anxiety, depression, addictions, eating disorders, and other emotional disorders are designed to meet the specific needs of each patient.

Full-time staff psychiatrists direct the treatment provided by teams of caring professionals, including nurses, occupational therapists, recreational therapists, and counselors. All have a common goal of working with families and patients to return them to productive lives.

The range of services includes inpatient stress and crisis care, adolescent services, chemical dependency, and complex medical-psychiatric care, as well as outpatient counseling and acute partial hospitalization for those clients not requiring inpatient services.

Orthopedic, Neurosurgery, and Rehabilitation Services

Complex surgical procedures including total joint replacements of hips and knees, as well as neurosurgery for diseases affecting the brain and spinal cord, are considered routine for the skilled surgeons on Bloomington Hospital's medical staff. Patients recovering from surgery or other orthopedic or neurological problems, including stroke, receive expert and compassionate care during the acute, transitional, and rehabilitative phases of treatment.

Orthopedists, neurologists, and neurosurgeons confidently rely on an experienced team of rehabilitation professionals to get patients back on the road to normal activities as quickly as possible.

Outpatient therapy for speech, mobility, or adaptive daily living skills is also available in several locations. These comprehensive rehabilitative facilities include two REBOUND Sports

Owen
- Advanced Home Health Care
- Diabetes Education Outreach Program
- Dialysis Center
- Hometown Healthcare Family Practice
- Medical Specialist Program
- Pacemaker Clinic
- Residence at McCormicks Creek*

Brown
- Advanced Home Health Care
- Diabetes Education Outreach Program
- Medical Specialist Program
- Nashville Hometown Healthcare Family Practice

Monroe

Greene
- Advanced Home Health Care
- Diabetes Education Outreach Program
- Hospice of Greene County
- LaneTree Medical Center

Lawrence
- Advanced Home Health Care
- Bedford Radiation Oncology and Imaging*
- Mitchell Family Practice and Outpatient Diagnostic Center (joint venture with Orange County Hospital)

Daviess
- Advanced Home Health Care
- Odon Hometown Healthcare Family Practice

* Planned services

Today, Bloomington Hospital & Healthcare System's physical presence far exceeds city limits. Committed to bringing a broader range of quality services to the residents of south central Indiana, above are new services started in 1997 and planned services for 1998.

Medicine Centers for athletic and work-related injuries and a Children's Therapy Clinic. The children's clinic is the only multidisciplinary program in southern Indiana for children with developmental disorders.

Leading Edge Cancer Services

Fighting cancer should not include fighting traffic to get treatment. The most technologically advanced and personalized care is expertly delivered close to home at Bloomington Hospital. The cancer program encompasses a full range of the latest treatment methods, including radiation therapy, biotherapy, chemotherapy, and surgical procedures.

Specially trained physicians, nurses, pharmacists, dietitians, and counselors work together to meet the physical and psychological needs of patients. The compassion of the staff is nowhere more apparent than through their treatment of cancer patients and families as they provide therapy, supportive education, and discharge planning services.

As a community hospital, Bloomington Hospital believes it has a responsibility to build awareness among residents that will assist in the prevention and early detection of cancer. Each year the hospital provides free cancer screenings and education programs to help achieve that goal.

Regional Expansion Increasing Rural Access to Care

"Taking care of you—close to home" is a commitment Bloomington Hospital takes very seriously. No longer just a large limestone building at the corner of Second and Rogers Streets, Bloomington Hospital now has a physical presence in six other counties of the service area. For example, it has placed nurse practitioners at strategic sites in south central Indiana where they can bring convenient

health care to rural communities. Both Linton and Odon, located in medically underserved areas, now have stand-alone clinics where nurse practitioners can diagnose, treat, and prescribe medications for many primary care health problems typically handled by physicians. In Spencer and Nashville, nurse practitioners work in the offices of local physicians to help them expand the services they can bring to their patients.

A prime example of taking care to the people is Owen County Hometown Health Care in Spencer. This medical complex not only houses Bloomington Hospital primary care physicians and visiting specialists, but also offers hospital services including dialysis, radiology, physical/occupational/speech therapies, cardiac rehabilitation, and pacemaker checks.

A unique addition to Owen County's health services is a new extended care facility built by Bloomington Hospital called The Residence at McCormick's Creek. The Residence offers 36 assisted living units for those residents requiring a little help with their normal activities of daily life, in addition to 30 beds for those requiring skilled nursing care.

Having recognized a need for a hospice for the care of terminally ill patients, Greene County residents asked Hospice of Bloomington, a department of Bloomington Hospital, to open a satellite office in their community. All hospice care is directed by the patient's primary care physician. The Hospice of Greene County team also includes two registered nurses, a social worker, chaplain, and 20 volunteers.

Partnering with Other Providers

A joint venture between Bloomington Hospital and Orange County Hospital has made medical services conveniently available to residents in southern Lawrence and northern Orange Counties. The Mitchell Family Health Center provides the services of a family practice physician as well as several diagnostic and therapeutic services usually provided in a hospital setting. Among the available hospital services will be physical and occupational therapies, cardiac rehabilitation, cardiac diagnosis through stress and echocardiology testing, obstetric ultrasound, and radiology.

Emphasizing Health Education

Bloomington Hospital is expanding its efforts to provide health education to the community, expecting not only to improve the quality of life of residents but to lower health care costs as well. It is much less expensive to prevent illness and injuries than to treat them.

Promoting Healthy Lifestyle Choices

The old saying "an ounce of prevention is worth a pound of cure" is often true, and Bloomington Hospital has taken it to heart. Helping people prevent disease is just as important to the hospital's health care professionals as taking care of patients when they are sick or injured.

To help prevent illness, Bloomington Hospital is collaborating with local organizations to target many segments of the community. A few specific goals include reaching children and adolescents at risk for forming bad health habits, vulnerable children and adults who don't have easy access to health care, and seniors who may be developing more health problems and who need social support as well as health care. Activities include health fairs and screenings, special programs featuring health care experts as speakers, and counseling or support groups.

Targeting Major Health Concerns

Because heart disease is the number one killer in this community, Bloomington Hospital has created a chest pain educational video designed to help people recognize the symptoms of a heart attack. The first few minutes of a heart attack are a critical time, and knowing when to call 911 can be a lifesaver. The educational video is available, free of charge, to groups and individuals.

Eating disorders are prevalent in many communities, and our area is no exception. To encourage early detection and successful treatment of eating disorders such as anorexia and bulimia, Bloomington Hospital has participated in the creation of another educational video called "Eating Disorders: a Reality Check." The video features interviews with the psychologists who direct the Bloomington Hospital Eating Disorders Program.

Investing in Families

To meet the needs of a broader group of new parents for childbirth education, Bloomington Hospital has expanded its traditional Baby Basics class to include a special class for adoptive parents. This class provides information not just on the newborn but on the child up to 12 months, with an emphasis on growth, development, and safety.

Another new class for couples planning a family is the Maybe Baby class, a series of three sessions, beginning with a preconception class for couples interested in starting a family.

A Teaching Hospital

While educating patients and raising community awareness of health issues is a top priority for Bloomington Hospital, it is also proud to be a teaching hospital. As such, it provides clinical experience for first- and second-year Indiana University medical students, as well as for Indiana University and Ivy Tech nursing, radiology, and surgery tech students. The hospital also operates a training center for paramedics and other emergency medical technicians.

Looking Toward the Future

As the community's health care needs continue to change, Bloomington Hospital will continue to strive to meet them—whether that means further expansion of primary care access in rural areas, schools, or churches; creating more community health education opportunities; or enhancing existing and developing new inpatient and outpatient services. Bloomington Hospital will be "taking care of you—close to home." ⚐

Opened in spring 1998, The Residence at McCormick's Creek is Bloomington Hospital & Healthcare System's fourth extended care facility. The Residence at McCormick's Creek is home to 96 individuals, including half in assisted living units, in nearby Owen County.

Children smile for their new bicycle helmets at the Crestmont Safety Fair, part of the Community Health Education initiative of Bloomington Hospital & Healthcare System.

Cook Family Health Center Inc.

While other companies have been bemoaning the rising cost and declining quality of health care, the Cook Group has done something about it. In July of 1993, Cook Group took a major step forward by becoming the first company in Indiana to offer its own health care clinic. The Cook Family Health Center has quickly become one of the most important benefits offered to the almost 4,500 area Cook Group employees and their dependents.

Under the medical direction of Dr. William D. Cutshall, and staffed by area physicians, the center provides a wide array of medical services, including routine physicals, treatment of illnesses, minor surgeries, and maintenance checks for certain chronic conditions. The in-house pharmacy offers medication at dramatically reduced prices. But best of all, the center provides a continuum of medical care much like the traditional "family doctor" once offered. Cook Group employees and their families know they will be seen by a center physician who is familiar with their medical records and has their best interests at heart.

"The clinic has been a monumental move in providing comprehensive quality health care," says nurse manager Francie Hurst. "It has reduced the cost to the patient and improved the medical care."

No longer must Cook Group employees head to the emergency room as a primary care provider. The Cook employer-owned clinic makes it easier to see a doctor when necessary—and to pay only a nominal fee per visit, with no deductibles or co-payments. Employees continue to have health insurance but, with such financial incentives, convenient hours, and quality care, Cook Group employees have found the center to be an outstanding service.

A major emphasis at Cook Family Health Center is a dedication to education and preventive medicine. Free immunizations are provided for children, and annual flu shots are offered at a minimal $5. A nutritionist is available to help patients learn how to deal with medical conditions like diabetes and hypertension. The center has developed information sheets on exercises and techniques to prevent such problems as carpal tunnel syndrome from repetitive motions.

"We are patient advocates," says business manager Becky Easton. "We try to make the clinic as accessible as possible and we take care of the whole family at one convenient location."

The clinic is easily accessible off North Rogers Street, a main Bloomington thoroughfare, and offers ample, ground-level parking for easy entry. From the time a patient enters the center, the receptionist, nurses, physicians, and other medical personnel strive to make the visit as stress-free and timely as possible. The colorful and relaxing waiting room features a homey atmosphere, instead of the cold, sterile surroundings of many health facilities. At Cook Family Health Center, patients come first, and serving the needs of Cook Group people is a top priority.

Patients are treated with respect. They are listened to and become partners with doctors in maintaining their own health. Patients are seen promptly; no appointment is necessary. The staff is polite and professional and devoted to making follow-up calls to be certain that advice is being heeded and patients are making a good recovery.

The primary care offered by Cook Family Health Center is the wave of the future with the friendliness and warmth of the past. It is caring, comprehensive, high-quality, and cost-efficient. Since its opening, the Cook Family Health Center has been on the cutting edge of the evolution in modern health care with its reliance on courteous patient service and its devotion to healthy lifestyles and preventive care. At Cook Family Health Center, patients know they will find the latest in technological advances and can count on something else that adds immensely to their sense of well-being and trust—the compassion and concern that comes from being a valued part of a family. ⚕

Cook Group took a major step forward by becoming the first company in Indiana to offer its own health care clinic. The Cook Family Health Center has quickly become one of the most important benefits offered to the almost 4,500 area Cook Group employees and their dependents.

At Cook Family Health Center, patients come first, and serving the needs of Cook Group people is a top priority.

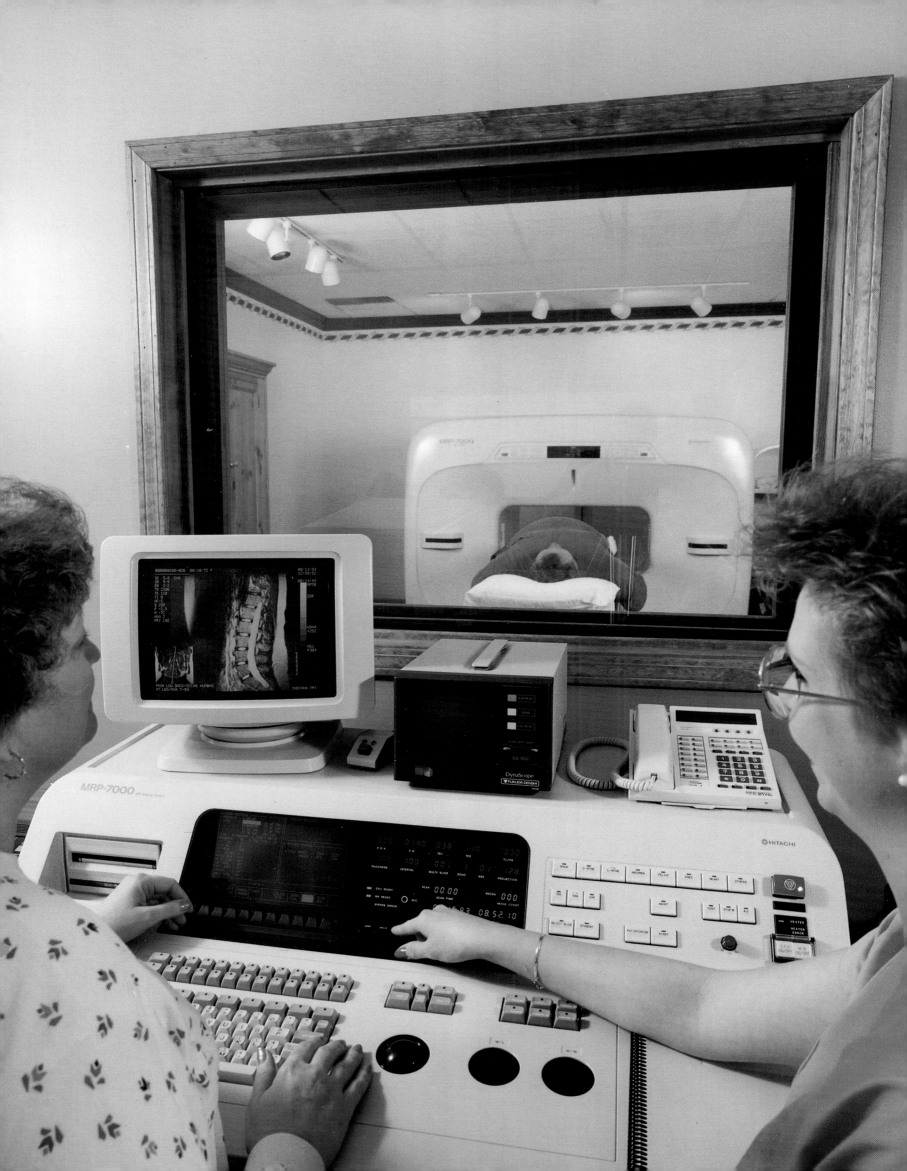

Chapter

17

The Marketplace

Curry Buick Cadillac Pontiac GMC Truck, Inc.

The four-generation story of the Curry family begins at the dawn of the auto age in America. When W. S. Curry sold his first car in 1915, he launched a family operation based on the simple, time-honored principle that satisfied customers will return. He was right.

Today, Curry Buick Cadillac Pontiac GMC Truck, Inc. still carries that same enthusiasm and dedication to customer service. As proof of that, the Curry dealership has been honored with the highest award that Buick bestows. For 13 consecutive years, Curry has received the prestigious Best in Class award, based on customer satisfaction—one of only 10 of the country's 3,000 Buick dealerships to achieve this record.

Few family businesses have ever gotten to the point of celebrating almost a century of continuous operation in the Bloomington community. It takes a strong family foundation built on solid business principles, a good product, perseverance, and the abiding philosophy that the customer comes first.

Travel back to the early 1900s when William S. Curry was a farmer and dairyman by trade. In 1912 he went to California with his wife and four children, settling in the town of Santa Anna. After starting a taxi business and operating it for a year or so, he decided to move back to his Hoosier roots.

In 1914, the cross-country return trip was made in his 1912 Buick Model C-73B, a touring car, pulling a large trailer. The trip took about 45 days. The car was decorated with advertising for the town of Santa Anna, and along the way back to Indiana the advertising created quite a stir—and publicity for Buick.

After seeing a story about the Currys' trip in the *Kansas City Star,* an official from Buick Motor Co. came to Bloomington to interest W. S. Curry in a dealership. So in June of 1915, the dealership was opened in combination with a horse and carriage stable.

Usually W. S. Curry had only one car at a time to sell. When it was purchased, he would travel to Indianapolis, board a train to Michigan to buy another model, and drive it back to Bloomington.

Eventually, Curry Buick moved to Seventh Street, in what is now an office building, still called the Curry Building. At that location, the dealership really began to grow as Americans began their love affair with automobiles.

The second generation saw Glenn Barnhill Curry manage the dealership—from 1924 to 1928, while his father W. S. Curry was the county sheriff. While other businesses were closing their doors during the Great Depression, the Curry dealership survived.

Pontiac was added to the Curry line in 1930, GMC Truck in 1932, and Cadillac in 1935. Then came World War II, when auto manufacturing came to a standstill, and dealerships everywhere had to find some kind of activity to fill the void. Some shut down altogether.

W. S. and Glenn survived on service, washing cars, and storing cars for the Graham Hotel. After the war, business boomed with customers on a "wait list" to purchase a vehicle.

Over the years, certain Curry traditions remained. For instance, in the father-to-son ownership, sons have had to work from their teen years at the dealership, starting out with the mundane task of washing cars. They were expected to prove themselves, including attending college. A dealership career could last long beyond retirement age, too. W. S. died in 1963, still a dealer at 83 years old.

The business torch was then passed through Glenn Curry to his son Richard Curry, who has now passed it on to his son Cary K. Curry. In an inconspicuous corner behind Cary Curry's work desk is a small auto track and some kiddie cars played with by the next generation, Cary Curry's small son Joseph.

In the late 1960s, Richard Curry began thinking about moving the dealership. He decided the farmland around the new College Mall might be a good place to locate a brand-new, modern facility.

Richard S. Curry is president of Curry Buick Cadillac Pontiac GMC Truck, Inc.

(Left to right) General Manager Craig Richards and Cary Curry are shown in front of the IU Auditorium. Curry has served as a trailblazer by working as a partner with the Indiana University Auditorium to underwrite an entire theater season.

Taken in 1954, this picture shows the first three generations of the Curry family: (left to right) Richard S. Curry, Glenn B. Curry, and W. S. Curry.

Automotive officials scoffed, warning that people wouldn't drive out to the country to buy a car and that shopping malls might be a flash in the pan. They were wrong. Richard Curry was right.

Today, the location at Auto Mall Road and Buick-Cadillac Boulevard is surrounded by strip malls and an expanded College Mall, one of the busiest shopping areas in the several county area. Curry has expanded and added on twice to the existing facility to accommodate growing business and customer needs. The company employs more than 60 people, 35 percent of whom have been with Curry for a decade or more.

The company has come a long way since its picturesque beginnings, but it still enjoys the kind of reputation for quality that it takes a century to earn.

The Curry business strategy has been one of gradual sustained growth emphasizing "one location—one commitment" to its customers. Curry believes that, in a business where an owner can take on many different dealerships spread over a vast area, it is important for customers to protect themselves by knowing from whom they are buying.

But Curry is more than an automotive dealership. It is an integral part of the community emphasizing a broad-based "good neighbor" policy. Working to be a positive presence, Curry supports a range of local charitable organizations and efforts, including the United Way, Girls and Boys Inc., the Indiana University Foundation, the Bloomington Hospital Foundation, and the area school systems.

Curry believes in leading by example. That means many things, including serving as a trailblazer by working as a partner with the Indiana University Auditorium to underwrite an entire theater season. Through its financial support, Curry has enabled the community to enjoy such quality performances as *A Chorus Line, Joseph and the Amazing Technicolor Dream Coat,* and an appearance by Bill Cosby.

"We are very excited to have Curry as one of our primary sponsors," says Winston Shindell, executive director of the Indiana University Memorial Union/IU Auditorium. "Cary Curry has just been incredible. His energy, his enthusiasm have led us to other partnerships. As a result, we have been able to upgrade our entire program."

In the fall of 1997, Curry was also the first local business to make a major financial contribution towards the renovation of the downtown Indiana Theater.

Whether considering product quality, professional sales staff, service backed by years of experience and training, or community involvement, Curry Buick Cadillac Pontiac GMC Truck, Inc. leads the field. ⚠

Shown here is the current location of Curry Buick Cadillac Pontiac GMC Truck, Inc. Photographed in 1971, who would have ever guessed what development would take place in the next 27 years?

Scholars Inn

Step into the stately brick mansion and turn back the clock to another time, an era when innkeepers offered gracious hospitality and country-fresh gourmet breakfasts.

For over a century, the Scholars Inn has watched the world go by from its convenient location close to downtown Bloomington and Indiana University.

But it took a young couple to breathe new life into the circa 1892 home. As Indiana University graduates, Lyle and Kerry Feigenbaum fell in love with the timeless grace of Bloomington. But they moved to Lyle's home in New York after graduation. The idea was to work in the Big Apple for several years and then come back to Bloomington to raise a family.

However, their old college town kept tugging at their heartstrings. The Feigenbaums decided not to wait. Shortly after marrying on November 2, 1996, Kerry and Lyle began looking around for a way to return to Bloomington. Then they heard the historic Scholars Inn was for sale.

Making a quick trip on December 10, the newlyweds saw the Scholars Inn and immediately felt at home. It would be Bloomington's premier bed-and-breakfast and their own marvelous residence, they vowed.

After making an offer, the Feigenbaums closed a deal on December 27, and the landmark inn with its antique furnishings was theirs. Loading a U-Haul with their belongings, Kerry and Lyle drove from New York, arriving back in Bloomington on New Year's Eve of 1996. Their first guests were set to arrive January 2, and after an exciting whirlwind of activity, the new owners were ready.

So impressed were those initial visitors that they scheduled another stay for that March. The Scholars Inn was launched on its new life, and the Feigenbaums—along with their golden canine mascot Brandy—have been happily welcoming people into their home ever since. "We both like to entertain. We like having people here," Kerry says.

Guests have five interesting rooms to choose from, each individually decorated and named after a famed Indiana scholar. All rooms are richly appointed with oriental rugs, antique furnishings, and king-sized beds with pillow-top mattresses.

Rooms are equipped with private baths, telephones, cable television, and VCRs for viewing videos from the inn's collection. A fax machine and modem hook-ups in guests' rooms offer convenience for the many business travelers who choose to make the Scholars Inn their home away from home.

The Caleb Mills Room, named after the founder of the public school system in Indiana, is a garden suite with a hand-carved limestone fountain, Jacuzzi tub, and French doors with a private access to the patio. A brick tile floor, white wicker furnishings, and a blue and white lily of the valley bedspread add a French garden touch.

The Charles Austin Beard Room, in honor of the prolific author on history and foreign policy, is a spacious master bedroom offering a marble bath, marble-topped desk, and the schoolmaster's armoire from the movie *Hoosiers*.

The Henry Ward Beecher Room, commemorating the eloquent and witty Protestant preacher, is delightfully decorated in blue delft, complete with a romantic fireplace and warm hardwood floors.

The Gene Stratton Porter Room in a quaint corner is quiet and relaxing with an antique armoire, Jacuzzi bathtub, an old school bell, and copies of the author's most popular works, *Girl of the Limberlost, Freckles,* and *The Keeper of the Bees.*

The Robert Dale Owen Room, created for the social theorist and American legislator, is a charming setting on the back side of the house with a soothing view of the grounds and a sitting area with an antique writing desk.

Guests at the Scholar's Inn step into the stately brick mansion and turn back the clock to a time when innkeepers offered gracious hospitality. Photo by Gene Howard, courtesy of the Bloomington/Monroe County Convention & Visitors Bureau.

The great room with its fireplace and plump sofas is available for showers and parties, weddings, receptions, and prenuptial dinners. Photo by Gene Howard, courtesy of the Bloomington/Monroe County Convention & Visitors Bureau.

The Scholars Inn offers special events throughout the year, including murder mystery weekends, IU football tickets with tailgate lunch, IU basketball or auditorium theater tickets, and afternoon teas.

The great room with its fireplace and plump sofas also is available for showers and parties, weddings, receptions, and prenuptial dinners.

The Scholars Inn is close to the campus and all university activities. It is only a gentle walk to downtown shops, superb restaurants, and a wealth of entertainment, including some evenings when Lyle might be seen in the leading role of a local theater production.

Guests at the Scholars Inn can leave behind the hustle and bustle of the world. Day begins with fresh-brewed coffee or tea, while tempting breakfast smells waft up from below. Guests can wander down to the cheery dining room at leisure or enjoy eating on the sunny patio.

A luxurious breakfast in bed also can be part of a visitor's stay. It's a time to browse through the morning paper, sip fresh juice, and savor fruit compote, homemade cinnamon rolls, and a special egg, cheese, and spinach casserole prepared by hostess Kerry Feigenbaum.

"I enjoy cooking," she says. "And this is a chance for me to pull our old family recipes and fix them for our guests."

The beautifully landscaped backyard is a good place to cuddle up with a good book in a gently swaying hammock. Or guests can sit back with a soothing cup of tea, a dainty scone, and some soft music in the great room.

History, romance, antiques, and elegance combine in the Scholars Inn. The mahogany paneling and hardwood floors speak of proud workmanship. The French doors and hand-carved limestone foundation tell stories of an opulent past.

At the Scholars Inn, guests find the warmth and charm of yesteryear combined with the comfort and convenience of today. Visitors also make a pleasant discovery in this fast-paced world.

"You'll arrive at the Scholars Inn as a guest," Lyle Feigenbaum says. "And you'll leave as a friend." ⚎

The Caleb Mills Room was named after the founder of the public school system in Indiana. Photo by Gene Howard, courtesy of the Bloomington/ Monroe County Convention & Visitors Bureau.

Guests can choose from individually decorated rooms, richly appointed with oriental rugs, antique furnishings, and king-sized beds. Photo by Gene Howard, courtesy of the Bloomington/Monroe County Convention & Visitors Bureau.

Huse Food Group

Under the direction of (left to right) Stephen M. Huse, Chairman of the Board and CEO, and Thomas R. Browne, President, Huse Food Group strives to provide quality service to its customers.

The "Friends of the West" photo wall at the Arby's restaurant on Bloomington's west side tells the story.

It is family that is important to the Huse Food Group—the family of employees, customers, and the community it serves. Face after smiling face beams from the photographs of people who enjoy coming to Arby's. They return time and again for the delicious food, fair prices, excellent service, comfortable surroundings, and warm friendliness of the Arby's family.

Many of the customers are known by name to the Arby's staff, who look forward to their often daily visits. Long-time guests have singled out their own personal seating spot and their menu favorites, like the Cookie Man, who comes in each day for dinner, always ending with a chocolate chip cookie for dessert.

That commitment to family and individualized attention isn't surprising for those who know the man behind Huse Food Group. The story of the company seems to epitomize the American dream.

Stephen M. Huse, now one of Indiana's most successful restaurant owners and operators, started out in a poor inner-city section of Indianapolis. He worked as a janitor and mailboy during high school and sold cookware to put himself through Indiana University.

His first job out of college was in sales. Given one of the toughest territories in the Dakotas, Nebraska, and Iowa, Huse knew it would be impossible to cover that area by car. So he learned how to fly.

Although he became the company's top salesman, Huse didn't like living on the road, nor did he want to spend his life working for someone else. So when the opportunity arose in 1967 to buy into an Arby's restaurant in Bloomington, Huse jumped at the chance.

Since then, the Huse Food Group has grown by leaps and bounds. With perseverance, self-discipline, and loyal employees, Huse also turned a failing Little Caesar's franchise into the independent giant that Noble Roman's eventually became. He later opened the popular Mustard's restaurant on Bloomington's east side. Those concepts were sold in the 1980s, subsequent to Noble Roman's going public. When Mustard's became part of Consoli-dated Products, Inc., the parent company of Steak 'n Shake, Huse assumed the presidency of that company for a period of time.

Today, the Huse Food Group has 14 Indiana Arby's—four in Bloomington, six in Indianapolis, two in Columbus, one in Washington, and one in Linton, as well as St. Elmo Steakhouse in Indianapolis. The Huse Food Group, Inc. is a growing management corporation that handles construction, operations, marketing, insurance, extensive public relations, and accounting functions for its family of restaurants and real estate investments.

It's the personal touch that helps set Huse Food Group's Arby's apart from other restaurants. For example, when Arby's in Columbus, Indiana, received a letter from a military base in Iwakuni, Japan, the employees set about satisfying a homesick American's longings.

A young woman wrote how much she loved Arby's sandwiches and, in particular, Arby's sauce. Would it be asking too much, she wrote, to send her a few packets? No problem! The Arby's manager and crew put together a care package with 50 packets of Arby's sauce, a T-shirt, Frisbee, sipper cup, and lots of good wishes.

Part of the philosophy Huse has lived by in building the business is that

The Huse Food Group is a growing management corporation that handles construction, operations, marketing, insurance, extensive public relations, and accounting functions for its family of restaurants and real estate investments.

The Huse Food Group operates 14 Indiana Arby's—four in Bloomington, six in Indianapolis, two in Columbus, one in Washington, and one in Linton.

success flows from an ability to attract and keep good people. The company has been blessed with associates who have worked alongside Huse from the very beginning. Much of the company's management and leadership are long-time associates.

At its Arby's restaurants, the Huse Food Group believes in promoting good service and rewarding achievements among its employees. A regular newsletter recognizes accomplishments by individuals as well as units. Ongoing competitions and annual banquets also honor employees with awards and cash prizes. Lorenzo Acuno, an immigrant Mexican and an employee of St. Elmo Steakhouse for over 20 years, received the highly coveted Rose Award of 1997 honoring his contributions to the restaurant and hospitality industry. He is representative of the calibre of employee sought after and valued by this organization.

From its corporate offices on Walnut Street, the Huse Food Group promotes the maxim that customers should be treated as guests in a home. Do whatever it takes to create total satisfaction and the desire to return.

The secret of success is really no surprise, the company believes. Give customers a quality product and treat them with respect and dignity. It's that simple.

But the Huse philosophy does not stop only with the company and its restaurants. The spirit of giving and family cooperation extend into the community as well.

"Show me a corporation involved in the community and I'll show you a corporation with a heart," a Huse newsletter notes. Along those lines, Huse Food Group personnel put their efforts into helping make Bloomington a better place to live.

From top executives to hourly employees at Arby's, Huse Food Group people have touched the community. They have reached a helping hand to Middle Way House, a shelter for abused women and children. They have raised money for local charities and pitched in with literacy efforts, helping to create a learn-to-read program. They have worked as Big Brothers/Big Sisters. One of Arby's favorite employees is a young woman from the Stonebelt Center in Bloomington, where people with physical and mental disabilities are trained to function in the world.

Once a week for an hour, three Huse Food Group volunteers—President Thomas R. Browne, Vice President of Marketing Anne Pollard, and Executive Assistant Kitty Wooldridge—have tutored and acted as mentors for elementary school students through the Good Friends program.

Other community involvements include the American Red Cross, Bloomington Economic Development Council (BEDC), MCCSC—School to Careers, United Way, Leukemia Society, Convention & Visitors Bureau, Monroe County Airport, Hospitality House, and the Chamber of Commerce.

The Huse Food Group isn't content to let the American dream end with financial success. Striving to provide quality service and offer more benefits for the Bloomington community is part of their ongoing efforts to make their family even stronger and better. ⚶

Once a week, Huse Food Group volunteers, such as Anne Pollard, Vice President of Marketing, tutor and act as mentors for elementary school students, like Kyla Langley, through the Good Friends program.

Star Travel Services Inc.

Star Travel Services was created in 1988 to provide worldwide travel services, including business, leisure, and group travel arrangements.

Imagine taking 260 high school students and their musical instruments to New York. Add to that almost 150 adults going along as sponsors, chaperones, and instructors.

The goal is to get the whole bunch aboard motor coaches from Indiana to Macy's Thanksgiving Day Parade and back home. While in New York City, the job involves taking care of hotel rooms, meals, entertainment, tours, and dozens of big and little details.

It's all in a day's work for Star Travel Services Inc. Or rather, it's the most enjoyable part of business, says company president Mike Attebury.

A Cook Group Company, Star Travel Services was created in 1988 to provide worldwide travel services, including business, leisure, and group travel arrangements. Star Travel experts can plan an entire event—from airline and hotel reservations to menus, speakers, entertainment—even theme parties.

Star Travel Services was born of necessity. When Cook Group pioneered the Star of Indiana Drum and Bugle Crops and its myriad other companies, it became obvious that travel arrangements were going to be a very important task.

Why risk assigning those travel needs to an outside agency? Why not have an in-house agency with top-notch travel experts who know all the ins and outs of travel?

So Star Travel Services came aboard, and the road has been much smoother for Cook Group companies, as well as other clients who have discovered the joys of traveling with Star. Ninety-five percent of group clients are repeat business—the highest vote of confidence a company can have.

Star Travel offers assistance in specialty areas such as educational group travel and corporate meeting and convention planning. Whether arranging vacation trips, business travel, or custom-designed tours, the staff members of Star Travel strive for excellence in customer service.

A member of the American Society of Travel Agents, Star Travel boasts three certified travel counselors. Certification takes nearly five years of job experience, plus 18 months of training.

Attention to detail is a key component of all the company's services. Whether it is a large group going to a popular destination such as the

Caribbean, or a couple going on an unusual European bed-and-breakfast vacation, clients need only name the time and place, and Star Travel will work with them for an unforgettable experience.

Star Travel tries to stay "three steps ahead" throughout a trip. As "point man" for the Concord School band trip from Elkhart to New York, Attebury flies into the Big Apple the day before the group arrives. He double checks everything—from the hotel room assignments to any special requirements, such as making sure a refrigerator is available for a diabetic's insulin.

When the group arrives, Attebury is waiting. Each guest is preregistered, rooms are ready, and the New York City fun can begin. "Our job is to organize everything and be prepared for any changes," Attebury says.

One of the biggest misconceptions in the travel field is that going through an agency to make travel arrangements is a very costly proposition. "That's not true," Attebury says. "It doesn't cost a dime more for us to do it. In fact, we can do it cheaper."

No matter the destination or purpose, Star Travel leads the way with its commitment to personalized service and dedication to making travel the enjoyable experience it should be. ◢

Whether arranging vacation trips, business travel, or custom-designed tours, the staff members of Star Travel strive for excellence in customer service.

The home of the Hoosiers has produced yet another star—this time in the transportation industry. With their blue stars and gold, orange, and red stripes, the motor coaches of the Star of Indiana Charter Service are a familiar sight on highways and byways across the United States. The vehicles represent comfort, convenience, and safety, along with the friendliest and most professional drivers on the road.

Established in 1986, the Star of Indiana Charter Service has racked up an impressive number of miles and a growing list of repeat customers. To say that Star of Indiana Charter Service is on the move refers to much more than its top-notch motor coaches. Its progressive philosophy combines teamwork and levels of service well beyond conventional standards.

In the beginning, Star of Indiana Charter Service was formed as a bus line to carry the Star of Indiana Drum and Bugle Corps to competitions. However, the buses sat idle several months a year when the drum and bugle corps wasn't traveling. At the same time, the Bloomington area needed a charter bus company.

The logical solution, of course, was the Star of Indiana Charter Service, a Cook Group company. The charter service started out with three employees and four middle-aged motor coaches. The vehicles were reliable and clean but totally without frills.

The fleet now has grown to 40 employees and 17 motor coaches—16 conventional ones and a deluxe entertainer coach. Each coach is equipped with a lavatory, VCR, public address system, and reclining seats.

In 1986, the customer base was largely a young one. Group travel consisted mainly of organizations like high school bands and college athletic programs. These customers are still a significant component of the Star market, but the growth of the industry, both regionally and nationally, has come from a very different type of passenger.

The explosive increase in leisure travel among retirees has changed the nature of the charter business dramatically. To cater to a choosier and more affluent customer base, the characteristics of tour motor coaches changed more in the last few years than they had in the previous two decades.

For example, in 1987 Star purchased a VCR-equipped coach, quite possibly the first one in Indiana. By early 1991, the entire fleet was so equipped and was almost certainly the first all VCR fleet in the Midwest.

It takes an unrelenting commitment to excellence to maintain the consistent quality for which Star of Indiana Charter Service is known. Since 1989, Star has purchased only new vehicles custom built to the company's specifications. The deluxe entertainer coach is dark green with gold stripes. A roomy inside allows for maximum comfort with tables, a kitchenette, sofas, and bunk beds.

"Our company philosophy is to do the job right, and we are given the equipment to do it right," says general business manager, Ian Patton.

In 1993, the company moved its headquarters to Indiana Highway 37, north of Bloomington. At this convenient location, Star of Indiana Charter Service operates a completely equipped maintenance facility. Under the supervision of fleet operations manager Everett Farley, the firm services its own vehicles and provides emergency maintenance services to other commercial operators.

Professional, careful, and efficient. Star of Indiana Charter Service is a company that knows what it is doing and hustles to meet the needs of its customers. No matter what the travelers' purpose or where the road leads, the Star shines. ⚑

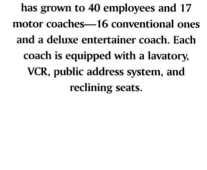

The Star of Indiana Charter Service has grown to 40 employees and 17 motor coaches—16 conventional ones and a deluxe entertainer coach. Each coach is equipped with a lavatory, VCR, public address system, and reclining seats.

In 1993, the company moved its headquarters to Indiana Highway 37, north of Bloomington. At this convenient location, Star of Indiana Charter Service operates a completely equipped maintenance facility.

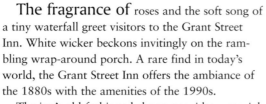

Each of the 24 rooms at the Grant Street Inn is unique and provides the utmost in privacy. All rooms have color televisions, phones, and private baths.

The fragrance of roses and the soft song of a tiny waterfall greet visitors to the Grant Street Inn. White wicker beckons invitingly on the rambling wrap-around porch. A rare find in today's world, the Grant Street Inn offers the ambiance of the 1880s with the amenities of the 1990s.

The inn's old-fashioned charm provides a special place for people who like their travel to be tranquil and soul-restoring. A gracious remnant of a bygone era, the Grant Street Inn combines all the conveniences of a world-class hotel and the friendly services of a small country inn.

Located in the historic section of Bloomington, the Grant Street Inn has a fascinating history. Built in 1883, the main section of the inn was owned by Charles and Martha Zeigler and acquired by the First Presbyterian Church of Bloomington in 1987.

Because of its historic significance, the fate of the house was of great concern when it was no longer needed by the church. CFC, an arm of the Cook Group, purchased the house and relocated it to its new home. The community watched on March 19, 1990, as the Zeigler House was moved under adverse technical and weather-related conditions.

In December 1990, the house—now restored to its original beauty and connected by an enclosed breezeway to the historic Gilstrap House on the adjoining lot—became the Grant Street Inn. Each of the 24 rooms is unique and provides the utmost in privacy. All rooms have color televisions, phones, and private baths. Some have fireplaces and many boast separate entrances for extra privacy. Suites are equipped with fireplaces and large whirlpool Jacuzzis™. The parlor is just right for relaxing with a good book by the fireplace.

"What we have tried to do is create a comfortable, homelike atmosphere away from home," says President Donna Harbstreit. "Our guests are encouraged to help themselves to our homemade pastries and desserts and coffee and tea in the main parlor."

In the original section of the inn, brass plates on the spacious rooms echo the

history of the city, and each room has its own charm.

Guests wake up every morning to a superb breakfast, featuring breads and pastries, fresh fruit, and several hot dishes. Along with the homemade baked goods, the daily menu includes a variety of breads from The Bakehouse, providing European hearth-style breads made in the old-world tradition. Served on the lovely enclosed breezeway, breakfast is such a delightful experience it's no wonder guests linger and find it difficult to leave.

The inn is minutes away from Bloomington's most popular spots, including the Indiana University campus, Fountain Square Mall, Bloomington Antique Mall, Courthouse Square, College Mall, Convention Center, Bryan Park, IU Golf Course, IU Memorial Stadium, and Assembly Hall.

The Grant Street Inn surrounds its guests with a sense of tranquillity and warm, caring service. Each season brings something new to admire—the first yellow crocus of spring, the lush profusion of summer, the brilliant colors of autumn, the luminous snow blanketing the landscape of winter. Whatever the time, the Grant Street Inn is a welcome retreat to relish memories and renew dreams. ▲

A gracious remnant of a bygone era, the Grant Street Inn combines all the conveniences of a world-class hotel and the friendly services of a small country inn.

Fountain Fabrics

The employees of Fountain Fabrics understand that choosing an upholstery fabric or window covering sometimes can be a frustrating and expensive task. But at Fountain Fabrics, the talented staff makes the job into the exciting and rewarding experience it should be.

"Often, customers have an idea what they want but aren't really sure how it will look or if it will suit their needs," says business President Donna Harbstreit. "We help them see what the choices are and decide what will work best."

Fountain Fabrics also takes the expense and guesswork out of buying fabric for area residents. People no longer have to drive out of town to save on upholstery fabric or order expensive material based on seeing just a small swatch of fabric in a book.

"The fabrics are all at about half price," Harbstreit says. "The savings are made possible by buying in bulk from New York wholesale houses." Fountain Fabrics offers consumers an extensive in-stock selection of fine decorator fabrics. Thousands of yards, which are displayed on racks especially designed for large bolts, include tapestry, velvet, lace, sheer, chenille, jacquard, cotton, and damask. Sample books from various companies also are available for special orders. The shop serves clients who want to fully redecorate or may just need to make a pillow in a certain fabric that will enhance their decor. For those who desire custom plans, Fountain Fabrics provides a designer to help select the concept that best suits the client's needs with

combinations that won't be mass produced and duplicated in chain markets.

Professional decorators also save money by being able to purchase only the quantity of material needed for their projects. To further enhance the offerings of fabrics for residential and commercial decorating, an outstanding selection of trims, hardware, upholstery supplies, decorator accessories, books, and patterns, as well as a custom furniture line, is available.

Part of the purpose of the popular shop was to provide a service that wasn't offered and to add another attraction to draw shoppers downtown, and it worked. Opened in 1990 in Fountain Square by the Cook Group, Fountain Fabrics quickly outgrew its original home and moved to the historic former railroad depot in downtown Bloomington. The depot with its unmistakable railway look was renovated in 1983. The long, lean building at Morton and Seventh Streets was built in 1906 and is listed on the National Register of Historic Places.

In 1996, Fountain Fabrics added yet another service when it purchased The Quilter's Patch, a long-time Bloomington business. Quilting fabrics, supplies, and classes have proven a hit with people who like to make quilts or other items for home use, gifts, sales, or future family heirlooms.

"It's been phenomenal," Harbstreit says. "Quilt-making has had a real resurgence, and so many people are interested in making something they can pass down from generation to generation."

Fountain Fabrics is located in the historic former railroad depot in downtown Bloomington. The long, lean depot building at Morton and Seventh Streets was built in 1906 and is listed on the National Register of Historic Places.

Fountain Fabrics offers consumers an extensive in-stock selection of fine decorator fabrics. Thousands of yards include tapestry, velvet, lace, sheer, chenille, jacquard, cotton, and damask.

Bloomington Antique Mall

The Bloomington Antique Mall is not only in the heart of downtown Bloomington, but it also is the wellspring for unusual gifts, quality home furnishings, and memories of a bygone era.

Feathered hats from the 1940s nestle alongside sparkling brooches. A walnut rocker burnished to a warm patina from years of loving use sits beside a brocade fainting couch. A round brown crock perches on a tall maple dresser with filigreed handles. A *Little Red Riding Hood* cookie jar waits atop a beautifully kept Hoosier kitchen cabinet.

From top to bottom, the Bloomington Antique Mall is chock-full of enough lovely items to keep browsers happy for hours. And shoppers have been flocking to its door since the huge facility opened in 1988.

"It's a major drawing card for the downtown area," says President Donna Harbstreit. "We get 10,000 or more visitors a month." The brick and wood building is itself a part of Bloomington's interesting past. Once a wholesale foods warehouse, the circa 1890 facility was deteriorating when CFC Inc. stepped in. As the development arm of the Cook Group of companies, CFC is responsible for much of the downtown renovation and progress.

In order to attract more people downtown and preserve a part of the city's history, CFC Inc. renovated the warehouse and turned it into the Bloomington Antique Mall. With three floors and 25,000 square feet of space, the mall has 120 booths and a waiting list of antique dealers who would like to have space in the popular spot.

"We still have 75 percent of our original dealers, which seems a good testimonial to how successful the venture has been," Harbstreit says. The Bloomington Antique Mall has set high standards for the dealers it accepts and the merchandise it allows. Thus the mall has earned in a short time a reputation as a top-notch establishment and a favorite destination for antique lovers who enjoy quality, reasonable prices, and the intrigue of the hunt.

From top to bottom, the Bloomington Antique Mall is chock-full of enough lovely items to keep browsers happy for hours.

The antique mall concept is a growing trend across the country. The mall arrangement allows multiple antique dealers to have booths, which operate like small shops under one roof. The mall is supervised by a manager who handles sales. Individual antique dealers do not have to be present at all times, but only have to collect and display their wares. In return, the mall management receives rent and a percent of sales from each booth.

The Bloomington Antique Mall is an important attraction not only for antique buffs who travel long distances to go "antiquing," but also for tourists and convention attendees. The mall's strolling distance to downtown restaurants and other stores provides added appeal.

The interior of the building still reveals touches of its former life, such as exposed bricks and wood. The large open spaces of the former warehouse lend themselves to versatile booth size and arrangement for convenient shopping. The mall is equipped with security protection, a loading dock, an elevator, ramp access, air-conditioning, restrooms, reception area, and parking.

Browsing through the Bloomington Antique Mall, shoppers can uncover memories by finding a piece "just like Grandma used to have" and take home a part of the past to create new family memories. ⚞

The Bloomington Antique Mall is not only in the heart of downtown Bloomington, but it also is the wellspring for unusual gifts, quality home furnishings, and memories of a bygone era.

Bibliography

Baker, Ronald. *From Needmore to Prosperity; Hoosier Place Names in Folklore History.* Indiana University Press, 1995.

Blanchard, Charles. *Counties of Morgan, Monroe, and Brown, Indiana. Historical and Biographical.* 1884.

Cook, Gayle and Diana Hawes. *Monroe County in Focus.* Discovery Press, 1990.

The Ellettsville History 1837-1987. 1987.

Gilliam, Frances V. Halsell. *A Time to Speak; A Brief History of the Afro-Americans of Bloomington, Indiana 1865-1965.* Pinus Strobus Press, 1985.

Harding, Samuel Bannister, ed. *Indiana University 1820-1904.* Indiana University, 1904.

List, George. *Singing About It; Folk Song in Southern Indiana.* Indiana Historical Society, 1991.

McDonald, Bill. *A Short History of Indiana Limestone.* 1995.

McEntire, Nancy C., Grey Larsen, and Janne Henshaw, eds. *The Lotus Dickey Songbook.* Indiana University Press, 1995.

Sanders, Scott R. *Stone Country.* Indiana University Press, 1985.

Taylor, Robert M., Jr., Errol Wayne Stevens, Mary Ann Ponder, and Paul Brockman. *Indiana: A New Historical Guide.* Indiana Historical Society, 1989.

Wilson, D. Ray. *Indiana Historical Tour Guide.* Crossroads Communications, 1994.

Enterprise Index

Index

Photos on pages 6, 8, 10, 12, 146, 152, 180, 198, 207, 208, 235, 236, 243, and 244 by Kendall Reeves.
Photos on pages 5, 14, 179, 197, and 222 by Rich Remsberg.